Mexico's Recent Economic Growth

THE MEXICAN VIEW

T0324341

Latin American Monographs, No. 10

Institute of Latin American Studies

The University of Texas

Mexico's Recent Economic Growth

THE MEXICAN VIEW

Essays by
Enrique Pérez López • Ernesto Fernández Hurtado
Mario Ramón Beteta • Alfredo Navarrete R.
Ifigenia M. de Navarrete • Victor L. Urquidi

INTRODUCTION BY TOM E. DAVIS

TRANSLATED BY MARJORY URQUIDI

Published for the INSTITUTE OF LATIN AMERICAN STUDIES
by the UNIVERSITY OF TEXAS PRESS, Austin

Acknowledgments

The present volume of six essays on the recent economic growth of Mexico represents a selection of the more significant contributions over the last few years by outstanding Mexican economists. Marjory Urquidi performed the strenuous task of translation. Tom E. Davis, economist and director of the Latin American Studies Program at Cornell University, has provided a stimulating introduction in which he compares the growth of the Mexican economy with those of Argentina and Chile over roughly the same time period, indicating important research paths to be explored in the field of comparative Latin American economic development.

The purpose of this work is to make readily accessible to the English-reading audience these penetrating studies in one volume. The original conception of this work is that of Victor Urquidi, president of El Colegio de México, who, in collaboration with the Institute of Latin American Studies of The University of Texas, secured the necessary permission for the translation and publication of these essays. In the long course of preparing the manuscript for publication a number of individuals have lent their expertise, and their valuable assistance is gratefully acknowledged by the Institute of Latin American Studies: Calvin P. Blair, associate professor of business administration, The University of Texas at Austin; Robert B. Freithaler, economist with the Rand Corporation; Manuel Cuellar, professor of business administration, Instituto Tecnológico y de Estudios Superiores de Monterrey.

Special thanks are due to Enrique Pérez López for providing us with an up-dated version of his original essay, "The National Product of Mexico."

John P. Harrison, Director
Institute of Latin American Studies

Richard P. Schaedel, Editor
Institute of Latin American Studies Monograph Series

About the Contributors

ENRIQUE PÉREZ LÓPEZ: graduate of the School of Economics, National University of Mexico; M.A. degree from the School of Business Administration, Harvard University; formerly, director of Department of Economic Research, Bank of Mexico; present position: director of Commercial Policy, Ministry of Foreign Affairs.

ERNESTO FERNÁNDEZ HURTADO: graduate of the School of Economics, National University of Mexico; M.A. degree from the School of Public Administration, Harvard University; present position: deputy-director of the Bank of Mexico.

MARIO RAMÓN BETETA: graduate of the School of Law, National University of Mexico; M.A. degree in economics, University of Wisconsin; formerly held posts with the Bank of Mexico; present positions: director general of Credit and Banking, Ministry of Finance; lecturer in the School of Economics, National University of Mexico.

ALFREDO NAVARRETE R.: graduate of the School of Economics, National University of Mexico; Ph.D. degree from Harvard University; formerly, director of Department of Financial Research, Nacional Financiera; present position: deputy-director of Nacional Financiera.

IFIGENIA M. DE NAVARRETE: graduate of the School of Economics, National University of Mexico; M.A. degree from the School of Public Administration, Harvard University; present positions: economic adviser to Ministry of President; lecturer in the School of Economics, National University of Mexico.

VICTOR URQUIDI: graduate of London School of Economics and Political Science, University of London; formerly, economist with the Bank of Mexico, director of the Mexican Office of the United Nations Economic Commission for Latin America, and economic adviser to the Ministry of Finance; present positions: director of the Economic and Demographic Research Program, El Colegio de México; president, El Colegio de México.

MARJORY URQUIDI: translator of the present volume of essays and wife of Victor Urquidi. Mrs. Urquidi, who has translated several works from Spanish into English in recent years, has a background of graduate studies in the United States and a firsthand acquaintance with Mexican economists.

Tom E. Davis: Dr. Davis, who wrote the Introduction for this volume, was formerly an assistant professor of economics at the University of Chicago. He is presently professor of economics and director of the Latin American Program at Cornell University.

Contents

Tables

Figures

Introduction

BY TOM E. DAVIS

Introduction

TOM E. DAVIS

Three decades of continuous, rapid growth differentiates the performance of the Mexican economy from that of the other Latin American nations. During each quinquennium in the period 1934–1964, total product has grown at a rate in excess of 4 per cent per annum, and has averaged more than 6 per cent per annum over the entire period. Various Latin American countries expanded their industrial sectors at virtually comparable rates, and Venezuela's overall development was even more rapid than Mexico's through the mid–1950's; but Mexico alone not only sustained, but accelerated, this growth during the decade 1954–1964. In the case of Mexico and, to a lesser extent, Venezuela, agricultural output increased dramatically, in sharp distinction to that of Argentina, Chile, and Colombia where, since 1948, output of crops has barely exceeded the growth of population.[1]

The sustained economic expansion of Mexico surpasses even that of the presently developed countries during the period of their most rapid growth (see Table 1). During the thirty-five years prior to the First World War, the United States grew 56.0 per cent per decade; Japan, 49.3 per cent per decade, and Canada, 47.1 per cent per decade. By comparison, from 1935 to 1963, Mexico increased at a rate of approximately 70.0 per cent per decade. Crop output, which between 1948 and 1963 progressed even more rapidly than total output, greatly surpassed the rates "achieved by now economically advanced nations during comparable periods of time." [2]

[1] U.S. Department of Agriculture, Economic Research Service, *Changes in Agriculture in 26 Developing Nations: 1948 to 1963* (Washington, D.C., Foreign Agricultural Economic Report No. 27, 1965), p. 6.
[2] *Ibid.*, p. v.

TABLE 1

The Growth of Population, Net National Product, and Net National Product per Capita in Ten Developed Countries

Country	Initial Period	Terminal Period	Population	Percentage Change per Decade in Net National Product	NNP per Capita
United Kingdom	1860–1869	1949–1953	8.0	21.5	12.5
	1860–1869	1905–1914	11.1	25.0	12.5
France	1841–1850	1949–1953	1.3	15.3	13.8
	1841–1850	1901–1910	1.9	18.6	16.3
Germany	1860–1869	1950–1954	10.1	27.4	15.1
	1860–1869	1905–1914	11.5	35.6	21.6
Denmark	1870–1878	1950–1954	11.5	30.1	16.7
	1870–1878	1904–1913	11.3	32.7	19.3
Sweden	1861–1868	1950–1954	6.6	36.0	27.6
	1861–1868	1904–1913	6.8	34.8	26.2
Italy	1862–1868	1950–1954	6.9	18.0	10.4
	1862–1868	1904–1913	7.0	15.7	8.1
Russia/ U.S.S.R.	1870	1954	13.4	31.0	15.4
	1870	1913	15.7	27.7	10.4
U.S.A.	1869–1878	1950–1954	17.4	41.2	20.3
	1869–1878	1904–1913	22.3	56.0	27.5
Canada	1870–1879	1950–1954	18.3	41.3	19.3
	1870–1879	1905–1914	17.8	47.1	24.7
Japan	1878–1887	1950–1954	12.7	42.3	26.3
	1878–1887	1903–1912	11.6	49.3	33.7

Source: Simon Kuznets, "Quantitative Aspects of the Economic Growth of Nations. I. Levels and Variability of Growth Rates," *Economic Development and Cultural Change*, Vol. V, No. 1 (October, 1956), p. 13. See also the discussion in Ernesto Fernández Hurtado, "Private Enterprise and Government in Mexican Development," in this volume.

Accelerating population growth, averaging approximately 30 per cent per decade, contributed to the growth of aggregate output, as did the increasing degree of female participation in the labor force. Even in terms of output per capita and output per worker, however, Mexico has equaled Sweden's and Japan's performances; clearly exceeded those of the United States, Canada, and Germany; and vastly surpassed those of Denmark, France, the United Kingdom, Russia, and Italy. Benefiting from the accumulation of technology and knowledge amassed over five consecutive decades, Mexico advances at a pace hitherto unknown, though a pace paralleled, and perhaps even exceeded, in postwar Japan and Europe.

In any event, the Mexican experience, as described and analyzed in this volume by a group of leading Mexican economists, clearly warrants the attention of those concerned with economic growth, as well as those interested in the particular process by which specialized institutions—e.g., the development banks—emerged and functioned successfully to reinforce the growth process in a Hispanic-American cultural context.[3]

Why has Mexico been capable of marshaling knowledge and technology to the service of the nation while the other Latin American countries have succeeded to varying, but lesser, degrees? In other words, what is unique in the Mexican experience?

One approach to the problem of identifying the principal factor (or factors) is to determine the point at which the economic history of modern Mexico diverges significantly from those of Argentina and Chile. These countries, whose economies are now practically stagnant, share with Mexico the distinction of having attained a high degree of political unification during the nineteenth century (albeit under dictatorial regimes which were far more pronounced in Argentina and Mexico than in Chile).

Contemporary research, conducted under the general auspices of the noted historian Daniel Cosío Villegas, demonstrates that Mexico witnessed three decades of moderate growth during the period 1877–1911.[4] Total product grew at an average annual rate of 2.7 per cent, and population, 1.4 per cent. More significant is the fact that during the period capital formation as a proportion of gross output rose as high as 13 per cent, a figure seldom exceeded subsequently and above the level frequently assumed to be necessary, if not sufficient, to sustain economic growth.

This experience, while by no means common to the Latin Amer-

---

[3] A penetrating analysis of the functioning of the development banks as part of the Mexican *political* framework is presented by Charles W. Anderson's "Bankers as Revolutionaries: Politics and Development Banking in Mexico," in William P. Glade, Jr., and Charles Anderson, *The Political Economy of Mexico* (Madison, Wis., University of Wisconsin Press, 1963). For a discussion of the operations of the Central Bank, and the commercial banking system, see the essay by M. R. Beteta, "The Central Bank, Instrument of Economic Development in Mexico," in this volume.

[4] Fernando Rosenzweig "El desarrollo económico de México de 1877 a 1911," *El Trimestre Económico*, Vol. XXXII, No. 3 (julio-septiembre, 1965), p. 405; and Enrique Pérez López, "The National Product of Mexico: 1895 to 1964," Table 2, in this volume.

ican nations, was repeated in Chile and Argentina.[5] As in Mexico, the impetus was provided by foreign investment in railroads designed to facilitate the extraction of primary products, and by loans to cooperating governments that provided title to vast land areas.[6] The resulting expansion of exports created additional demand for labor and manufactured products. In Mexico, the manufacturing sector expanded at a rate of 5 per cent per annum, only slightly below that of exports. Nevertheless, the increase in real minimum daily wages appears to have been confined to the mining sector (see Table 2).

TABLE 2

Minimum Real Daily Wages in
Various Mexican Industries, 1877–1911
(in Pesos, 1900 Prices)

Year	Aggregate	Agriculture	Manufacturing	Mining
1877	32	32	32	32
1885	29	27	34	31
1892	28	26	26	30
1898	39	37	50	47
1902	33	32	36	43
1911	30	27	36	72

Source: Fernando Rosenzweig, "El desarrollo económico de México de 1877 a 1911," *El Trimestre Económico,* Vol. XXXII, No. 3 (julio–septiembre, 1965), p. 447.

In all three countries, "liberal" governments placed large tracts of public land in private (including foreign) hands, but, whereas in Argentina and Chile this land was largely unoccupied (or very sparsely populated), in Mexico it was being cultivated or grazed by individual holders *(comunidades indigenas),* whose title was deemed deficient in the eyes of the State. This difference, plus a higher degree in Mexico of concentration of assets in foreign hands,

[5] Marto Ballesteros and Tom E. Davis, "The Growth of Output and Employment in Basic Sectors of the Chilean Economy, 1908–57," *Economic Development and Cultural Change,* Vol. XI, No. 2 (January, 1963); and Marto Ballesteros, "Argentine Agriculture, 1908–1954: A Study in Growth and Decline" (Doctoral dissertation, University of Chicago, 1958).

[6] For the distribution of foreign investment in Mexico in 1911, see Alfredo Navarrete R., "The Financing of Economic Development," Table 1, in this volume.

appears to offer a more satisfactory explanation for the fact that the Mexican peasants alone revolted in 1910 than does the explanation of a high rate of growth of total output vis-à-vis a limited increase in real wages, factors common to Chile and Argentina as well.

This agrarian revolution slowed the rate of growth in Mexico to less than 1 per cent per annum during the next decade, despite substantial foreign investment in the petroleum industry, whose growth accounted for virtually all the increase in gross national product (including commerce, government, and services). The decade of the 1920's brought little improvement in economic performance as agriculture stagnated and the recovery of mining output merely compensated for the decline in petroleum production; manufacturing and transportation accounted for the increments in output in the basic sectors of the economy.[7] Elsewhere in Latin America, manufacturing was also expanding rapidly as a result of the disruption in imports caused by the First World War. With the cessation of hostilities and the resumption of the gold-exchange standard, despite violent fluctuations in the prices of primary products, additional capital from abroad flowed into the extractive industries. Not only did Argentina and Chile grow rapidly, but per capita income, well reflected in such indicators as the number of automobiles per inhabitant, was higher in Buenos Aires than in some of the European capitals where governments and private bankers were eagerly funneling capital into Latin America.

The onslaught of the great depression of the 1930's eliminated the buoyancy provided by the inflow of foreign capital, and foreign-exchange availabilities were further curtailed by drastic declines in export prices. In Mexico and throughout Latin America the common response was an intensification of efforts to limit imports to essentials, mainly capital goods and raw materials for domestic industries producing import substitutes. The degree of initiative taken by the State in fostering investment in these industries, the amount of continuing protection afforded to the "import substitution" industries (by curtailing imports of final products after export prices had recovered and foreign–exchange receipts had increased), and the extent to which the price of foreign exchange was prevented from rising were a measure of the political vitality

---

[7] Tables 2 and 3 in Pérez López, in this volume.

of the domestic producers and the degree of labor intensity in the export industries. This situation is well illustrated by comparing the treatment accorded to foreign-owned, capital-intensive mineral exports of Chile with the domestically owned, labor-intensive agricultural exports of Argentina. As a result of these measures, however, the decline in gross national product, which offset the real growth in income that had occurred since the end of the First World War, had been erased by 1934 in Mexico and even in Chile, the most sorely affected of all the Latin American countries.[8]

The aftermath of the great depression, almost universally, was increased participation in, and control of, economic activity by the State. In this respect, the "mixed economy" of Mexico was not fundamentally different from that of Chile, or, for that matter, even from that of Argentina. In fact, the Chilean Development Corporation was created only some five years after the establishment of the Nacional Financiera in Mexico, and in the fields of labor and social-security legislation, Chile and Argentina were second only to Uruguay.

The characteristic that truly distinguishes Mexico from the three countries comprising the southern cone, after the recovery, was the extent of the land-redistribution program and the fact that industrial growth was complemented by increases in agricultural output that accelerated after the Second World War.[9] At a time when acreage and irrigation had approached their maximum extent in Chile, and increased inputs into Argentine agriculture were subject to sharply diminishing returns to scale, Mexico was investing in irrigation, transportation, and electrification that contributed directly to the expansion of agricultural output, albeit in certain instances with a relatively extended period of gestation.[10] Public expenditures in Chile and Argentina, in contrast, were being devoted to an expansion of the government bureaucracy, to defraying the costs of a comprehensive social-security system (complete with full pension benefits for white-collar employees after thirty to thirty-five

[8] *Ibid.*, Table 3; and Ballesteros and Davis, "The Growth of Output and Employment in Basic Sectors of the Chilean Economy, 1908–57," p. 160.

[9] For a survey of the entire period 1930–1954, see Section IV, "Progress in Agriculture," of the essay by Ernesto Fernández Hurtado, "Private Enterprise and Government in Mexican Development," and Victor L. Urquidi's essay, "Fundamental Problems of the Mexican Economy," both in this volume.

[10] Fernández Hurtado, Table 5, in this volume.

years of service), and to constructing middle-income housing, primarily for public employees.[11]

The ability of the government to postpone demands for immediate implementation of the social goals of the Revolution and to push forward with this investment program was strengthened by the elimination, as a political force, of the pre-Revolutionary traditional elites and service-middle class (with their similar origins, values, and aspirations) and by the formation of a single, dominant political party, P.R.I.[12] The vast program of land redistribution assured the P.R.I. of a broad popular base of political support that enabled successive governments to resist the immediate consumption demands of the fragmented middle classes and the direct political action of urban pressure groups. Organized labor exercised its influence within the party structure, where its influence never exceeded that of the agrarian sector, and public employees (including the armed forces), were ultimately submerged into a "popular sector" that also included representatives from industry and commerce. The degree of political consensus maintained within the P.R.I. stands in sharp contrast to the internecine struggles of fragmented, class-oriented parties in Argentina and Chile, particularly after the Second World War.

This political consensus served Mexico well during the two critical periods confronted by all the Latin American countries—the aftermath of the Korean War, when the demand for primary products declined, and the period of the early 1960's, when governments faced the political challenge presented by Fidel Castro. Mexico devalued its peso in 1954, well before there was a serious loss of confidence in the government's ability to maintain convertibility. The result was a temporary constriction in imports coupled with a vast expansion of tourism, which subsequently pushed foreign-exchange earnings and international reserves to new heights. Prices rose throughout the economy; the initial reduction in imports, however,

[11] See Tom E. Davis, "Dualism, Stagnation and Inequality: The Impact of Pension Legislation in the Chilean Labor Market," *Industrial and Labor Relations Review*, Vol. 17, No. 3 (April, 1964).

[12] Housing and other social investment seldom constituted more than 15 per cent and occasionally less than 10 per cent of public capital formation in the period 1939–1954. See Raymond Vernon, *The Dilemma of Mexico's Development* (Cambridge, Mass., Harvard University Press, 1963), Table A-2, p. 198.

directed demand toward import substitutes; the pace of economic activity, especially industrial production, accelerated. By 1958, price increases had restored the real price of foreign exchange to the pre-devaluation level. The successful implementation of this policy attested to the ability of the Mexican government, with its broad base of political support, to adopt the economic measures required to ensure that the future growth of the Mexican economy would not be compromised in the interest of a higher immediate level of consumption.[13] In contrast, Chile and Argentina, in response to political pressures, postponed devaluation until reserves were virtually exhausted (a process that was found to be repeated in Brazil and Colombia in 1963/1964), and then failed in their attempt to devalue successfully. In these countries, economic growth virtually ceased, and at this point the path of the Mexican economy diverged even more radically from that of these more highly industrialized and politically fragmented countries.

The Mexican economy again paused for breath in the early 1960's. The peak inflow of net foreign capital occurred in 1957 in Mexico and Latin America generally. After New Year's Day, 1959, it appeared obvious that Latin American governments, irrespective

---

[13] The Mexican dilemma, Raymond Vernon argues, stems precisely from the requirement of maintaining broad consensus, which will limit the ability of future Mexican governments to make the decisions required to sustain the rate of growth. On the basis of past experience, however, two conclusions appear evident: (1) that successive Mexican governments have been willing to risk offending individuals and groups in the process of implementing economic policy; and (2) that a sustained rate of economic growth greatly assists in the restoration (and preservation) of political consensus when economic-policy decisions do alienate particular groups. Charles W. Anderson says that "the Mexican chief executive would seem to have considerably more autonomy in decision-making (in comparison to the U.S. President). He need not be immediately responsive to pressures from below; for the decision of a group (and here we include the components of the P.R.I. as interest-groups), feeling itself mistreated, to bolt the Revolutionary coalition is far more perilous than would be a comparable decision of a U.S. group to utilize the ultimate bargaining sanction and withdraw into the opposition. The Mexican President must be constantly aware of the margins of toleration of the components of the Revolutionary coalition, for his power is ultimately dependent upon the maintenance of that coalition; but in comparison to his United States counterpart, he can count on greater leeway for independent decision-making before a group will confront, as a real question, the fateful choice of whether to endure or to oppose," *Political Economy of Mexico*, p. 133.

of the direct threat to their viability or to the concept of private property posed by *Castrismo,* would be compelled to allocate a larger fraction of the public budget to wages, salaries, and welfare expenditures and to press the private sector to follow a similar course. The Mexican government recognized the legitimate and forceful appeal of the ideals of the Cuban Revolution, particularly to many in the lower socio-economic groups who had yet to benefit significantly from the rapid growth of the Mexican economy.[14] Public statements that the policy of López Mateos' government would incline toward the "extreme left within the constitution" nevertheless disturbed the business community. Real wages, which had actually declined in three of the four years in the period 1955–1958, advanced at a rate approximating 9 per cent per annum in the quinquennium 1959–1964. [15] Savings in the private sector declined and gross investment remained constant in real terms during the period 1960–1962. [16] Taking advantage of the rapid decline in the popularity of the Cuban experiment during 1961–1962, government leaders acted energetically to restore the confidence of the business community, and to accelerate the rate of "productive" public capital formation with the proceeds of foreign loans. The private sector, reassured by public pronouncements and impressed by the evidence of continuing confidence of international banking circles in the future of the Mexican economy, reentered the capital markets in such volume that not only did gross investment as a fraction of gross national product rise to a historic high in 1964, but the public sector was compelled to curtail its own expenditure program in early 1965 to prevent the reemergence of inflationary pressures.

Elsewhere in Latin America, and especially in Chile, public funds

[14] Even before the appearance of Ifigenia M. de Navarrete's *La distribución del ingreso y el desarrollo económico de México* (México, D.F., Instituto de Investigaciones Económicas, Escuela Nacional de Economía, 1960), of which Chapters III and IV are presented in this volume under the title "Income Distribution in Mexico," an article titled "Los salarios reales en México, 1939–1950" was published in *El Trimestre Económico,* Vol. 18, No. 2 (abril-julio, 1951) by Diego G. López Rosado and Juan F. Noyola Vásquez, presenting evidence that real wages in selected industries had declined.

[15] This estimate is based on the data presented in Table 3. The marked increase in 1960 and 1961 in housing and other social investment as a fraction of public capital formation can be observed in Vernon, *Dilemma of Mexico's Development,* Table A-2, p. 198.

[16] Pérez López, Table 5, in this volume.

TABLE 3

*Annual Rates of Change in Price and
Wage Indexes, 1955–1964*

Year	(Year-end) Wholesale Prices	(Year-end) Cost of Living	(Fourth Quarter) Wages
1955	17.1	16.9	16.2
1956	2.2	− 2.4	4.6
1957	5.5	13.6	11.1
1958	4.2	8.6	4.0
1959	0.0	0.0	13.5
1960	6.0	8.0	8.5
1961	0.0	− 2.8	6.3
1962	1.9	2.9	7.4
1963	0.9	0.0	18.5
1964	5.5	3.6	9.8

Sources: Bank of Mexico, *Annual Reports,* and International Monetary Fund, *International Financial Statistics.*

continue to be channeled toward housing and urban facilities to some extent as the result of pressure to meet the social-development objectives of the Alliance for Progress. The current dynamism of the private sector in Mexico, stimulated in no small degree by the volume and directly productive character of public investment, is without peer in the more industrialized countries. The result is that at this second critical turning point the economic-policy decisions reached by the Mexican government appear destined to advance the economy at a pace well in excess of that likely to be attained by Argentina, Brazil, Chile, Colombia, or Uruguay.

Many Mexicans, as well as the vast majority of foreign commentators on Mexican affairs, are deeply disturbed because more of the tangible benefits of three decades of sustained growth have not filtered down to the masses within the industrialized sector of the economy, not to mention the persistence of the culturally "dual" society.[17] To help to place this phenomenon in comparative historical perspective, however, it is well to note the following comment: ". . . the last three decades of the eighteenth century, that is the

[17] Jesús Silva Herzog, *La revolución mexicana en crisis* (México, Cuadernos Americanos, 1944); Daniel Cosío Villegas, *Change in Latin America: The Mexican and Cuban Revolutions* (Lincoln, Neb., University of Nebraska Press, 1961); and Oscar Lewis, "Mexico since Cárdenas," *Social Research,* Vol. 26, No. 1 (Spring, 1959).

period which saw the unmistakable beginnings of rapid industrialization in England, the rate of increase in average real income was
apparently negligible, if indeed there was not a positive decline. . . .
There seems to have been a perceptible increase in the inequality
of incomes . . ." [18] Thus, despite the more rapid rate of Mexican
economic advance, direct action may be required in the near future
to induce significant changes in the income distribution.

An argument in support of such action, frequently heard during
periods when private investment lags, contends that investment opportunities in Mexico are increasingly limited by the extent of the
market, and that increased real wages and a more equitable income
distribution are requisites for continuing expansion in market dimensions.[19] Secularly, however, the basic limitation on investment—
and particularly public capital formation—appears to have been the
lack of saving in the Mexican economy. This phenomenon stands
in sharp contrast with the situation in Argentina and Chile, where
profitable investment opportunities in the industrial sector in the
past fifteen years have appeared limited, and where urban real
estate has come to constitute a favored depository for private, as
well as public, funds. The two dimensions limiting market size
most frequently of concern to observers of the Mexican scene—inequality in income distribution and lack of cultural homogeneity—
are clearly less in evidence. Furthermore, Simon Kuznets, summariz-
ing the results of his exhaustive statistical study of comparative
economic growth, observes that "the pattern of size distribution of
income characterizing underdeveloped countries today is not too
different from that observed in the presently developed countries in
the 1920's and 1930's, or at the beginning of the century—before
the recent trend toward narrower inequality," and he concludes
that "the unequal distribution of income in the presently developed
countries did not prevent rapid economic growth." [20] Thus the

[18] Phyllis Deane, "The Industrial Revolution and Economic Growth: The
Evidence of Early British National Income Estimates," *Economic Development
and Cultural Change*, Vol. V, No. 2 (January, 1957), pp. 167–168.

[19] See Adolph Strumthal, "Economic Development, Income Distribution, and
Capital Formation in Mexico," *Journal of Political Economy*, Vol. LXIII, No.
3 (June, 1955).

[20] Simon Kuznets, "Quantitative Aspects of the Economic Growth of Nations. VIII. Distribution of Income by Size," *Economic Development and Cultural Change*, Vol. XI, No. 2, Pt. II (January, 1963), pp. 68–69.

threat to the continued growth of the Mexican economy deriving from income inequality, as well as the stimulus to growth that would emerge as a result of measures that would increase equality, may be somewhat exaggerated in the recent discussion.

Concern for the future growth of the Mexican economy is a recurrent theme, however, that is by no means limited to preoccupations concerning the income distribution and the rate of expansion in market size. Absolute market size (or the national income) is frequently assumed to be an impediment to the development of capital-goods industries in Mexico, a logical "next step" in the process of industrialization. The present rate of growth (3.3 per cent per annum), however, will result in a doubling of the population of Mexico in two decades, and if the past rate of increase in per capita income persists, gross national product will surpass that of the European countries during the interwar period, when their capital-goods industries developed rapidly. Thus the development of these industries would not appear to be totally dependent upon the success of efforts to integrate Latin America economically.

The failure of export earnings and net long-term capital inflows to continue to increase could require that Mexico extend "import substitution" to capital goods "prematurely." Heretofore these products have been obtained more cheaply (in terms of labor and capital) by expanding exports and using the proceeds to acquire capital goods as well as industrial raw materials. The increased volume of capital that will be required to produce this equipment domestically presumably will result in a fall in the private (as well as the social) rate of return on investment, at least until such time as the market for capital goods expands to provide a market for the most economical scale of production. The government may thus be required to take the initiative in the development of the capital-goods industry through the Nacional Financiera and then await the day when the return on the invested capital will rise to the point where the industry can be sold to private investors at a price that will recover the initial investment. Otherwise it may protect the industry from foreign competition, permitting the price of capital goods to rise, in the hope of thus raising the private rate of return on investment to attract private interests into the industry. In either event, the development of these industries will tend to raise the marginal capital-output ratio and lower the rate of growth in the absence of an increase in the savings ratio. Heretofore, the Mexican economy has advanced very rapidly despite the fact that gross investment has never accounted for as much as 15 per cent of the gross national product; whereas numerous countries (including Argentina) whose rate of growth is significantly lower invest more than 20 per cent of their gross national product.[21] A low marginal capital-output ratio could reflect the fact that investment has been highly productive, or that technological advance and improvement in the quality of factor inputs, particularly labor, has increased output in enterprises where little or no investment occurs.[22]

The low marginal capital-output ratio in Mexico, however, may reflect the highly productive character of certain major capital projects in electrification, irrigation, transportation, and communication. In that event, since the superior investment opportunities have already been exploited, future investment will contribute progressively less to sustaining the rate of growth. Furthermore, as the economy eliminates progressively pockets of extremely low labor productivity (or "disguised unemployment"), the increase in output resulting from investment in modern plants and equipment can be expected to decline. Both factors are frequently cited to account for the retardation in the rate of growth that has been observed in the developed countries (see Table 1). Retardation, however, need not result in stagnation, as is apparent from the historical experience: "The industrial economy of the United Kingdom grew at an annual rate of between 2 and 3 per cent per annum in the period 1793–1817, between 3 and 4 per cent in the period 1818–1855, between 2 and 3 per cent in the period 1856-1876 and by less than 2 per cent in the period 1877–1935."[23] Thus, to judge by the symp-

[21] Another way of expressing this relationship between investment and the rate of growth of total output is that the marginal capital out-put coefficient has been substantially lower in Mexico than in Argentina. For values of this coefficient, see Pérez López, Table 5, in this volume. Victor Urquidi ("Fundamental Problems of the Mexican Economy," in this volume) calls for an increase in the investment ratio to 18–20 per cent of gross national product.

[22] As a result of technological advance and related means to improved efficiency, output per unit of tangible capital has risen by about 1 per cent per annum in the United States economy. See J. W. Kendrick, *Productivity Trends in the United States* (Princeton, N.J., Princeton University Press, 1961).

In Mexico, the next generation of industrial workers will have been reared in an urban environment and received more education than their parents. To judge by their basic endowments, labor productivity should increase.

[23] Phyllis Deane, "The Industrial Revolution," p. 170.

toms, the malady which afflicts Argentina and Chile is not that historically associated with industrial "old age" and, hence, is not inevitably the fate of the Mexican economy.

The maintenance of political consensus is clearly one factor that will influence both public and private investment and labor productivity as well as the continuing ability of governments to forestall demands for higher immediate levels of consumption. Despite the continuing efforts of Mexican intellectuals to sustain allegiance to principles of the Revolution and the political party currently recognized as its contemporary institutional counterpart, the cement binding the two and the vast majority of Mexico may deteriorate with the passage of time. Even in this event, however, the Revolution will have served as the cohesive force that was required to provide the political consensus necessary to launch the Mexican economy into a prolonged period of rapid economic growth. If the experience of the developed countries is relevant, then the economic institutions created in the process, the value orientation of those who have risen to form this new establishment, the common interest in the maintenance of the rate of growth, and the shared belief derived from the historical experience that the economy can grow rapidly should provide the cohesion required to sustain growth.

The length of the period of sustained growth required for the complete demolition of traditional, hierarchical values; for competition to eliminate adscription as a basis for selection; and for individuals to rely upon a competitive labor market for the requisite degree of economic security in lieu of the *patrón* (a role played by the State under "popular" Fascism) is yet to be determined, particularly for Mediterranean and non-Western cultures. The experience of Argentina indicates that it is longer than two decades, even though gross investment constitutes 15 per cent or more of the gross national product. Perhaps another necessary condition is that the demand for labor press hard enough on the available supply to raise labor's share in the total product.

In the following essays, six Mexican economists discuss the structure, performance, and problems of their economy. The emphasis is institutional rather than theoretical. The authors concentrate on the Mexican experience, and where comparative material is introduced, it relates to the developed countries, not generally to Latin America.

Three of these essays were written to be included in a memorial volume marking the fiftieth anniversary of the Mexican Revolution (1960), an event that consequently figures frequently in the text. The reader might easily gain the impression that five decades were devoted to the systematic construction of institutions, political as well as economic, designed to carry forward to the stage of bricks, mortar, and human organization a blueprint fashioned in 1917. Whether this happened in fact, or whether the spirit of the Revolution was successfully invoked to cloak with legitimacy institutional development and policies dictated by enfolding circumstances will be debated by Mexican intellectuals long after the term "traitor to the Revolution" has lost its pejorative connotation.[24] The fact remains that the blueprint was not so clearly drawn as to prevent successive Mexican governments from employing considerable latitude within which to reach decisions on matters of economic policy consistent with the principles of the Revolution. The economists represented here have, and will continue to have, influence, as *tecnicos*, in helping to set the limits within which the political decisions will ultimately be taken.

Despite the cohesion provided by these Revolutionary principles, several issues appear to divide this group (and economists generally). One such issue concerns the relationship between the maintenance of price stability and economic growth, and particularly the question as to whether or not restrictive monetary policy during the 1950's resulted in a lower rate of economic growth. Those who hold with the classical economists that the supply of capital limits the volume of investment are inclined to see monetary stability as a requisite for sustained economic growth. Those who believe, with the Keynesian economists, that investment demand frequently, if not generally, will fall short of the volume of capital supplied will view monetary restraint as a depressive factor limiting investment demand and hence capital formation and growth. Less conventional is the defense, by those economists who view capital as scarce, of

[24] In the meantime, foreign observers will offer their opinions as to whether the last year of the Cárdenas administration was a watershed in Mexican history. For the continuity hypothesis, see William P. Glade, Jr., "Revolution and Economic Development," in Glade and Anderson, *Political Economy in Mexico;* for the divergent view, Oscar Lewis, "Mexico since Cárdenas."

the efforts of the Bank of Mexico to allocate the available supply but to insist that the task becomes easier when inflation is not working to distort the investment pattern. Those who see the demand for investment falling short of the availability of capital are inclined to see less merit in the allocation system, insisting that the needs that are not met through the banking system are ultimately served through the *financieras* and other financial intermediaries.

With respect to taxation, the advocates of increases in public revenues and expenditures are those who consider that increased taxation would occur at the expense of private savings that are frequently untapped and that the expansion of public investment is required to provide a necessary additional stimulus to private investment. Rather than press the case for domestic taxation, those who view investment as retarded by shortage of savings are inclined to favor public borrowing abroad and are even tolerant of direct foreign investment. Probably no other subject elicits stronger feelings—for reasons that are readily apparent in the following quotation:

One misconstrues the real situation by thinking in terms of a fixed aggregate supply of capital, partly foreign and partly domestic, so that a sacrifice of foreign capital contributions is equated with a corresponding reduction in the total capital available to the economy. Were this the case, many of the measures of the Revolution would stand indicted as an uneconomic sacrifice of already scarce resources.[25]

The ultimate Mexicanization of enterprise constitutes a broadly shared objective. Any disagreement arises simply with respect to the rapidity with which this objective can be attained without compromising the rate of growth. Harmony depends to a large extent upon the continued success of public borrowing abroad, i.e., upon the replacement of direct, with portfolio, investment.[26] This replace-

[25] William P. Glade, Jr., in *Political Economy in Mexico*, p. 100.

[26] Mexico's net drawing on U.S. banks in 1963–1964 approximated $480 million and now exceeds $1 billion. In addition, long-term Mexican securities (amounting to $85 million face value) have been sold successfully in the New York financial market at gradually declining yields (7.00, 6.75, and 6.43 per cent, respectively). Even with unprecedented levels of foreign borrowing, however, the investment plans of the public sector had to be curtailed in early 1965 to avoid resurgence of inflationary pressures. Hence, full implementation of the capital budget of the public sector would appear to require additional tax revenues, which increasingly have been forthcoming from direct (and particularly income) taxes.

ment of direct investment with portfolio investment, with fixed schedules for the payment of interest and amortization, implies a steady growth of exports and foreign-exchange earnings, which in a world where so many currencies are not freely convertible, implies that markets must be found in the principal creditor countries. As a result optimism or pessimism concerning trade prospects, as well as consideration of domestic capital shortage or surplus, is necessarily linked to the length of the horizon envisaged for complete Mexicanization of enterprise.

Other examples of divergence will emerge clearly in these essays but the dominant impression is one of broad agreement—both with respect to the road that has been traversed and the decisions made along the way, as well as to the main outline of the map on which the future course is to be plotted.

The essays appear in the following order:

1. Enrique Pérez López ("The National Product of Mexico: 1895 to 1964") provides an overview of the development of the GNP in the Mexican economy and the structural changes that were imperative if basic social goals were to be implemented and the optimal adjustments to changing world conditions effected.

2. Ernesto Fernández Hurtado ("Private Enterprise and Government in Mexican Development") discusses the process of accommodation and cooperation between the private and public sectors that has contributed significantly to economic growth; he particularly stresses the role of agriculture.

3. Mario Ramón Beteta ("The Central Bank, Instrument of Economic Development in Mexico") describes central-bank policy and the functioning of the Central Bank. Control over credit and the banking system has the twin objectives of assuring stability and accelerating growth by optimally helping to allocate the supply of real savings among investment alternatives through its credit rationing.

4. Alfredo Navarrete R. ("The Financing of Economic Development") traces the sources of domestic savings that have provided 90 per cent of the capital employed in the Mexican economy since the Revolution.

5. Ifigenia M. de Navarrete ("Income Distribution in Mexico") demonstrates that rapid economic growth has not resulted in a more equitable income distribution.

6. Victor L. Urquidi ("Fundamental Problems of the Mexican

Economy") stresses the balanced growth that has been achieved by virtue of allocating public capital formation to basic infrastructure that aided in the development of agriculture as well as industry, and indicates the nature of the structural change that must occur if the economy is to continue to expand rapidly.

I. THE RECORD

The National Product of Mexico: 1895 to 1964
BY ENRIQUE PÉREZ LÓPEZ

Private Enterprise and Government in Mexican Development
BY ERNESTO FERNÁNDEZ HURTADO

The National Product of Mexico: 1895 to 1964*

ENRIQUE PÉREZ LÓPEZ

The aim of economic policy in Mexico is constantly to improve the welfare of the population through more efficient use of the country's productive capacity and through an increase in such capacity. Only within an expanding economy is it possible to solve the problems arising from the efforts of different social groups to obtain a larger share of the national product.

However, growth in the production of a nation's goods and services—as measured by national product—is not merely an economic phenomenon. Social, political, and cultural motivations also create and keep alive the impetus. The interdependence of factors is so complex even within the realm usually defined as economic that it is difficult to distinguish between cause and effect and even more difficult to evaluate the relative importance of each factor.

The purpose of this study is to give only a brief general view of the growth in Mexico's national product from 1895 to 1964 and of the changes in its composition by main activities, although some of the problems that Mexico has had to face will also be pointed out.

I. THE NATURE OF ECONOMIC DEVELOPMENT

The traditional structure of the economic, political, and social institutions within which economic activity takes place in the underdeveloped countries frequently leads to stagnation rather than to progress. One of the main reasons for this is the low level of income, which keeps savings and investment at a low rate, which in turn prevents income from rising.

* A revised text of the essay "El producto nacional," which appeared in *La Economía*, Vol. 1, *México: 50 años de revolución* (Mexico, D. F., Fondo de Cultura Económica, 1960), pp. 571–592.

Other factors are also responsible for stagnation or slow growth: a lack of entrepreneurship and of ability to organize and administer; a paucity of institutions providing financial capital; the tendency of high-income groups to spend on luxury consumption and non-productive investment; the use of primitive and inefficient techniques of production; and the limited exploitation of existing productive resources.

A primary condition for economic development has been the capacity of agriculture to produce a surplus of food for the consumption of those engaged in capital formation for the community. Because the latifundium system is not adapted to the need to create an agricultural surplus, it has become necessary to change land-tenure systems and farming methods.

The rate of economic development is also determined by the rate of population increase, by the rate of capital accumulation, by technical progress, and by shifts within the labor force—especially from agriculture to industry where productivity is higher—all of which raise production per capita.

Although there is no single way to speed up development, it can be said that the rate of capital formation is vital to sustained growth. Given favorable social, cultural, and political conditions, increases in output per capita depend on the expansion of productive equipment available to the labor force. In other words, to achieve the economic objectives of full employment, growth, and price stability, total output must exceed consumption.

When the rate of investment reaches a certain level, forces emerge which make possible an autonomous maintenance of the new levels of output, while unemployment or underemployment diminishes. The volume of investment must reach a point at which the rate of growth in total output outstrips the rate of population increase, thereby permitting a steady rise in real product per capita.

The marginal capital-output ratio is a crude indicator of the productivity of capital. This is the ratio between an increase in existing capital and an increase in output.

Thus, it can in general be stated that in order to accelerate the rate of growth, the amount of net investment in relation to the net national product obtained—that is, after allowance for depreciation of capital equipment—must be 10 per cent, for if the capital-output ratio is assumed to be 2, output will then grow more rapidly than population even though population may also increase substantially. This also means an increase in consumption per capita, subject to the pattern of income distribution, the rate of population increase, and the magnitude, type, and productivity of investment.

Furthermore, a higher level of investment provides more opportunities to improve productive techniques, because technological and scientific progress is usually incorporated into the productive process through capital formation.

One form of investment that is essential to a higher rate of economic development is the establishment of social overhead capital: energy, railroads, highways, irrigation, education, health, etc. It is usually the responsibility of governments to provide this economic infrastructure so that business enterprises may benefit from external economies and thereby raise their productivity.

From the standpoint of the general structure of output, the acceleration of development requires a sharp increase in the output of one or several sectors, where the very speed of growth may facilitate a take-off into sustained growth.

The construction of railroads, by reducing transportation costs, opening up new areas, and helping to market production, frequently has been the main energizer in economic growth. Similarly, the initial thrust toward steady growth in investment and production has been furnished in many countries by the impact of expanding exports on aggregate income, the result of which in turn has permitted higher domestic investment.

Once the economic take-off is accomplished, the community must reallocate its resources in order to continue to progress in other important sectors. Flexibility in reallocation of resources is a sign that sustained growth has actually been reached.

II. THE STAGES OF ECONOMIC GROWTH

A country's national product may be taken as a measure of its economic growth. However, study of the economic development of Mexico from 1895 to 1964 has been handicapped by the absence of systematic data until 1939, when the Bank of Mexico began to prepare such information. Therefore it has been necessary to link this series with other estimates of the national product for the years 1895 to 1910 and 1921 to 1938.[1]

[1] See the appended Methodological Note.

TABLE 1

Gross National Product, 1895–1964
(At 1950 Prices)

	1895	1910	1921	1929	1934	1945	1964
National product (millions of pesos)	8,863	13,524	14,560	16,666	15,927	30,494	93,200
Population (thousands)	12,632	15,160	14,335	16,296	17,776	22,233	39,643
Product per capita (pesos)	702	892	1,016	1,023	896	1,372	2,351
Indexes (base: preceding column = 100)							
Aggregate product		152.6	107.7	114.5	95.6	191.5	305.6
Agriculture		127.8	96.8	89.1	97.9	167.8	286.4
Livestock		120.0	105.8	104.0	113.4	186.5	214.2
Mining		237.1	59.7	259.8	67.9	117.3	133.0
Petroleum		......	5,300.0	32.4	108.6	182.5	477.2
Manufacturing		206.3	90.9	145.4	100.0	269.0	395.2
Transportation		144.6	139.3	174.5	101.3	182.9	305.7
Annual rates of growth (%)							
Product per capita		1.6	1.0	0.1	−2.6	3.9	2.9
Aggregate product		2.9	0.7	1.7	−0.9	6.1	6.1
Agriculture		1.6	−0.3	−1.4	−0.4	4.8	5.7
Livestock		1.2	0.5	0.4	2.5	5.8	4.1
Mining		5.9	−4.6	12.6	−7.5	1.5	1.5
Petroleum		...	43.0	−13.1	1.7	5.6	8.6
Manufacturing		5.0	−0.8	4.8	0.0	9.4	7.5
Transportation		2.5	3.1	7.2	0.3	5.6	6.1
Share in aggregate product (%)							
Agriculture	23.8	19.9	17.9	13.9	14.3	12.5	11.7
Livestock	9.6	7.5	7.4	6.7	8.0	7.8	5.5
Mining	4.9	7.5	4.2	9.5	6.8	4.1	1.8
Petroleum	...	0.1	6.9	2.0	2.2	2.1	3.3
Manufacturing	9.1	12.3	10.4	13.2	13.8	19.4	25.1
Transportation	2.3	2.2	2.8	4.3	4.6	4.4	4.4

Although it is not always advisable to divide the history of a nation's economic growth into strictly defined stages, in this case secular trends may more easily be traced through six separate periods: the first, prior to the Revolution, from 1895 to 1910; the second, corresponding to the establishment of the new regime, from 1910 to 1921; the third, mainly one of reconstruction, from 1921 to 1929; the fourth, covering the years of the world economic depression, from 1929 to 1934; the fifth, a time of accelerating development, from 1934 to 1945; the sixth and last, from 1945 to 1964, devoted to consolidation of development.

From 1895 to 1910, Mexico's national product increased at an annual rate of 2.9 per cent or at a per capita rate of 1.6 per cent. However, this was a period of rising rates of growth. Railroad construction had greatly encouraged economic activity through lowered transportation costs and expanded output for the market economy. It also helped to develop the export sector, principally mining, which grew at an annual rate of 5.9 per cent from 1895 to 1910.

Manufacturing increased at a rate of 5 per cent and transportation at 2.5 per cent per year. Agriculture and cattle raising, in spite of the stimulus provided by improved communications, went up at much lower rates—1.6 per cent and 1.2 per cent per year, respectively.

The share of agricultural and livestock output in national product declined during this period from 33 per cent to 27 per cent; that of mining, chiefly for export, rose from 5 per cent to 8 per cent; and that of manufacturing, notwithstanding a significant change in structure—from an essentially handicraft production to the first large-scale industries—went up only from 9 per cent to 12 per cent. The trends in this period already showed that agriculture was losing importance in Mexico and that mining, albeit subject to external market fluctuations, was coming to dominate the economy as a whole.

Although lack of statistical information for the period 1910-1921 does not permit an analysis of the annual changes in output by sectors, a comparison is possible of the initial and final years.

The weaknesses of the economic structure existing in 1910, which for some time had adversely affected Mexico's rate of growth, and the armed struggle that engulfed this period interrupted the country's economic development. Mining appears to have suffered most, owing especially to the disruption of railroads, and its output in

TABLE 2

Gross National Product, 1895–1910
(Millions of Pesos at 1950 Prices)

Year	Agricul- ture	Live- stock	Min- ing	Petro- leum	Manu- factur- ing	Transpor- tation	Sum of Preced- ing columns	Other Activ- ities	Total
1895	2,107	850	431	....	806	204	4,398	4,465	8,863
1896	2,093	862	442	....	937	200	4,534	4,603	9,137
1897	2,263	875	485	....	1,005	210	4,838	4,912	9,750
1898	2,461	887	531	....	1,016	225	5,120	5,198	10,318
1899	2,043	903	556	....	1,153	215	4,870	4,944	9,814
1900	1,991	907	541	....	1,232	237	4,908	4,983	9,891
1901	2,100	925	634	(0) [1]	1,444	227	5,330	5,411	10,741
1902	1,942	925	693	(0)	1,146	244	4,950	5,025	9,975
1903	2,157	964	746	(0)	1,379	258	5,504	5,588	11,092
1904	2,106	1,027	771	1	1,425	271	5,601	5,686	11,287
1905	2,543	1,017	848	1	1,475	299	6,183	6,277	12,460
1906	2,445	999	826	2	1,542	299	6,113	6,206	12,319
1907	2,716	1,005	858	5	1,591	297	6,472	6,570	13,042
1908	2,707	1,010	907	21	1,520	297	6,462	6,560	13,022
1909	2,701	1,016	961	14	1,664	296	6,652	6,753	13,405
1910	2,692	1,020	1,022	19	1,663	295	6,711	6,813	13,524

[1] (0) indicates less than 500,000 pesos.

1921 was not more than 60 per cent of the 1910 level. Manufacturing production declined by 9 per cent and agricultural output by 3 per cent.

In spite of the physical destruction of railroad equipment during the violent phase of the Revolution, transportation increased by 39 per cent, which is 3.1 per cent per year, because during this time internal combustion engines began to be widely used.

The most striking development of this period was the rapid growth of the petroleum industry, which hardly existed in 1910. By 1921, the industry's peak year until 1956, its output amounted to 7 per cent of the national product.

During this stage, aggregate national product increased by 7.7 per cent, or at a rate of just 0.7 per cent per year. Nevertheless, because population actually declined, the per capita product went up at a rate of 1 per cent per year.

During the eight years of reconstruction, Mexico barely recovered from the devastation of the Revolution. National product increased by 14.5 per cent, which is an annual average of 1.7 per cent, and the per capita product rose only slightly.

Recovery (1921–1929) permitted mining to increase its activity very rapidly—by 160 per cent—so that by 1929 its output had reached a record level. On the other hand, by 1929 the volume of activity in the petroleum industry had fallen to one-third of the 1921 level. Agricultural output declined by 11 per cent over the period. The reconstruction of railroads resulted in an unprecedented volume of transportation services, which increased 7.2 per cent annually. The output of the manufacturing industry expanded 4.8 per cent and that of the livestock industry 0.4 per cent per year.

In the midst of its slow recovery, Mexico's economy was hit by the world depression that started in the United States at the end of 1929. The five-year depression period, from 1929 to 1934, must be examined separately in order not to introduce a short-term cyclical fluctuation into the long-run trend of the economy and thereby distort the analysis.

National product dropped sharply and by 1932 had fallen below

TABLE 3

Gross National Product, 1921–1939
(Millions of Pesos at 1950 Prices)

Year	Agriculture	Livestock	Mining	Petroleum	Manufacturing	Transportation	Sum of Preceding columns	Other Activities	Total
1921	2,606	1,079	610	1,007	1,512	411	7,225	7,335	14,560
1922	2,599	1,085	829	949	1,522	410	7,394	7,505	14,899
1923	2,590	1,090	1,062	937	1,528	441	7,648	7,763	15,411
1924	2,582	1,096	1,064	851	1,466	464	7,523	7,636	15,159
1925	2,575	1,101	1,168	737	1,889	521	7,991	8,111	16,102
1926	2,917	1,106	1,299	647	2,111	523	8,603	8,732	17,335
1927	2,758	1,111	1,418	436	2,137	543	8,403	8,529	16,932
1928	2,947	1,117	1,484	359	2,082	567	8,556	8,684	17,240
1929	2,322	1,122	1,585	326	2,199	717	8,271	8,395	16,666
1930	1,975	1,081	1,435	321	2,189	710	7,711	7,827	15,538
1931	2,612	1,119	1,252	261	2,080	669	7,993	8,113	16,106
1932	2,320	1,109	868	269	1,524	606	6,696	6,798	13,494
1933	2,565	1,099	905	297	2,025	525	7,416	7,527	14,943
1934	2,273	1,275	1,077	354	2,199	726	7,904	8,023	15,927
1935	2,399	1,342	1,118	362	2,555	680	8,456	8,583	17,039
1936	2,623	1,407	1,172	338	2,896	741	9,177	9,314	18,491
1937	2,527	1,443	1,338	387	2,972	822	9,489	9,631	19,120
1938	2,612	1,418	1,345	375	3,100	814	9,664	9,809	19,473
1939	3,239	2,035	1,263	603	3,999	827	11,966	10,373	22,339

TABLE 4

Gross National Product, 1939–1959
(Millions of Pesos at 1950 Prices)

Year	Agriculture	Livestock	Mining	Petroleum	Manufacturing	Transportation	Construction	Electricity	Other Activities	Total
1939	2,926	1,434	1,220	383	3,348	864	488	110	9,732	20,505
1940	2,739	1,526	1,190	371	3,629	871	460	112	9,833	20,721
1941	3,185	1,574	1,209	398	4,058	897	512	112	11,344	23,289
1942	3,776	1,652	1,376	352	4,637	1,009	594	117	12,860	26,373
1943	3,607	1,639	1,387	363	4,882	1,169	672	122	13,517	27,358
1944	3,852	1,598	1,235	392	5,257	1,257	761	122	15,216	29,690
1945	3,703	1,494	1,319	487	5,732	1,244	846	137	17,047	31,959
1946	3,787	1,639	948	490	5,846	1,367	862	148	18,997	34,084
1947	4,250	1,778	1,239	551	5,681	1,378	887	160	18,593	34,517
1948	4,768	1,784	1,127	566	6,183	1,345	833	177	19,347	36,080
1949	5,249	1,805	1,117	611	6,676	1,557	781	193	19,638	37,627
1950	5,912	1,972	1,223	656	7,643	1,780	756	197	21,361	41,500
1951	6,273	1,952	1,162	724	8,100	1,852	846	219	23,372	44,500
1952	6,039	2,019	1,249	787	7,949	2,007	928	238	23,784	45,000
1953	6,385	2,049	1,209	825	1,968	2,064	871	254	22,775	44,400
1954	7,570	2,278	1,107	870	8,666	2,274	916	280	23,839	47,800
1955	7,750	2,416	1,198	1,003	9,623	2,388	1,009	312	26,801	52,500
1956	7,863	2,552	1,297	1,101	10,567	2,599	1,135	349	28,537	56,000
1957	8,178	2,642	1,345	1,219	11,234	2,786	1,273	376	28,947	58,000
1958	8,925	2,760	1,240	1,393	11,775	2,854	1,252	405	29,996	60,600
1959	8,700	2,888	1,297	1,625	12,644	2,945	1,307	435	31,559	63,400

its 1910 level. In 1933 it began to recover and by 1934 it was only 4 per cent lower than in 1929.

During those five years, mining and agricultural output declined by 32 per cent and 2 per cent, respectively. On the other hand, live-stock output went up by 13 per cent and petroleum production by 9 per cent. Manufacturing output and transportation services in 1934 were at the levels they had reached in 1929.

From 1934 to 1945, Mexico's economic development was more rapid, thanks to three sets of circumstances: recovery in the industrially developed countries, which increased demand for Mexico's exports; the land-reform policy and the expansion of public works; and the enormous stimulus to aggregate demand resulting from the Second World War.

The highest rate of growth was in manufacturing. With no war-time foreign competition at home and with new export prospects, its output during those eleven years increased by 169 per cent. By 1935, manufacturing accounted for 19 per cent of national product, while the share of agriculture and livestock had fallen to 20 per cent and that of mining and petroleum to 6 per cent. This meant that Mexico's economic structure had begun to change as its secondary activities gained and its primary activities declined in importance.

The steady increase in national product made it possible to accumulate savings that helped raise the rate of capital formation in the following stage.

Consolidation of economic development began after 1945. The advances in national production during the previous stage were the result of the profound structural changes—not only economic, but also political and social—brought about by the Mexican Revolution. Since the end of the Second World War, Mexico's national product has increased autonomously. The economic progress of the country has been solid. During this period, all the major sectors of the economy expanded substantially. Agricultural and livestock production went up by 159 per cent, petroleum output by 377 per cent, electric-power generation by 413 per cent, and manufacturing by 295 per cent. On the whole, national output, including services, increased by 206 per cent during the nineteen years of the period— an average annual rate of 6.1 per cent and twice the annual population increase of 3 per cent. This means that from 1945 to 1964, real per capita income expanded by 3 per cent per year.

TABLE 5

Gross National Product and Gross Domestic Investment, 1939–1964
(Millions of Pesos at 1950 Prices)

Year	Gross Product		Gross Investment[1]	Ratio of Investment to Product (%)	Marginal Capital-Output Ratio[2]
	Total	Increase			
1939	22,339	....	1,169	5.2	......
1940	22,588	249	1,600	7.1	......
1941	24,751	2,163	2,006	8.1	1.25
1942	26,291	1,540	1,728	6.6	1.14
1943	27,471	1,180	1,730	6.3	1.22
1944	29,676	2,205	2,206	7.4	1.47
1945	30,494	818	3,191	10.5	2.33
1946	32,319	1,825	4,391	13.6	3.00
1947	33,496	1,177	5,034	15.0	3.40
1948	34,987	1,491	4,712	13.5	3.07
1949	37,108	2,121	4,240	11.4	2.05
1950	40,577	3,469	4,828	11.9	1.66
1951	43,621	3,044	6,242	14.3	2.18
1952	45,366	1,745	6,483	14.3	4.52
1953	45,618	252	6,243	13.7	4.46
1954	50,391	4,773	6,509	12.9	2.02
1955	54,767	4,376	7,288	13.3	1.77
1956	58,214	3,447	8,605	14.8	2.13
1957	62,708	4,494	9,116	14.5	2.23
1958	66,177	3,469	8,652	13.1	2.72
1959	68,119	1,942	8,699	12.8	2.88
1960	73,482	5,363	10,008	13.6	2.55
1961	76,038	2,556	10,141	13.3	2.90
1962	79,691	3,653	10,044	12.6	2.84
1963	84,700	5,009	11,056	13.0	2.13
1964	93,200	8,500	13,631	14.6	....

[1] Preliminary data estimated by Bank of Mexico.
[2] Adjusted by means of moving averages.

This rate of growth is largely attributable to the increase in capital formation, which accounted for 15 per cent of gross national product, that is, approximately 10 per cent of net national product. From 1945 to 1964, gross domestic investment went up by 327 per cent in real terms, at an annual rate of 7.9 per cent. The private sector carried out 60 per cent of such investment and the public sector supplied the remainder. Nevertheless, this rapid increase in investment has not prevented growth in real consumption per inhabitant.

To achieve these basic changes in the relationship of the different sectors of production and to promote growth, it has been necessary to follow a policy of active government intervention. In a country such as Mexico, just as in the large industrial countries, the price mechanism cannot be exclusively relied upon to counteract market forces leading to stagnation. Public investment in Mexico has not been simply the compensatory device usually employed in developed countries, but has been decisive in increasing overall investment and, in turn, raising the rate of growth.

Public funds have been allocated mainly to investment in the economic infrastructure needed to augment general productivity and to induce expansion of private enterprise throughout the economy. In investing in social overhead capital, the government has deliberately created surplus capacity—a characteristic of this type of investment—because in the long run it is more economic. If a country undertakes a large number of major infrastructure projects that require several years to be completed and even longer to be fully utilized, the capital-output ratio will tend to be high at the outset; but this does not mean that these investments are less efficient for economic development.

The Mexican government has gone even further and promoted the establishment of many essential manufacturing industries which, given the size of the investment or the initial risk involved, do not attract private investment.

On the other hand, apart from the creation of basic facilities leading to external economies, private investment has been encouraged by several other means: by tariff protection for import replacement, by tax exemption, and by public loans. The government has also favored domestic industry in its purchases of goods and services. Domestic savings have financed most investment in Mexico; foreign savings have been only supplementary.

Public investment has been financed primarily out of tax revenues and other current receipts of the federal government and its agencies. Private investment has been largely financed out of business savings, including depreciation allowances, and out of individual savings. Only a small part of the resources needed to finance the increase in fixed capital has been obtained from the banking system through an expansion in the money supply.

Capital formation, which steadily raised productive capacity, enabled Mexico to maintain a rate of growth of 6.1 per cent per year in spite of a series of unfavorable circumstances, such as the United

States recessions of 1946, 1949, 1954, and 1958; the decline in the international prices of Mexico's leading exports; and the bad crop years of 1952, 1953, and 1957.

From 1945 to 1964, the rates of growth by sectors were as follows: petroleum, 8.6 per cent, mostly to meet mounting domestic demand; manufacturing industries, 7.5 per cent; transportation, 6.1 per cent; agriculture, 5.7 per cent; and cattle raising, 4.1 per cent. The last two sectors grew at a higher rate than in any previous period. Agriculture has become Mexico's principal source of foreign exchange, while mining has stagnated.

By 1964, agricultural and livestock production accounted for 17 per cent of national product, whereas in 1895 and 1921 they represented 33 per cent and 25 per cent, respectively. The share of the extractive industries has fallen to 5 per cent of national product, petroleum production has gone up, and mining has remained unchanged. The share of manufacturing output in the total has reached 25 per cent. It is evident that Mexico's economic structure has been changing gradually, with a larger participation of secondary activity and a steady trend to diversification. This trend, conspicuous in exports, has permitted Mexico in recent years to offset fluctuations in external demand.

To summarize: The rate of growth of Mexico's national product accelerated after 1934 and a high rate has been sustained on the average since 1945. This has made it possible for the rate of capital formation and the diversification of output to continue to raise per capita product. As the latter has gone up, Mexico's economic structure has come to resemble that of an industrialized country, a status creating different economic problems. How Mexico approaches these new problems and solves them will determine whether its income and standard of living will go on improving or will stagnate.

III. THE PROBLEMS OF ECONOMIC DEVELOPMENT

Economic development involves a whole series of very complex problems. Mexico's problems will now be discussed in terms of three main considerations: imbalance between different sectors of output; growth and monetary stability; and dependence on foreign countries, or the external sector. The following sections analyze in a general manner the problems now confronting Mexico.

Imbalance between Sectors

In the underdeveloped countries, especially because their principal sectors are not very well integrated, utilization of the surplus output available to raise productive capacity presents a number of serious problems.

Imports aside, the proportion of total output allocated to investment can be increased only by expanding the capital-goods industries at a higher rate than the consumer-goods industries. If the structure of supply does not change appropriately, the rate of growth will decline, not because of the community's inability to generate sufficient savings to finance an adequate rate of investment, but because of rigidity in the structure of investment, which prevents the system from supplying itself with the capital goods required.

This problem arises because investment plays a dual role in the increase in output. On the one hand, expenditure on buildings, plants, and equipment is one of the components of demand for current output; on the other hand, it expands existing productive capacity. If during a given period, the structure of demand does not respond to that of the supply made possible by existing capital, some sectors of the economy will have excess capacity whereas others with insufficient productive capacity will be subject to scarcities.

The structure of output in underdeveloped countries adapts only slowly and imperfectly to changes in the rate and composition of demand, so that resources, manpower, land, and even industrial plants are not fully utilized.

The supply of certain basic goods is constricted by the immobility of productive resources, which in turn results mainly from an inadequate rate of capital formation, although it is also affected by social and cultural conditions.

In Mexico the structure of production has changed gradually and adapted itself to the needs of growth according to the different rates of investment in the several sectors of the economy. But given the different capital-output ratios prevailing in the various sectors, the ratio of aggregate investment to aggregate output depends on the distribution of investment by economic sectors. These ratios are higher in energy, transportation, and communications and lower in manufacturing, commerce, and services.

Because the output of some sectors is the input of others, the rate of growth of total output is largely contingent upon maintaining a suitable equilibrium between the rates of the growth of the different sectors.

Consequently, Mexico's economic development requires a policy aimed at achieving a dynamic equilibrium between the rates of growth of output in the principal sectors of economic activity, that is, between agriculture and manufacturing, between consumer-goods industries and capital-goods industries, and especially between exports and imports.

Growth and Monetary Stability

Obviously a sound economic policy must have as its objectives both growth and stability. Mexico does not need to choose between a higher rate of growth without monetary stability and a lower rate of growth with monetary stability. A policy of inflation not only will not increase the amount of real resources but will actually lead to misuse of resources and therefore will retard rather than accelerate growth.

Inflation does great damage to economic development. It raises the share of national income going to the sectors that receive profits and reduces the share of the fixed-income sectors, thus confining the market and creating social unrest. It also stimulates those investments that are least desirable for economic development, for example, speculation with inventories, real estate, and foreign exchange. Furthermore, it reduces voluntary savings, discourages expansion of the securities market, and leads to inefficient utilization of resources. Finally, inflation itself tends to turn into a wage-price spiral.

Price stabilization eliminates an artificial stimulus to production and, as the experience of many underdeveloped and developing countries shows, a stable price level is not inconsistent with a rapid rate of growth.

Inflation in underdeveloped countries is a very complex phenomenon. Although it may have some specific origin, once underway it is usually subject to a combination of influences.

On the one hand, the maladjustment between consumption and investment needs, within the limits set by productive capacity, may on certain occasions bring about inflationary pressures. That is, differences in the rates of growth of the various sectors of production induce inflationary pressures on the supply side. Difficulties in the supply of consumers goods, especially foodstuffs—which do not respond immediately to increases in demand—frequently have resulted in higher prices for foodstuffs and a fall in real wages, thereby hindering the growth of investment and output.

On the demand side, inflationary pressures in the underdeveloped countries arise mainly from efforts to raise real income as development takes place. Often these efforts have led to inflationary financing of investment through the banking system. When the latter has financed an increase in the gold and exchange reserves and in the working capital of business enterprises, there is usually very little surplus of funds for noninflationary long-term financing. Consequently, aggregate demand outstrips existing productive capacity.

The basic problem of economic development is the attainment of a large volume of investment in order to maintain growth in the face of insufficient savings.

There is no doubt that Mexico's productive resources are not fully utilized, that there are resources that are not used at all, and others that are only partially used. In industrial countries, an increase in investment is not necessarily inflationary when there are idle resources available, because it generates higher incomes that provide the marginal savings required. In the case of Mexico, such unutilized resources are to be considered as only potential resources and are not real capacity ready to be used whenever effective demand increases through monetary expansion.

In other words, the problem is not a lack of effective demand, but an insufficiency of productive capacity. This capacity can be raised, especially through further investment, but only if inflation is avoided by means of an increase in real savings.

Investment has to be financed out of real savings, chiefly domestic, supplemented by foreign savings within the country's payments capacity. Real savings should originate mainly outside the banking system.

Mexico must also take into account the effect that a policy of monetary expansion will have on its balance of payments and on its exchange stability. The experience of underdeveloped countries has confirmed the close relationship between domestic price level and balance of payments. Inflation is a cumulative process that leads to external imbalance. Because of higher costs, exporters cut back output of exportable products, while these products tend to rise in price and become less competitive in the world market; imports of consumer goods increase and domestic output of import substitutes is adversely affected; foreign investment is discouraged and the hoarding of gold and foreign exchange is induced. The resultant balance-of-payments deficit drains the monetary reserves of the country and makes it difficult to maintain the exchange rate. However, devaluation alone is not likely to reestablish a lasting equilibrium between internal and external prices.

In the short run, economic stability is dependent on monetary and fiscal policy. If sectoral pressures on prices are to be avoided, a balance between the structure of demand and that of existing productive capacity is essential. This requires a reallocation of resources over a long period which, to preserve the flexibility of the economic system, should be done without resorting to direct government price-and-wage controls and without stimulating uneconomic industries.

Monetary policy is only a part of a country's general economic policy for limiting total expenditure to the capacity for growth implied in available real resources. This general policy also includes fiscal policy as well as nonfinancial measures that may help to adjust demand to supply. Monetary policy is a more flexible instrument, because it can be adapted to immediate requirements. However, just as any other measure aimed at changing the level of aggregate expenditure, it is not effective at once.

Undoubtedly a country needs monetary stability to attain its growth targets and to sustain economic expansion free from artificial distortions that may adversely affect output and the distribution of goods and services.

The External Sector

In Mexico, the export sector has played an important role in encouraging domestic investment and, therefore, the growth of national product.

The problems of maintaining external equilibrium are much more complex than those of achieving growth with domestic stability. Mexico, like all underdeveloped countries, contends with a special problem in raising the rate of its capital formation, because a large part of investment takes place through foreign trade. Capital goods must be imported and paid for with foreign-exchange receipts derived chiefly from exports of raw materials. The limited capacity of domestic industry to produce capital goods means that resources must be allocated to exports with which to finance imports. But it is not always easy to transfer production resources to the export sector, owing to the rigidity of the economic structure and the low rate of investment.

Furthermore, an increase in exports depends not only on a country's ability to expand its output of exportable commodities, but also on its export prospects. Therefore, a higher rate of savings may result in less output or in an accumulation of unsold stocks, instead of in more foreign-exchange earnings.

This means that even if a country allocates sufficient resources to produce the export goods needed to finance its investment demand as represented by imports of capital goods, the size of foreign demand will still determine the growth of its exports.

Should the domestic supply of foodstuffs not respond adequately to the increase in demand generated by the higher rate of investment, it will become necessary to import such foodstuffs in order to support consumption levels. The consequent decline in imports of capital goods will depress national economic activity. Mexico has almost completely overcome this difficulty by concentrating on the development of its agricultural sector.

The domestic and external aspects of these complicated problems are interwoven. The domestic solution lies in a satisfactory rate of development and diversification of economic activity to offset the effects of unfavorable factors and prevent them from becoming cumulative. But the lack of diversification of output and exports is compounded by the instability of external markets. As is well known, the terms of trade of underdeveloped countries that export primary products and import manufactured goods have deteriorated.

The sharp fluctuations in world prices of raw materials upset the internal equilibrium of underdeveloped countries. When prices go up, inflationary pressures are transmitted from the developed to the underdeveloped countries. When prices decline, inflationary pressures are intensified, because ordinarily it is not possible to readjust the domestic economy to the falling export prices.

Since the Second World War, the underdeveloped countries have found it increasingly difficult to maintain their balance-of-payments equilibrium. World demand for raw materials has fallen behind world demand for manufactures because output in the industrial countries has increased more rapidly than their demand for imported raw materials. In these conditions, maintaining external equilibrium widens the gap between the living standards of underdeveloped and developed countries. Furthermore, in their need and desire to progress, the underdeveloped countries have augmented their imports of capital goods, industrial raw materials, and even foodstuffs more rapidly than they have expanded their national output.

Therefore, international equilibrium has been disrupted, and it will not be restored so long as a country's rate of development does not permit its mounting demand for imports to be matched by a greater world demand for its exports. Underdeveloped countries like Mexico will not achieve internal equilibrium unless they curtail imports of capital goods and industrial raw materials. External equilibrium will thus be at the expense of a country's economic progress and its share in world trade.

The stabilization of world prices and demand for primary products is complicated by the following contingencies: climatic conditions affecting the supply of some agricultural products; increments in industrial or agricultural productivity; methods of disposal of agricultural surpluses; the lag in demand for food as incomes rise; the increasing self-sufficiency of industrial countries in respect of primary products; structural changes in supply and demand resulting from technological progress that reduces the utilization of primary products and promotes the competition of substitutes; and fluctuations in the economic activity of the industrial countries.

Economic stability in industrial countries, though of cardinal importance, does not ensure a firm demand for primary products, for even slight changes in final demand or in stocks in the developed countries may have serious repercussions on the exchange receipts of the countries producing the raw materials.

For the underdeveloped countries, a relatively small change in foreign markets for basic products may mean the difference between prosperity and depression, between inflation and deflation, and between adequate exchange reserves and the need to impose trade and exchange restrictions. Comparatively moderate price fluctuations in primary products may mean the difference between a rising or a declining capacity to import, between a balanced budget or a government deficit, and between expanding or contracting consumption or investment.

The fundamental solution is to progressively replace imports as an element of aggregate expenditure. This process has had more success with foodstuffs because domestic output of manufactures cannot be increased without further imports of not only capital goods but of fuel, raw materials, and intermediate products. Countries like Mexico, which have already reached a middle level of industrialization, find it very difficult to keep their imports from rising excessively—and even more so if their industrial organization is not well balanced. They also encounter difficulties in exporting their manufactures, owing to the protectionist reaction of the developed countries.

International loans and direct foreign investment have brought relief to a number of countries, but, in general, the volume and direction of these long-term capital movements during the postwar period have not sufficed to meet the trade deficits of most of the underdeveloped countries. These countries have lost gold and foreign exchange and have had to restrict imports. In fact, underdeveloped countries have presently a much lower ratio of net inflow of private long-term capital to value of exports than thirty years ago, and most of that capital has gone into the petroleum industry.

Public loans and grants have more than offset the relative decline of private capital, but since the 1920's public funds have contributed barely over two dollars per year per inhabitant to the capacity to import and therefore to the economic development of the underdeveloped nations, where two-thirds of the world's population live.

External capital is only a temporary solution. In the final analysis, a country cannot grow at a satisfactory rate and achieve a diversified economic structure unless it can finance investment out of its own savings without inflationary pressures and adapt its economy to world demand as well as to changes in domestic demand. Mexico has already diversified its exports and receives additional foreign earnings from tourism to help it counteract fluctuations in external markets.

The underdeveloped countries will not be able by themselves to stabilize world demand and prices for their primary products. The solution to this problem must come through international cooperation.

Admittedly, deficit countries should take measures to balance their payments by correcting maladjustments in their economies, for steady growth involves more than the international prices of raw materials. Disequilibrium becomes more serious when resources are not used rationally and also when inflationary financing of investment is resorted to as a means of accelerating growth.

It seems clear, however, that the developed countries are in a much better position to make the readjustments needed to avoid excessive fluctuations in prices and demand for basic products. This is only a marginal problem for the industrial countries, where the rate of growth derives mainly from domestic output of manufactured goods and not from exports to underdeveloped countries. Any reduction in domestic output that might result from lifting restrictions on imports would affect a relatively small proportion of domestic consumption and, on the other hand, would substantially increase purchases of basic products from abroad.

The principal economic concern of the world today is to create favorable conditions for long-term growth, especially in the poor nations. Therefore the economic policy of the large industrial countries should be guided by national and international considerations benefiting both themselves and the underdeveloped countries. They should abolish restrictions on imports from the underdeveloped countries, give up the protection of certain domestic products, reduce excise taxes on basic products, and increase the flow of capital to developing nations.

Gradually the industrial countries have come to recognize that the problems relating to basic products are closely linked to economic development in the underdeveloped countries, and they have become persuaded that the progress of these countries is not only a desirable international goal but also a condition for their own progress and security.

To strengthen and expand national economies throughout the world and to solve both the external and internal problems of economic growth, a means must be found to bring about multilateral cooperation between nations.

Methodological Note on the Estimates of Mexico's Gross National Product, 1895–1964

Throughout this study, gross national product and its composition by sectors are given at 1950 prices. National income has not been estimated owing to the lack of reliable data on depreciation and indirect taxes. For the same reason, factoral income distribution by wages, profits, rent, etc. has not been analyzed.

Although the aggregate corresponds to gross national product, data for sectors refer to gross domestic product. An overall adjustment for net factor payments to the rest of the world has been made implicitly in the column headed "Other Activities."

A. Methodology for the Period 1895–1939

These estimates are based on published data for 1939. The proportional distribution of the 1939 total domestic product by sectors, as given in the Combined Mexican Working Party's report (*The Economic Development of Mexico* [Baltimore, The Johns Hopkins Press, 1953]), was assumed to be valid also for gross national product.

Each of the sectors was then extrapolated back to 1895 by means of indices of the volume of output in the different activities. Activities for which no estimates were available were calculated annually on the assumption that their ratio to total product remained unchanged.

Production-volume indices were calculated for agriculture, livestock, mining, petroleum, the manufacturing industry, and transportation.

In the almost complete absence of information for the period 1911 to 1920, no estimates were attempted for these years. Furthermore, when no data were available for certain items in the years approximating this period, a simple linear interpolation was made.

All the indices were Laspeyres indices with changing weights. They were suitably linked whenever the number of items included had to be reduced because of lack of information.

The index of agricultural output was calculated from data for 1924–1939 published by the Office of Rural Economy of the Ministry of Agriculture; and for the years prior to 1910, from data in the *Anuarios Estadísticos de Peñafiel*. These figures were adjusted to eliminate errors in the output of corn and beans. The adjustments were made on the basis of the 1929, 1939, and 1949 agricultural censuses as well as on the basis of a consumption survey carried out in 1942 and an agricultural survey conducted in 1954.

Estimates of livestock output were based on the slaughter of cattle for consumption in the post-Revolutionary period and were linked with estimates made by the Colegio de México for 1895 to 1911.

The index of mining production was prepared with data from the statistical yearbooks on mining.

Petroleum output was calculated in two stages: from 1900 to 1922, a simple index of production of crude; and from 1922 to 1929, an index including the principal processed products together with exports of crude petroleum.

The index of industrial production was computed on the basis of industrial commodities produced in Mexico according to data in the 1939 and 1940 statistical yearbooks (General Bureau of Statistics). The necessary links were introduced in carrying the calculation backward to earlier years when the number of commodities was smaller.

For transportation, an index of volume of services in each means of transport was prepared with weights taken from the 1939 transportation census. This index includes an independent estimate of haulage by draft animals.

All calculations for this period were prepared by Miguel Flores Márquez and should be considered provisional.

B. Methodology for the Period 1939–1964

Use was made of preliminary data prepared by the Bank of Mexico on the basis of its input-output table for 1950.

For the period after 1951 and for 1939–1949, annual changes in product were estimated by extrapolating value added in each of the economic activities by means of indices of volume of output of goods and services. These indices were calculated from various statistics from official and private sources, supplemented by data from the censuses and direct surveys.

In the case of commerce, the flow-of-goods method was adopted. A computation of commercial transactions was made from data on production and imports, classified according to the final use of the goods.

The Laspeyres formula was used for the calculation of all indices.

For additional details on methodology and sources of information employed by the Bank of Mexico, see "Revisión preliminar de las estimaciones del producto nacional de México" ("Preliminary Revision of Estimates of Mexico's National Product") in *Comercio Exterior* (Banco Nacional de Comercio Exterior, México, D.F., September, 1963).

All estimates by the Bank of Mexico are preliminary and are subject to change in the light of research now in progress.

Private Enterprise and Government in Mexican Development*

ERNESTO FERNÁNDEZ HURTADO

The Mexican Revolution, which began in 1910, was the nation's most important attempt to modify and give new vitality to a social and economic order that had been characterized by agrarian feudalism, a slowly evolving industrial structure, and an all-powerful political group who permitted the country to progress only to the extent that existing forces would be maintained without any significant change in structure and balance.

A study of the roles played by private enterprise and government in development should single out the factors that determine the behavior of the private and public sectors in economic activity, in order to analyze the changes that those factors have undergone. Of course, political, social, and economic elements are interdependent in an endless circle of cause and effect. But an analysis of this interrelation, if it is to lead to any valid conclusion, must identify fundamental causes and clearly and precisely connect them with their corresponding effects.

In Mexico, investment and economic activity—both public and private—are closely linked to persons or groups whose attitudes, though largely decided by their circumstances and resources, basically depend on their concept of the way in which a desired objective should be achieved.

I. MEXICO GLIMPSES PROGRESS

After the internal wars and foreign invasions of the nineteenth century, Mexico appeared, at least superficially, to be ready to begin

*Originally published as "La iniciative privada y el Estado como promotores del desarrollo," in *La Economía*, Vol. I, *México: 50 años de revolución* (México, D.F., Fonda de Cultura Económica, 1960) , pp. 593–619.

capitalistic development, a stage already reached in Europe and in more than one American country.

Mexico's vast territory was supposed to offer great mining and agricultural possibilities in areas still sparsely populated or hardly explored. Public security and respect for the law had been established and were zealously maintained. Other nations considered the government of Porfirio Díaz to be stable and, above all, respectable. Recently discovered riches in oil and nonferrous metals opened up important sources of, and new prospects for, economic activity and exports.

At that time, a thriving mining industry in the interior that had to be connected with its external markets attracted foreign investment, especially in railroad lines, communications, urban transport, and electric energy.

Economic philosophy was at its peak and nations joyously practiced a policy of *laissez faire*. The success of the spectacular industrial development of the nineteenth century was attributed wholly to economic liberalism. The governments of Latin America, overwhelmed by the problems of pacifying and consolidating their territories, did not realize that Europe's industrialization was tied to the existence of powerful national economies.

In Europe, industrialization rested on a broad base of farmers and on large urban populations whose standard of living was very high compared to that of Latin America's indigenous population. This standard of living was supported by high agricultural yields, the highest in the world; by incomes and markets furnished by colonial possessions acquired in preceding centuries; and by Europe's absolute control of world trade.

In one after another of the European countries and in those massive transplants of European populations, the United States and the English provinces of Canada, with the culture and production and consumption habits of their mother country, the pattern was repeated: steady industrial development, sustained by a domestic demand for consumer and producer goods and by the demand of the raw-materials-producing countries on the economic periphery.

The "Porfirian" Concept of Development

Porfirio Díaz applied in Mexico the economic liberalism that he saw triumph as a reality in the civilized European world of his time.

The group that directed his policies, in the face of opposition—sometimes violent—from members of the legislature, assumed that by attracting foreign capital to develop mining, to construct an extensive network of railways, to provide electric power, and to establish consumer industries, the entire country automatically would embark on an industrialization not very different from that of the most advanced nations.

In agriculture, it appeared necessary to protect the hacienda system and maintain a peaceful countryside so that the new techniques of crop rotation, fertilizers, and mechanized farming would improve yields and raise rural incomes as dramatically in Mexico as they had in the temperate-zone countries of the Old and New Worlds.

Foreign Investment Does Not End Stagnation

The regime resolved to attract foreign capital in amounts never before witnessed in Latin America, and it was successful.

Although figures on foreign investment during that period are uncertain, it is estimated that from 1870 to 1908 United States investment in Mexico amounted to $800 million.[1] In 1911, an American observer[2] calculated that United States capital in Mexico reached $1,044.6 million, representing approximately 40 per cent of some $2,343 million of aggregate investment in the country.[3] British investment, which at the end of 1880 was estimated at 32.7 million pounds sterling, by 1910 had tripled to 98.4 million.[4]

Even taking into account the tendency of foreign investors—or commentators—to include the value of concessions and subsoil rights with that of capital actually imported from abroad, there is no doubt that during the regime of Porfirio Díaz foreign capital flowed into the country in quantities proportionately much greater—in relation to national capital and the natural and human resources of Mexico—than the volume of European capital that entered the United States during its period of most intensive development. Not-

[1] Jorge Espinosa de los Reyes, *Relaciones económicas entre México y los Estados Unidos, 1870–1910* (México, D.F., Nacional Financiera, 1951) .

[2] William H. Seamon, in the *Daily Consular Reports* of the U.S. Government.

[3] Other estimates arrive at $750 million for United States investment in Mexico in 1907.

[4] J. Fred Rippy, *British Investments in Latin America, 1922–1945* (Minneapolis, University of Minnesota Press, 1959) .

withstanding all this, the regime of Porfirio Díaz failed completely in its objective of industrializing the country and of increasing the productivity and income of the rural masses.

In industrialization, national industrial enterprises were not expanded and diversified. Foreign capital went principally into the exploitation of natural resources—mining and oil—and the construction of railways: in 1908, 82 per cent of United States investment was in mining, petroleum, and railways. These investments created only a small demand for domestic manufactures; and even the industries established in the country to manufacture such goods as textiles, foodstuffs, shoes, and iron and steel products were largely financed by foreign capital and were limited to the production of the most indispensable consumer goods and raw materials. In fact, they were isolated enterprises that did not spread to the rest of the economy.

The middle and upper classes in Mexico hardly participated in the establishment of new enterprises. The wealthy Mexican occupied himself only in the absentee administration of his hacienda, and the bourgeois, educated mainly in the liberal professions, had neither the technical training nor the incentive to apply, to any appreciable extent, his modest experiences in the field of industry.

The Mexican economy did not respond as expected to the huge inflow of foreign capital, nor did it succeed in creating a broad domestic demand for manufactured goods. Therefore the country was unable to "take off" into the process of industrial growth.

The stagnation was derived, fundamentally, from the failure of the Porfirio Díaz regime to solve the problem of Mexico's extremely low agricultural productivity—to a large extent the same problem that faces the Mexico of today and tomorrow. The rural population, cultivating land with very low yields per hectare, made up 80 per cent of the total population in 1910—at present it represents 55 per cent—and raised almost exclusively corn, beans, sugarcane, and other foodstuffs.

Progress in agriculture, which until that time had been carried on with primitive techniques and, for the most part, in mountainous and arid soil, required an approach and a solution carefully thought out and resolutely applied. Agriculture was not likely to be affected by investment concentrated in the extractive or urban industries. Neither could the country be industrialized so long as its economy depended solely on its small urban mining centers. The semifeudal system of the Mexican hacienda was aided and abetted by the government of that period. Once moderate output had been achieved through the extensive cultivation of large holdings—thanks to a subdued countryside—no attempt was made to ensure progressive increments in yield per hectare or in average rural income. Rural income even lagged behind levels of agricultural productivity, because of low wages and a system of servitude based on the exploitation of surplus labor.

Many of the railway enterprises soon found themselves in difficulties for lack of freight, although they had been planned primarily for the export of minerals and other raw materials. The little impact made on the national economy by the mining and petroleum industries, which paid poor wages in line with the low incomes of villages in agricultural regions, was limited to the taxes they paid the government. The rest of the economy continued to be rural, with a standard of living comparable to that of certain Asian colonies and, unless Mexico's economic and social policies changed completely, apparently without hope of improvement.

As seen now, this was the situation in Mexico in 1910. When, in that year, the first shots of the great drama were fired, it was evident that the regime of Porfirio Díaz had failed not only politically, but, above all, economically.

After thirty years of peace, of extensive foreign investment, of economic liberalism and the protection of large landholdings, the average annual per capita income of the Mexican people was equivalent to only about $80 (at 1950 U.S. prices). This situation could not continue without causing a great social upheaval in a nation that shared a 2,500-kilometer border with the United States, a country that already enjoyed the highest standard of living and level of economic development in the world. Nowhere else at the beginning of the twentieth century did a common border join two nations with such disparate standards of living. It was not by mere chance that the armed rebellion drew upon men from the northern part of the country.

Before and After

The year 1930 marks the point when, after twenty years of armed conflict, the country began to heal its wounds and fulfill the objectives of the Revolution; beginning with that date, therefore, the Revolution's achievements can be analyzed statistically.

At 1950 prices, Mexico's gross national income in 1910 is estimated at 13,429 million pesos—almost the same amount, 14,733 million pesos, that represented the gross national product in 1930. On the other hand, in 1959, [5] the gross national product reached, also at 1950 prices, 63,430 million pesos, which represents a real increase to five times the gross product of 1910 or 1930, with only a doubling of the population. In 1959, the gross product of the manufacturing industry had increased in real terms to more than seven times the 1930 level, whereas urban population had grown only two and a half times (see Table 1).

Other activities engaged in by the urban population increased in similar proportions: transport multiplied its services and income four and a half times; trade, electric power, finance, and government quadrupled their activities in real terms; the petroleum industry expanded its producing and processing volumes sixfold; only the extraction of minerals remained stagnant, for reasons that are well known.

Agricultural production and livestock raising also increased dramatically over the 1930 level: the first, to four and a half times; and the second, to two and a half times. Since rural population only grew 66 per cent, there was an important increase in per capita agricultural output. The significance of this increase in agricultural productivity per rural inhabitant should be carefully considered in the light of the problems that low rural incomes have placed in the way of national development.

As a result of the steady increase in the output of goods and services—both agricultural and industrial—proportionately much higher than population growth, the average per capita income of the country in 1959 was more than twice that of 1910 or 1930.

What happened to permit a very important increase in productivity and average income in the thirty years of Revolutionary peace following 1930 that did not occur in the thirty years of peace during the Porfirio Díaz regime?

In 1930 agricultural production had fallen, and the railway system had been largely disrupted. After twenty years of fighting and consequently of failure to pay debts, Mexico's external credit had

[5] Gross national product data quoted in this essay, written in 1960, for the period 1950–1959 have recently (1963) been revised. The changes do not materially alter conclusions in the text.

TABLE 1

Gross National Product[1]
(Millions of Pesos at 1950 Prices)

Sector	1910	1930	1959
Total	13,429	14,773	63,400
	—	—	—
Agriculture	2,308	1,800	8,193
Livestock raising	919	1,004	2,514
Mining	955	1,337	1,270
Petroleum	13	247	1,488
Manufacturing	1,653	1,776	13,062
Transport	369	582	2,687
Other[2]	7,212	8,027	34,186

[1] Preliminary data, subject to revision.
[2] Includes forestry, fishing, construction, electric power, trade, financial services, government, rents, interest, and indirect taxes and depreciation allowances.

deteriorated to the point that direct and indirect investment of foreign capital had ceased. Moreover, there had been a substantial emigration of the middle class to the southern United States, and the agrarian policy already initiated by the Revolutionary governments had caused not only the former large landowners but also many farmers with agricultural and marketing skills to seek refuge in the cities or flee abroad.

One of the more interesting aspects of the Revolutionary governments is the manner in which they worked out policies designed to complement and harmonize with private investment, in order to completely change the outlook for development, especially as regards prospects for the growth of the country in general, not limiting their designs to certain urban activities wholly dependent on foreign investment. Since 1930, the public and private sectors have played a paramount role, and their open or tacit collaboration has been essential to raising levels of investment in rural areas and in the cities.

In the first place, it must be remembered that the Mexican Revolution did not adopt a definite doctrine or norm of economic development. For this reason, its policies were not restricted by rigid, preconceived formulas of an economic or social character. Its influence on economic development depended on the effects of actions taken pragmatically to benefit urban labor and the farmer as the classes most likely to furnish future increases in national demand.

Its influence on the economic structure of the country, the distribution of population, and the reorientation of fields of activity attractive to private enterprise depended initially upon the effects of the armed conflict; later, its influence depended upon the effects of its policies of land reform and public works and of its constant effort to industrialize and actively participate in such basic industries as electric power and transport.

II. MIGRATION TO THE CITIES

Two of the effects of the Revolution, in its prolonged internecine warfare, were to determine in particular the course of Mexico's economic development. One was the substantial increase in urban population and the relative depopulation of the rural areas, and the other the resulting higher demand for manufactured goods and construction materials.

From 1910 to 1930, according to census data, the rural population decreased, in spite of a slight growth in the total population of the country. From 11,775,000 inhabitants in 1910, it was reduced by 763,000 to 11,012,000. On the other hand, the urban population, consisting of 3,385,000 inhabitants in 1910, rose to 5,541,000 in 1930, a net increase of 2,156,000 inhabitants (see Table 2).

TABLE 2

Urban and Rural Population
(Thousands)

	1910	Per Cent	1930	Per Cent	1959[1]	Per Cent	Percentage Increase 1930–1959	Increase or Decrease 1910–1930	1930–1959
Total	15,160	100.0	16,553	100.0	33,300	100.0	101	+1,393	+16,747
Urban	3,385	22.3	5,541	33.5	14,960	44.9	170	+2,156	+ 9,419
Rural	11,775	77.7	11,012	66.5	18,340	55.1	66	− 763	− 7,328

[1] Preliminary data.

This striking growth in urban population—important precisely because it was the first such increase since Mexico became independent—marked the beginning of a new trend in demand for articles of national industries and promoted an extraordinary expansion of the urban construction industry, a major consumer of domestic products. This increase in the population of Mexico's cities, which accelerated after 1930, was also a reflection of a phenomenon that had not occurred in the periods of peace that followed the wars of the nineteenth century.

The 1910 Revolution had agrarian roots that culminated in its policy of land reform. The uncertainty among large landowners and even among owners of smaller properties, once they realized that the Revolutionary governments were determined to carry out land distribution, led many of them to abandon farming and to attempt to recuperate their fortunes in commercial or industrial enterprises in the cities. The growth of these new activities was both cause and effect of the reorientation of interests of important sectors of the population. Most of these new city dwellers had a degree of education and skill that ensured their success in urban economic activities.

In time of peace, the process of urban concentration is usually due to increased yields in farming and to the consequent surplus of agricultural output over rural consumption. The experience of Mexico from 1910 to 1930 should be interpreted in a different light: the shift of population to cities, with its unquestionable stimulus to commercial and industrial activities, was provoked by the armed rebellion, since agricultural production during this period was arrested and even diminished, as was to be expected.

It is probable that if this massive movement from farm to city had not been initiated, the basis of Mexico's industrialism would have been weaker, for a rural population traditionally and universally consumes fewer manufactured articles than higher-income urban groups.

III. THE PRAGMATISM OF THE REVOLUTION

In order to achieve national economic development, the government of Porfirio Díaz relied on foreign investment and domestic private investment. It was assumed that domestic private investment would occur spontaneously and would not require constant incentives to relate its volume to the increasing investment needs of a country in the process of growth. It was also assumed that it would not be affected by the vicissitudes of climate in a predominately rural economy or by the fact that there was no steady improvement in the income of the population to spur industrial activity. The Revolutionary governments, on the contrary, quickly worked out a plan of action that encouraged private investment more effectively than had economic liberalism, at the same time eliminating excessive protection of private enterprise and protecting the laborer and the farmer.

The economic policy of the Revolutionary governments was swiftly applied in a series of public works and basic investments by the new State, which realized that such projects would not be carried out by domestic and foreign private investment. The government's feeling of responsibility was heightened by the absence of private investors, who were still fearful in this first phase of the Revolutionary period.

The government tried not only to remedy a fundamental deficiency in total investment but also to make sure that capital would be channeled into the real needs of the national economy instead of into fields that, for one reason or another, were acceptable to foreign investment. Its intensive effort in irrigation works, road construction, railways, and electric energy had tremendous impact on domestic and foreign private investments. It overcame the natural reluctance of the private sector—which had not forgotten the disastrous losses of capital suffered in twenty years of armed conflict—to invest in agriculture and industry. It proved that the demand generated by an increase in the real earnings of the consumer masses constituted a greater inducement for private investment than the unqualified protection of an industry not supported by a firm demand. And finally, it established a policy of economic development based not on theories valid for countries with different economic and social conditions and relationships, but on the observed behavior of the national economy.

Growth of Investment

The figures for the growth of development investment over the last thirty years are indeed dramatic. It is estimated that in 1930 aggregate investment, both public and private, reached only 216 million pesos ($102 million), of which public investment was 82 million pesos ($39 million), and private investment was 134 million pesos ($63 million) (see Table 3).

Three decades later, in 1959, total investment came to 17,243 million pesos ($1,379 million) of which 6,047 million pesos ($484 million) was public investment and 11,196 million pesos ($895 million) represented private investment.

TABLE 3

Public and Private Investment
(Millions of Pesos)

Year	Total	Public	Private
1930	216[1]	82[2]	134[3]
1935	377	143	234
1940	773	316	457
1945	2,276	928	1,348
1950	5,937	2,643	3,294
1955	11,829	4,229	7,600
1959[4]	17,243	6,047	11,196

[1] Estimated.
[2] Calculated as 38 per cent of aggregate investment based on the 1939 ratio as given in the report of the Combined Working Party of the Mexican Government and the *IBRD, The Economic Development of Mexico* (Baltimore, The Johns Hopkins Press, 1953).
[3] Estimated as a residual.
[4] Preliminary data.

Total investment, measured in dollars to facilitate calculation, multiplied approximately thirteen and one half times, with private investment increasing in the same proportion as public investment. The magnitude of the increase can be appreciated by considering that in 1959 the sum total of public and private investment in the country was almost equal to the total gross national product in 1930, at 1950 prices.

The favorable effect of public investment on all fields of national production can be explained not only by how much it has accomplished with scarce government resources, but by how it has been

TABLE 4

Public and Private Investment
(Millions of U.S. Dollars)

Year	Rate of Exchange (Annual Average)	Total	Public	Private
1930	2.12	101.9	38.7	63.2
1935	3.60	104.7	39.7	65.0
1940	5.40	143.1	58.5	84.6
1945	4.85	469.3	191.3	278.0
1950	8.65	686.4	305.6	380.8
1955	12.50	946.3	338.3	608.0
1959	12.50	1,379.4	483.8	895.6

channeled. Public works were given priority, first, to improve agricultural yields in regions where this was possible, and second, to give farm products rapid and cheap access to markets, a program of importance to a mountainous country with a potential to produce and export perishable tropical commodities.

An outstanding effort was made to supply electric energy and fuel to all the domestic industries by applying a policy that was not based on the principle of classical economics that an activity, no matter how important, should grow only in the measure that it might attract private investment: the policy applied was based on the realistic principle that private enterprise would not support industrialization unless there had been previously created, in terms of development possibilities and irrespective of the difficulties involved, ample and cheap sources of energy as well as easy access to raw materials and to national and international markets, through a basic development program.

Public investment stimulates private investment. Mexico does not have a classification of public investment going back to 1930; but according to figures available since 1939, public investment in agriculture and hydraulic resources rose from 39.7 million pesos in 1939 to 752.3 million in 1959, that is, it multiplied eighteen times, with a cumulative total of 8,477 million pesos over twenty-one years. Investment in transport and communication also multiplied eighteen times, increasing from 143.2 million pesos in 1939 to 2,790.3 million in 1959, adding up to 21,757.5 million pesos for that period, of which 8,837.5 million was used for the construction and maintenance of roads, 10,157.3 million for railways, and 2,762.7 million for related investments.

Investment in electric energy went up from 2.9 million pesos in 1939 to 762.9 million in 1959, an extraordinary twenty-sixfold increase, with a total outlay of 3,836.9 million pesos over the twenty years. Investment in petroleum, which had become a State industry, rose from 24.1 million pesos to 1,214.5 million, that is, it multiplied fifty times, with an aggregate of 9,213.5 million pesos for the period.

In all, public investment climbed from 264.6 million pesos in 1939 to 7,129.7 million in 1959, a twenty-sevenfold increase.

In all countries, capital formation involves improvements in educational levels, technical knowledge, and organizational ability, which cannot be measured statistically. Nevertheless, the volume of production equipment at a country's disposal, represented by material investments of a general economic character—roads, dams, railways, industrial and agricultural equipment, etc.—should steadily expand in relation to the number of inhabitants, in order to increase real per capita income and product. The Revolutionary governments have had a clear idea of this basic principle of economic development, and they have constantly bent their efforts toward making more economic equipment available to the productive sectors of the population. These efforts have proved fruitful in two ways: the amount of public investment per inhabitant has increased annually; and, as a direct result of the investment incentives provided to the private sector by the State program of public works and economic development, the amount of private investment per inhabitant has also risen.

Investments made in 1930 amounted to only $6.16 per capita.[6] Of this amount, $2.34 went into public investment and $3.82 into private; in 1959, total investment per inhabitant reached $41.42[7] of which $14.52 went into public investment and $26.90 into private.

Even considering that in 1959 the dollar had 53 per cent less purchasing power than in 1930, per capita investment in Mexico increased several times in real terms during that period, inasmuch as total investment per inhabitant went up to 6.7 times the 1930 level—in public investment, to 6.2 times, and in private investment, to 7.0 times.

The large increases in private investment, no smaller than in public investment, corroborate the theory, basic to Mexico's economic growth, that a development program resolutely carried out and broadly applied by the government plays a decisive role in the orientation and expansion of private investment.

IV. PROGRESS IN AGRICULTURE

The volume and nature of private investment are the best indicators of the country's confidence in the future policy of a government and in its ability to carry it out.

Undoubtedly, the acceleration of the agrarian-reform program

[6] The average total investment per capita in the five-year period from 1930 to 1934 was $3.33.

[7] The average total investment per capita in the five-year period from 1955 to 1959 was $37.96.

TABLE 5

Public Investment by Main Sectors
(Millions of Pesos)

Year	Grand Total	Agriculture and Resources			Transport and Communications				Electric Power	Petroleum	Other
		Total	Irrigation	Other	Total	Highways	Railroads	Other			
1939	264.6	39.7	38.1	1.6	143.2	51.3	88.6	3.3	2.9	24.1	54.7
1940	336.2	44.3	36.3	8.0	151.6	56.9	89.1	5.6	3.4	57.4	79.6
1941	383.7	58.7	56.7	2.0	188.3	88.7	94.0	5.6	4.0	24.4	108.3
1942	492.5	65.2	63.0	2.2	290.0	155.2	122.4	12.4	10.2	28.3	98.8
1943	626.1	86.0	83.0	3.0	384.7	180.6	175.0	29.1	9.5	26.5	119.4
1944	723.5	124.8	117.1	7.7	397.5	166.0	202.5	29.0	19.8	40.6	140.8
1945	952.6	148.0	139.6	8.4	455.6	183.8	250.2	21.6	16.2	113.4	219.4
1946	1,130.5	195.4	180.0	6.4	526.0	230.9	275.3	19.8	38.2	111.1	259.8
1947	1,431.1	266.1	228.3	37.8	671.1	233.6	417.0	20.5	77.5	85.3	331.1
1948	1,631.3	324.1	249.3	74.8	686.1	302.3	339.2	44.6	105.6	167.5	348.0
1949	1,964.2	504.2	260.7	343.5	756.7	332.6	352.5	71.6	176.6	246.7	280.0
1950	2,665.6	551.8	371.9	179.9	1,090.4	374.7	605.4	110.3	236.8	398.3	388.3
1951	2,981.4	685.8	565.8	120.0	1,084.6	394.1	608.5	82.0	245.2	425.0	540.3
1952	3,417.1	769.8	613.6	156.2	1,378.1	616.7	683.2	78.2	135.1	368.9	765.2
1953	3,253.6	570.3	513.7	56.6	1,392.8	592.4	661.1	189.3	252.8	456.1	581.6
1954	4,365.3	632.5	610.1	22.4	1,555.9	675.8	728.2	151.9	331.4	901.0	944.5
1955	4,959.7	611.9	608.6	3.3	1,485.8	655.2	661.8	168.8	368.6	1,055.3	1,138.1
1956	4,932.5	657.2	595.2	62.0	1,775.2	629.0	806.6	339.6	284.9	859.9	1,355.3
1957	5,946.3	679.7	650.4	29.3	2,101.4	872.3	849.7	379.4	293.6	1,282.6	1,589.0
1958	6,516.2	709.2	656.4	52.8	2,452.2	923.8	1,028.8	499.6	461.7	1,326.7	1,566.4
1959	7,129.7	752.3	710.6	41.7	2,790.3	1,121.6	1,118.2	550.5	762.9	1,214.5	1,609.7
TOTAL	55,803.7	8,477.0	7,357.4	1,119.6	21,757.5	8,887.5	10,157.3	2,762.7	3,886.9	9,213.5	12,518.8

Sources: Combined Working Party of the Mexican Government–IBRD; Dirección de Inversiones; Dirección General de Estadística.

TABLE 6

Investment per Inhabitant
(Dollars)

	Total	Public	Private
1930	6.16	2.34	3.82
1959	41.42	14.52	26.90
Ratios (1930 = 100)	672.40	620.51	704.19

initially caused private investment to withdraw from agricultural activities and livestock raising. This attitude was typical of the 1930's, becoming more marked when President Lázaro Cárdenas (1934–1940) intensified the program of land distribution. Nevertheless, as formerly stated, the lack of private investment in agriculture was partly offset by urban economic growth. After 1939, a general process of private investment, partly induced by the exceptional wartime demand, was initiated throughout the country in both urban and rural areas of activity. This process was aided by the administration of President Miguel Alemán, which consistently offered additional incentives to private investment, in order to satisfy the increased demand for the numerous consumer and producer goods required by Mexico's growing economy, while the government concentrated its efforts in basic industries and development works.

The distribution of public and private investment in Mexico shows once again the criteria, not dogmatic but pragmatic, by which the Revolutionary governments participated decisively in activities that in other countries, with different development criteria, might be considered exclusively within the terrain of private enterprise. Those activities received both public and private investment in order to produce the volume of goods needed for the country's expansion. In this way, a growing demand was not obstructed by rigid circumscription of which fields belonged to the State and which to private enterprise.

This philosophy was applied to agriculture as well as to electric energy and heavy industry, and to a certain extent, even to ordinary manufacturing.

In the agricultural sector, where efforts were concentrated on extending the amount of land under cultivation and especially of irrigated land, there was an appreciable increase in crop acreage—

TABLE 7

Area under Cultivation and Agricultural Output
(Area in Thousands of Hectares; Output in Tons)

	1930		1950		1959	
	Area	*Output*	*Area*	*Output*	*Area*	*Output*
TOTAL	5,337		8,614		12,042	
Sesame	24	6,391	189	86,688	205	120,950
Cotton	202	54,227	539	515,150	754	1,052,030
Rice	33	68,055	87	169,965	100	235,000
Sugar cane	103	3,621[1]	204	10,643[1]	238	16,301[1]
Beans	136	86,646	583	371,688	1,432	600,200
Corn	3,817	2,035[1]	5,745	4,850[1]	6,500	5,550[1]
Tomatoes	19	57,511	29	163,541	62	355,110
Wheat	544	276	538	519	946	1,400
Coffee	155	43,304	188	267,159	282	395,930
Other crops	304		512		1,523	

[1] Thousands of tons.
Source: Census data, Dirección General de Estadística.

more so in *ejidos,* financed and directed by the government, than in privately owned farms.

The 1930 census gives a total of 5,337,000 hectares under cultivation, rising in the 1959 census to 12,042,000. Despite the margin of error to be expected in figures of this type, the government's notable effort to expand irrigated areas indicates that the greatest increment occurred in such lands, which was an important factor in raising yields per hectare and the real per capita income of the rural population.

A comparison of the agricultural census of 1930 with that of 1950, which gives the most recent figures available for the *ejido,* shows that these communally owned lands expanded from 1.9 million to 8.8 million cultivated hectares. Privately owned farms were reduced from 12.7 million cultivated hectares in 1930 to 11.1 million in 1950. Irrespective of the relative yields of *ejidos* and of privately owned farms (a relationship that is meaningless because basically they raise different types of crops, depending upon the geographical areas in which they are located), the increase in production of various crops between 1930 and 1950 is not merely an index but a powerful demonstration that—with the exception of corn, which is raised on marginal, nonirrigated lands and is therefore less susceptible to improved yields—the policy of the government in agriculture has been very beneficial.

The increase in the volume of agricultural output was much greater than either the increase in cultivated land or in rural population. The high rates of growth bear ample testimony to the success of the general programs of agricultural development of the Revolutionary governments. Although there have been undoubted shortcomings and much still remains to be done, this is essentially because of Mexico's tortured geography and hazardous climate, against which human effort, no matter how well planned, can achieve only moderate results in the short run.

Table 8, which shows relative increases in agricultural output by product, clearly indicates that the growth in production and in yields is not only important but generalized. It is just as true of such foodstuffs as sesame, rice, sugar cane, corn, tomatoes, and wheat as it is of cotton, a fiber that has become the most extensively raised agricultural product for industrial use.

The rise in agricultural production is also much greater than the growth in rural population, an increase resulting in higher per capita productivity. Compared to an increase of 66 per cent in the rural populaton from 1930 to 1950, sesame production went up seventeen times; cotton, seventeen times; rice, one and a half times; sugar cane, two and a half times; beans, six times; tomatoes, four times; and corn production, 72 per cent.

Unquestionably, however land tenure may evolve, the Revolu-

TABLE 8

Percentage Increases in Agricultural Output and Yields

	Output 1930–1959	Yields per Hectare 1930–1959	Are under Cultivation 1930–1959
TOTAL			125.6
Sesame	1,792.5	116.9	754.2
Cotton	1,840.0	108.0	273.3
Rice	245.3	14.5	203.0
Sugar cane[1]	350.2	59.5	131.1
Beans	592.7	261.2	952.9
Corn[1]	172.7	95.8	70.3
Tomatoes	517.5	55.4	226.3
Wheat[1]	407.2	95.6	73.9
Coffee	814.3	−30.7	81.9
Other crops			401.0

[1] Thousands of tons.

tion's aim of raising the farmer's living standard can be more rapidly realized where land is moderately productive rather than arid, yielding the farmer nothing at all for his labor.

V. INDUSTRIAL PROGRESS AND INCREASING CAPITAL FORMATION

The government's efforts in the field of industry have given results as spectacular as those in agriculture.

Because of force of circumstance, or the reaffirmation of national sovereignty, or treatment as basic activities for the economic development of the country, there are fields that have been taken over by the government, others which the government has shared with private enterprise, and others that have belonged solely to private enterprise. In all these, both public and private investment has been mounting. There also has been an increase in the production of goods and services in all areas.

In activities like petroleum production, transport, and electric power—where growth is vital to development—as well as in manufacturing, the increase in output has equaled or surpassed the growth of the economy in general, as well as of total population and of urban population. The high relative rate of industrial growth is an indication that Mexico is embarked on the industrialization that has enabled other countries to raise steadily the real income of their inhabitants. Likewise, it definitely proves that Mexico's industrialization has not been achieved artificially—at a sacrifice of efficiency in the use of natural and human resources. Measured by its results, the process has been economically sound, one which has permitted the urban population to enjoy a constant rise in income and to absorb some, though still not enough, of the surplus rural population.

In activities basic to Mexico's industrial development like petroleum, electric power, the iron and steel industry, and transport, output expanded from 1930 to 1959 by ratios that fluctuated between 2.7 and 3.2, ratios that far outstripped the growth in population. The foregoing industries are either wholly or partly owned by the government.

Other manufacturing industries, chiefly in the hands of private enterprise, expanded production as much as sevenfold. In Table 9 a detailed analysis of the census figures for the 1930–1959 period reveals that production of almost all of the principal manufactured items increased by ratios appreciably higher than the population rate of growth.

TABLE 9

Industrial Development

	Units	1930	1959	Ratios (1930 = 100)
Crude petroleum	Thousands of cubic meters	6,285	16,814	267.5
Electric-power generation	Millions of KWH	1,425[1]	9,774	685.9
Iron and steel industry				
Steel ingots	Tons	57,826[2]	631,227	1,091.6
Pig iron	Tons	100,859[2]	1,327,752	1,316.4
Railroad transport	Millions of ton/ kilometers			
Freight		4,041	11,713	289.8
Passengers	Millions of passenger/ kilometers	1,448	3,314	228.9
Cotton ginning				
Cotton fiber	Tons	38,487	381,744	991.9
Textiles				
Crude (unbleached) muslin[a]	Tons	12,298[3]	49,206[4]	400.1
Soap	Tons	60,864[5]	170,113[c 6]	279.5
Vegetable oils and fats	Tons	38,918[5]	248,279[6]	638.0
Flour-milling				
Apparent wheat consumption	Tons	439,921	1,400,548	318.4
Beer	Thousands of liters	72,065	800,844	1,111.3
Sugar	Tons	215,600	1,264,137	586.3
Paper	Tons	46,017[5]	169,605[6]	368.6
Basic chemicals				
Sulfuric acid[7]	Tons	12,564	242,726	1,931.9
Glass[b]	Thousands of units			
Cement	Tons	224,768[8]	2,637,970	1,173.6

[a] In 1959, includes other types of unbleached cottons and dyed cloth.
[b] Includes containers and glassware of all kinds.
[c] Includes detergents.

Sources:
[1] (1932.) Anuario Estadístico de los Estados Unidos Mexicanos, 1938.
[2] Compañía Fundidora de Fierro y Acero de Monterrey, annual report, 1930.
[3] Anuario Estadístico de los Estados Unidos Mexicanos, 1941.
[4] Dirección General de Estadística.
[5] (1934.) Anuario Estadístico de los Estados Unidos Mexicanos, 1938.
[6] Dirección General de Estadística.
[7] (1935.) Banco de México, Departmento de Investigaciones Industriales.
[8] (1929.) Cámara Nacional del Cemento.

TABLE 10

Capital Investment in Manufacturing Industry
(Census Data; at 1930 Prices)

Industrial Manufacturing Branches	1930			1955			
	Persons Employed (Thousands) (1)	Capital Investment (Millions of Pesos) (2)	Capital per Person (Pesos) (3)	Persons Employed (Thousands) (4)	Capital Investment (Millions of Pesos) (5)	Capital per Person (Pesos) (6)	Ratio of Capital per Person (6/3) [1930 = 100]
Total	318.2	956.1	1,053	2,171.6	10,490.0	4,831	156.2
Cotton ginning and packing	2.4	10.1	4,208	11.3	110.6	8,788	208.8
Cotton textiles	40.0	133.5	3,338	118.6	366.6	2,963	— 11.2
Soap	2.5	18.4	7,360	19.1	188.7	9,880	134.2
Electric appliances, instruments, apparatus, machinery and equipment	0.1	0.1	1,000	47.4	251.6	5,308	530.8
Vegetable oils and fats	1.6	12.8	8,000	11.9	120.0	10,084	126.1
Mineral waters and soft drinks	3.2	3.9	1,219	44.8	150.0	3,348	274.7
Drugs and medicines	0.6	2.1	3,500	39.5	174.8	4,425	126.4
Rubber products	0.5	2.5	5,000	0.9	1.8	2,000	— 60.0
Electric-power generation and distribution	13.3	295.9	22,248	27.3	1,043.7	38,231	171.8
Flour milling	2.9	24.0	8,276	7.5	96.5	12,867	155.5
Beer	3.3	29.4	8,909	15.0	164.6	10,973	123.2
Corn dough (nixtamal)	10.1	7.2	712	39.1	17.9	451	— 36.7
Printing and engraving	7.0	16.4	2,343	39.4	94.8	2,406	102.7
Sugar	13.81	63.31	4,587	32.4	308.3	9,515	207.4
Iron and steel	4.2	23.4	5,571	7.8	184.4	23,410	420.2
Shoes	7.1	9.2	1,296	83.6	40.1	1,193	— 7.0
Paper	2.4	15.2	6,333	10.2	177.4	17,392	274.6

Woolen textiles	5.6	21.1	3,768	26.6	111.5	4,192	111.3
Cigarettes and tobacco	4.7	34.8	7,404	6.9	62.5	9,058	122.3
Basic chemicals	0.7	5.1	7,286	16.8	120.0	7,143	— 2.0
Glass	1.2	3.6	3,000	11.4	51.1	4,482	149.4
Cement	1.4	9.6	6,857	10.5	75.3	7,171	104.6
Heavy machinery and equipment	0.1	0.1	1,000	7.7	54.1	7,026	702.6
Matches	1.8	3.7	2,056	3.9	10.9	2,795	135.9
Other manufacturing industries	182.7	210.7		1,586.4	6,512.8		

1 1935 census.

Although figures are not available for the period from 1930 to 1950 that would show the increase in the output of consumer goods as compared to producer goods, there is a noticeable trend in the Mexican manufacturing industry to extend production beyond nondurable consumer goods to durable consumer goods and capital equipment.

The prospect of an industrialization that will include the production of durable consumer goods and industrial equipment favors not only a rise in the level of the country's real income but of its employment. Goods requiring a high degree of skilled labor can be produced domestically instead of being imported, and resources that formerly were used to pay for expensive imports can remain within the country to contribute to internal demand. The careful construction of a national industry to produce the equipment and machinery used by domestic enterprises better defines the interrelation of supply and demand that acted to bring about the continual expansion of the European countries during their great stage of economic growth from the end of the nineteenth century through the first half of the twentieth century.

The increases in industrial output reflect a parallel increase in the volume of capital invested in various industries.

In modern economies, higher efficiency and productivity are always tied to a rising ratio of capital to labor. During the twenty-five years between the industrial censuses of 1930 and 1955, there was a general and rather sharp increase in the amount of capital invested in basic industries and in domestic manufacturing industries. According to Table 10, total industrial capital in 1930 was 956.1 million pesos, with a labor force of 313,153 workers, representing an investment of approximately 3,050 pesos per worker. The census of 1955 shows a total capital investment of 10,490 million pesos, at 1930 prices, with 2,171,599 workers employed and an average capital investment of 4,820 pesos per worker.

According to the above-mentioned census figures, the average amount of capital invested per worker at constant prices was 58 per cent higher in 1955 than twenty-five years earlier, a fact that partly explains the increased industrial productivity of the country.

Even though census figures do not furnish strictly comparable data, owing to differences in methods, limitations in coverage, and variations in the concepts of capital investment, a comparative analysis of the capital and personnel employed in each of the various industries also reveals important growth by activity in the value of industrial investment per worker. Stated another way, the very substantial private investment made in the country during the quarter century covered by the two censuses referred to yielded an increase of total capital invested in each manufacturing activity that was much greater than the increase in the labor force.

According to the censuses, industrial employment totaled 313,153 in 1930, rising to 2,171,599 in 1955. This represents roughly a sevenfold increase, compared with an elevenfold increase in total capital invested, with figures adjusted to constant prices, from 956.1 million pesos in 1930 to 10,490.0 million pesos in 1955.

VI. REVOLUTIONARY MEXICO GOES FORWARD

Wholly valid or conclusive statements about economic development are not easily made. It is difficult to establish the causes of social and economic phenomena through mere statistical analysis. Nevertheless, the economic development of a country and the relative success of its public policies are determined to a large extent by economic programs and decisions. There are convincing figures to indicate that the efforts of the government in matters of public investment and the action of private investment, combined with elements of political stability and of specific State action in other economic and social fields, in general have had very favorable effects.

It is interesting to compare Mexico's growth in total product and improvement in per capita income in real terms during the period from 1930 to 1959 with that of many advanced countries during their stage of major development. Simon Kuznets[8] analyzes the ten-year growth rates of nineteen nations with average and high living standards. It may be noted that the rate of growth per decade of the total real product of such countries ranges from 12.8 per cent for Ireland to 49.7 per cent for the Union of South Africa, which has the highest. The total real product of the United Kingdom

---

[8] *Aspectos cuantitativos del desarrollo económico* (México, D.F., Centro de Estudios Latinoamericanos, 1959). This book has been published in English and references are to the English translation. See "Quantitative Aspects of the Economic Growth of Nations. I. Levels and Variability of Rates of Growth," *Economic Development and Cultural Change*, Vol. 5, No. 1 (October, 1956); "Quantitative Aspects of the Economic Growth of Nations. II. Industrial Distribution of National Product and Labor Force," *ibid.*, Vol. 5, No. 4, Supplement (July, 1957); and *ibid.*, Vol. 6, No. 4, Supplement (July, 1958).

went up 21.5 per cent per decade; of France, 15.3 per cent; of Germany, 27.4 per cent; of Russia, 31 per cent; of the United States, 41.2 per cent; of Japan, 42.3 per cent.

Dr. Kuznets estimates the growth per decade of Mexico's total real product at 78.4 per cent during the period 1925–1954. According to the Bank of Mexico data, growth per decade of the total national gross product from 1930 to 1959 was 64 per cent, a figure which substantiates the foregoing estimate.

Nevertheless, a more relevant comparison should be made in terms of per capita growth. For the nineteen industrial countries mentioned in the study, the rates of growth per decade in real per capita product during the period under discussion ranged from 5.6 per cent for Spain, the lowest, to 27.6 per cent for Sweden, the highest. The rate was 12.5 per cent for England, 16.8 per cent for France, 15.1 per cent for Germany, 15.4 per cent for Russia, 20.3 per cent for the United States, and 26.3 per cent for Japan. According to Dr. Kuznets, Mexico increased its per capita product 43.2 per cent per decade between 1925 and 1954, and the Bank of Mexico's estimate for the period 1930–1959 is 30 per cent per decade.

In Kuznets' study of the growth of real per capita product for various countries in Latin America, Mexico shows the greatest relative increase, notwithstanding its having one of the highest population rates of growth.

The rates of growth of the national economy, promoted since 1930 by the economic and social policies of the Revolutionary governments, not only bear comparison with, but surpass, those attained by other nations which, thanks to a steady rise in their living standards initiated earlier than Mexico's, are now known as developed countries.

It may be safely assumed that as the standard of living—and therefore the capacity to save—of the Mexican population improves, the proportion of annual income devoted to productive investment will substantially increase. Thus, although greater amounts of capital investment will be required per inhabitant, a rapid and continuous growth in per capita income can be maintained in the future and within the next thirty years Mexico's living standard will approach that currently enjoyed by the more advanced European countries.

II. FINANCING ECONOMIC DEVELOPMENT

The Central Bank,
Instrument of Economic Development in Mexico

BY MARIO RAMÓN BETETA

The Financing of Economic Development

BY ALFREDO NAVARRETE R.

The Central Bank,
Instrument of Economic Development in Mexico*

MARIO RAMÓN BETETA

The function of a central bank is to influence the financial institutions of the country to operate in a way that will fit into the general economic policy of the government. Its functioning will take the form most appropriate to the type of financial institutions that it must influence and to the economic policy that it is basically committed to develop. Therefore, there is no line of conduct common to all central banks. Actually, it is no exaggeration to say that there are as many kinds of central banks as there are countries in the world.[1]

The opening statement makes clear that the functions of a central bank go far beyond note issue and coinage. In fact, its issue of currency may be secondary to its control of credit and of operations in the financial and foreign-exchange markets. And even more important is how it applies these regulatory functions to achieve the objectives of the government's general economic policy.

One of the Mexican government's fundamental goals is to speed up the rate of economic development in order to raise the standard of living of the population as rapidly as possible. The responsibility of the central bank, as one of the elements of the economic process, is to maintain the value of the currency, or the purchasing power

* Paper presented by the author at the VI Operative Meeting of the Center of Latin American Monetary Studies, held in Buenos Aires, Argentina, in April, 1961. The text, revised and expanded with two appendixes, was published in M. R. Beteta, *Tres aspectos del desarrollo económico de México* (México, Publicaciones Especializadas, 1963) , pp. 76–133.

[1] R. S. Sayers, *Central Banking After Bagehot* (Oxford, England, Clarendon Press, 1957) , p. 47.

of wages and salaries, while this goal is being pursued; it also must try to prevent private enterprises and individuals from squandering their resources on speculations or activities of relatively low productivity. The central bank, therefore, must study and decide how great a volume of credit will stimulate economic activity by promoting industrial and agricultural development without at the same time causing a serious rise in prices or depreciation of the currency.

The purpose of this paper is to discuss in general terms some aspects of the role of the Bank of Mexico in contributing to the overall economic-development policy. The following pages will explain why central banks cannot follow an inflexible line of action irrespective of circumstances, and why, in the case of Mexico, the basic principles of central banking have been adapted to conditions in a country where capital is scarce and where the banking and financial system, although more advanced than in other countries at a similar level of development, still cannot be compared to that of the highly industrialized nations. For this reason, it has been necessary to establish selective credit-control measures in order to direct the limited loanable funds into production. In more developed countries, this is done through the ordinary financial mechanisms.

I. INTRODUCTION

In view of the substantial gains made by the Mexican economy, principally in industry, and of the significant increase in real national income from 1940 to 1960, Mexicans consider that theirs is a "developing," [2] rather than an underdeveloped, country. This description, however, does not seek to deny that a large sector of the population, still a little more than half, continues to be engaged in primary activities such as agriculture, cattle raising, and mining, which are on the average lower in productivity and, consequently,

[2] Real national income increased at an average rate of nearly 6 per cent per annum in the 1940–1961 period. The International Bank for Reconstruction and Development in one of its studies ("Current Economic Position and Prospects of Mexico," 1961) states that the annual rate of economic growth in the last two decades has been just over 5.6 per cent, a rate that it describes as "unusually rapid." In the last twenty years, the volume of industrial production has expanded at a rate of 8.3 per cent per annum.

yield less than do the secondary activities like industry and the services. This explains the concern of the government and, naturally, of the monetary and credit authorities with raising the living standard of the population.

All the administrations since 1910, guided by the principles of the Mexican Revolution, have bent their efforts, to a greater or lesser degree, toward establishing a solid economic infrastructure through the construction of roads, railways, irrigation systems, power plants, etc., and through broader education and technical training. Furthermore, they have worked hard to accelerate the process of industrialization, which would permit more rapid capital formation and the absorption into well-paid jobs of large numbers of workers displaced to urban centers by the increasing mechanization of agriculture.

Mexican authorities have taken both direct and indirect measures to stimulate economic development. The direct measures have consisted mainly of heavy investments in vast public works by the government itself and by the official sector. The indirect measures have included favorable tax treatment through tax exemptions for new and necessary industries and the provision of adequate financing, through a large group of official agencies, for activities essential to development but unable to secure support from private enterprise. The government also tries indirectly to speed up the rate of economic progress by channeling part of the savings held by the private banking system into the financing of those production activities that most immediately contribute to improving the standard of living. This paper will describe specifically the measures taken within this last line of action.

II. PRIVATE CREDIT INSTITUTIONS AND THE CENTRAL BANK

It might be thought that in Mexico there is a mixed banking system because, in practice, the various credit institutions parallel one another to some extent in their legal powers and, therefore, in their financial functions. However, the General Law on Credit Institutions and Auxiliary Organizations—the legal basis of our banking structure—adopts a system of specialized banks and lists seven types of credit institutions, each with its particular functions. The law

specifies deposit banks, *financieras* (private-development banks),
mortgage credit companies, capitalization companies, savings-and-
loan banks for family housing, savings banks, and trust companies.
The law expressly provides that the first five cannot be combined
and that only the last two can be operated as departments of the
other institutions. Nevertheless, the amendments enacted on December 31, 1962, permit capitalization companies to be operated in
conjunction with savings-and-loan banks, although in separate departments.[3]

The Bank of Mexico, which was established in 1925 but actually
began to operate as a central bank with the legal reform of 1932,
originally had jurisdiction over only the deposit banks. Jurisdiction
was later extended to the savings banks and recently to the *financieras*, which have come to play a progressively larger role in banking transactions, and to the mortgage credit companies, which issue
bonds and especially guarantee *cédulas* (mortgage bonds issued by
private individuals or firms and secured by real estate), representing a very important sector of Mexico's fixed-interest securities market.

Nevertheless, the other institutions mentioned, which are still outside the Bank of Mexico's sphere of direct action, are legally defined as credit institutions and therefore come under the jurisdiction of the monetary authorities and the supervision and control of
a bank-examining agency known in Mexico as the National Banking Commission. Although the Bank of Mexico does not specifically regulate the operation of these institutions, the banking law itself imposes a system establishing maximum percentages of investment in certain kinds of activities that the government considers less
desirable from a financial or socio-economic point of view; it also
establishes compulsory minimum percentages for other kinds of investment that will effectively finance economic development.

On the other hand, the very existence of credit institutions like
the savings-and-loan banks for family housing is in accord with the
Mexican program of action to solve the problem of low-cost housing, which has lagged behind the appreciable advances made in

---

[3] Appendix I of this paper is a study of the structure and operations of the
private banking system in Mexico. Each of the above institutions is briefly
described within the present framework of the law, and attention is drawn
to some of the basic amendments enacted on December 31, 1962.

other fields, such as food and clothing, that determine the standard of living.[4]

III. THE SYSTEM OF RESERVE REQUIREMENTS

The Bank of Mexico has found that economic reality limits its use of the instruments traditionally employed by central banks in countries of higher economic development. Confronted by a weak and unorganized securities market that reduces the efficiency of open-market operations and by rather irregular and high rates of interest that make variations in the discount rate ineffective as a monetary tool, Mexico's central bank has applied its policy of credit control both quantitatively and qualitatively by means of many indirect measures, but basically by changes in the reserve requirements.

On the other hand, as will be explained later on, the compulsory deposit is also the mechanism through which the Bank of Mexico chiefly carries out the purchase and sale of securities. In view of Mexico's present stage of development, these aspects of the reserve-requirements system—the channeling of credit and the purchase and sale of securities—are the result of the central bank's search for new ways to operate that are sometimes different from those used by central banks in highly industrialized countries.

Both the General Law on Credit Institutions and the Organic Law of The Bank of Mexico require deposit and savings banks—and under the legal amendment of December 31, 1962, the *financieras* as well—to maintain fractional reserves at the Bank of Mexico. In the case of deposit banks, the Bank of Mexico is empowered to impose reserve requirements of from 15 to 50 per cent of current liabilities; but, in the light of monetary and credit needs and at the discretion of the Bank of Mexico, the 50 per cent established as a maximum can be raised to 100 per cent of any increase in liabilities. Exercising this authority, Mexico's central bank has set maximum reserve requirements for deposit banks. However, in order to channel these resources into production activities, it has allowed the

[4] In 1962, a program was drawn up—to be initiated in 1963—that would channel vast amounts of internal and external resources into the construction of low-cost housing. This program has necessitated a series of legal amendments to permit the various credit institutions to participate actively in attracting domestic savings and directing them toward this specific end.

banks to maintain an interest-free cash deposit of only 15 per cent, which is the legal minimum, provided that they invest the remaining 85 per cent, after deduction of till money, partly in government securities, partly in industrial securities prescribed by the authorities, partly in certain types of loans to production activities also determined by the authorities, and partly in loans chosen by the banks and generally used for financing commercial activities. When the banks do not fulfill this compulsory-investment schedule, they must maintain the difference between the proportion fixed by the Bank of Mexico and the investment actually carried out, either in cash or in low-yield government securities. In the event that they do not meet any of these alternative requirements, the banks are obliged to pay a penalty interest established by the Bank of Mexico. At present, this rate of interest is 24 per cent per annum on the amount not deposited or not invested as required.

The operation of this system is regulated by having private banks send the central bank a weekly report with daily information on which to base the respective calculation and, as necessary, the penalty interest.

This admittedly complicated system, explained here only in outline, has served as the basis for a series of measures designed not only to control the money supply and the liquidity of the economy but also to channel part of the available savings into the promotion of economic development through the public and, primarily, the private sector.

IV. THE EFFECTIVENESS OF SELECTIVE CREDIT CONTROL

Before going on to describe specifically these measures, it should be stated that although the Bank of Mexico believes that their overall results are beneficial and that the effort made to apply them is therefore justified, it does not consider that the measures are of unqualified value or totally effective.

The practical worth of selective credit control has been discussed in numerous studies and special meetings. On the one hand, it is claimed that the use ultimately given a loan can seldom be ascertained, mainly because of the many intermediaries it must pass through before reaching its final destination, operations which make supervision almost impossible; and that it must be remembered that the different economic activities are not financially watertight compartments, a situation which means that frequently a loan extended to some will be transferred, at least in part, to others. On the other hand, it is stated that credit institutions find it relatively easy to reduce unattractive investments to a minimum. This matter was dealt with at the VI Meeting of Central Bank Experts of the American Continent, held in Guatemala City in November, 1960. At this meeting, where one body of opinion defended credit control and another was skeptical of its benefits, Mr. Javier Márquez, director of the Center of Latin American Monetary Studies (CEMLA) argued that the policy of selective credit seems to be more effective in the short run and particularly when it is applied to the promotion of given activities, whereas it is apparently less effective in the long run and for the purpose of discouraging certain activities. In the latter case, he maintained, credit institutions inevitably create "defense mechanisms" that tend to prevent the attainment of the established objectives.

The Mexican experience would demonstrate that selective credit control is useful, not only because it has directed large amounts of banking resources into activities needing them (see Table 1), but also because, through the application of these policies, it has been possible to break habits deeply rooted in the banking sectors, such as nonparticipation in branches of economic activity considered unprofitable or traditionally unattractive. Once forced by these policies to turn toward certain activities, banks find them to be lucrative and secure; and later on, under no pressure and of their own accord, they channel their loans into those fields. Furthermore, the

TABLE 1

Financing Granted by Private Banks to Production Activities,
1950–1961
(Millions of Pesos)

	1950	1961	Absolute Increase	Percentage Increase
Investments in public securities	460	3,937	3,477	756.00
Investments in industrial securities	408	1,932	1,524	374.00
Loans to agriculture	339	1,983	1,644	585.00
Loans to industry	1,143	6,985	5,842	511.10
Total financing to production	2,350	14,837	12,487	531.40

Source: Bank of Mexico.

purpose of the credit-control measures is by no means to divert resources of the private banking system into risky operations; it is
to encourage banks to establish sound and advantageous operations
in economic activities that they have not entered simply because of
inertia or tradition.

V. PRINCIPAL SPECIFIC MEASURES

The Bank of Mexico and other monetary authorities have adopted
specific measures to channel part of the savings held by the private
banking system into the financing of economic development. The
principal measures are discussed below:

1. Investments in Government Securities. The Bank of Mexico,
through its use of the compulsory instrument described above, has
channeled part of the investments of the country's credit institutions into the financing of the public sector. In fact, investments authorized to cover the compulsory deposit have included those made
in public securities such as highway, electric power, railway, irrigation, and other bonds.[5]

In addition to investments authorized in public securities for the
public works mentioned, there is another group of public securities
which finance private production activities and which are purchased
by deposit banks, savings banks, and *financieras* to cover their reserve requirements. This is presently true of the livestock bonds,
in which the banks invest part of their current liabilities.[6] Funds
obtained in this way by the federal government go to increase the
loanable resources of the Guarantee and Development Fund for
Agriculture and Livestock and Poultry Raising (discussed in de-

[5] At present, deposit banks, savings banks and departments, and *financieras*
can cover part of their reserve requirements with investments in public securities for the above-mentioned public works. For example, deposit banks in the
Federal District are authorized to buy these kinds of securities to cover 20 per
cent of their sight liabilities and 15 per cent of their time liabilities in national currency; and deposit banks throughout the rest of the country may
cover their peso deposits in proportions of 10 and 15 per cent, respectively
(Bank of Mexico Circulars, 1287, 1350, 1389, 1408, and 1420, dated in that
order August 31, 1955; January 15, 1958; July 15, 1959; May 20, 1960; and
January 1, 1961).

[6] Deposit banks in the Federal District must invest in these bonds up to 5
per cent of their demand liabilities as part of their compulsory deposits (Bank
of Mexico Circular 1389, July 15, 1959).

tail later on), and the fund, in turn, uses these resources to rediscount loans granted to cattle raising by the private banking system. This combination of deposit and rediscount policies has induced the country's banks, especially those outside the Federal District, to finance this important activity; at the same time, it has counteracted to some extent the concentration of financial resources in the capital city.

Channeling part of the savings held by the country's financial system into investment in public securities is the purpose not only of the compulsory-deposit mechanism but also of several legal provisions. For example, capitalization companies and insurance and bonding companies are required to maintain part of their resources in public securities.[7]

Compulsory investment in public securities of a part of the resources of the banking system has channeled savings held by it into the financing of the public sector and it has moderated the inflationary effect of occasional direct financing of the federal government by the Bank of Mexico. Furthermore, thanks to this system, the central bank has been able to bypass a shaky securities market and carry out what amounts to open-market operations in public securities.

It should be mentioned that in 1950 the private banking system held claims on the public sector totaling 460 million pesos and that by the end of 1961 this figure had risen to approximately 3,937 million pesos.

2. Medium-Term Investments. Since its amendment in 1949, the General Law on Credit Institutions permits deposit banks to make investments known as "medium-term," either in *avío* loans (backed by agricultural crops or industrial inventory) or *refaccionario* loans (for the purpose of buying machinery or equipment) with maturities of between two and five years,[8] or in securities with maturities

---

[7] As regards capitalization companies, see the General Law on Credit Institutions and Auxiliary Organizations, Art. 41, secs. VII and VII bis. Insurance companies must invest at least 30 per cent of their paid-up capital and reserves in public securities (General Law on Insurance Companies, Art. 86) ; bonding companies must invest at least 30 per cent of their capital and reserves, both capital and general, in securities of the government and of national credit institutions (Federal Law on Bonding Companies, Art. 41) .

[8] The 1962 amendments raised the period for *refaccionario* loans to ten years (see Appendixes I and II of this paper) .

of over two years, although limiting this type of investment to a maximum of 20 to 30 per cent of sight liabilities. This amendment took into consideration that, because certain proportions of demand deposits are not likely to be withdrawn, they could be invested, without affecting the banks' liquidity, in "medium-term" operations designed to promote production activities that particularly need this type of financing.[9]

In Mexico, *avío* loans are to finance working capital, and *refaccionario* loans are to finance fixed investment of production activities. In both types of credit, the lender, in order to safeguard the security of the loan and the priority of that guarantee over other debts, has the right to see to it that the funds are used precisely for the purposes for which they were contracted.

The monetary and credit authorities designate in general terms the branches of activity open to the above-described loans, as well as the securities available for this kind of investment.

The Bank of Mexico, under the legal provisions already mentioned, uses the compulsory deposit to induce deposit banks, savings banks, and *financieras* to invest specified proportions of their current liabilities in these medium-term operations, either in loans or securities.[10]

3. Minimum Portfolio in Production. The Bank of Mexico authorizes deposit and savings banks to cover their compulsory deposit with given amounts of loans or of investments in securities, on the condition that a minimum of 70 per cent of the total portfolio of such institutions be invested in production credits and 30 per cent in commercial credits. The same conditions tend to apply to the compulsory deposit of *financieras*, although not in proportions expressly established.

4. Channeling of Foreign-Currency Resources. For the double purpose of preventing the banking system from converting its re-

[9] The General Law on Credit Institutions and Auxiliary Organizations, Art. 11, sec. VI. The medium-loan portfolio of private banks amounted to 705.6 pesos in December, 1951; by December, 1960, this figure had risen to 2,703.7 million pesos, an increase of 283 per cent.

[10] At present, for example, deposit banks must invest 20 per cent of their sight liabilities in medium-term operations; 5 per cent in industrial securities and mortgage bonds designated by the Ministry of Finance; and 15 per cent in *avío* loans on terms of up to two years and in *refaccionario* loans on terms of up to ten years, for financing agriculture, livestock raising, fishing, and industry (Bank of Mexico Circulars 1287, 1350, 1389, 1408, and 1420, of dates given in n. 5).

sources into dollars—a tendency which intensified during periods of uncertainty about the exchange rate of the Mexican peso—and of exerting some degree of control over credit, the central bank, again making use of the compulsory deposit, has progressively frozen increases in foreign-currency resources, until 100 per cent has been reached for deposit banks and *financieras*. Moreover, since March, 1959, it has prohibited trust companies from performing the services of trusteeship, administration, or representation, by which they receive funds in domestic or foreign currency to be used for loans in foreign currency, as well as from accepting or expanding trust funds in foreign currency in order to grant loans in domestic currency.[11]

5. Financing of the Sugar Industry. The Bank of Mexico also has employed the compulsory-deposit mechanism to induce private banks to invest part of their liabilities in bonds issued by the Financiera Nacional Azucarera, an institution created expressly to aid the sugar industry. The growing importance of sugar in the national economy is evidenced by its present rank of third among Mexico's export commodities.[12]

6. Channeling of Resources Derived from Time Deposits. In order to encourage deposit banks—which form the most extensive network of credit institutions in the country—and *financieras* to channel more of the public's savings into financing production activities, the Bank of Mexico assigned to them a special schedule of reserve requirements for their peso time deposits at not less than ninety days. Under this schedule, they are permitted to pay higher interest rates than for deposits at under ninety days, but they also are granted relatively higher earnings on investments authorized to cover the compulsory deposit, 60 per cent of which must be made in production activities.[13]

7. Financing of Production by *Financieras*. It was observed that the *financieras*, which were supposed to base their operations in the

[11] Out of their frozen foreign-currency reserves, deposit banks and *financieras* are authorized to invest in dollar bonds issued by Nacional Financiera—Mexico's official development bank—as well as to grant short-term financing at low interest for the export of machinery, installations and equipment, or their parts, produced in Mexico (Bank of Mexico Circulars 1219 of February 16, 1953; 1310 of March 1, 1956; 1380 of January 15, 1958; and 1403 and 1404 of April 20, 1960).

[12] In 1962, private banks held approximately 230 million pesos in sugar bonds (Bank of Mexico Circular 1389, July 15, 1959).

[13] Bank of Mexico Circular 1408 of May 20, 1960.

capital market on medium- and long-term loans to production activities, were accepting large amounts of short-term resources. The Bank of Mexico, therefore, to correct this trend and restore the *financieras* to a more liquid position, decided to place a ceiling on the annual growth of their short-term obligations by subjecting such margins to a special schedule of reserve requirements under which loans and investments would be made principally in production activities and, to a lesser extent, in commercial activities. All such liabilities contracted in excess of the stipulated ceiling must be deposited without interest in the central bank.

The regulations for *financieras* permit them an unlimited increase in liabilities derived from the sale of their own bonds as well as in certain obligations maturing in more than a year, provided that their proceeds are invested in long-term financing of production activities.[14]

8. Rediscount Operations for Production Activities. The Bank of Mexico has been rediscounting short-term loans made by deposit banks to finance various crops like maize, beans, wheat, and sorghum. This operation is made attractive by granting the rediscount at a low rate of interest, thereby limiting the interest charged by the banks on the original loan.

This system of financial aid, restricted to small and medium farmers and farmers on *ejidos* (communal land holdings), not only has helped supply the domestic market with basic commodities but has also enabled the agricultural sectors to market their crops on favorable terms.[15]

In the same way, the central bank has used the rediscount system, combined with the compulsory deposit, to induce commercial banks to participate in the financing of Mexico's official commodity-supply agency—CONASUPO—which has obtained most of its funds from official credit institutions. CONASUPO, now partly supported by private financial resources, endeavors to keep the domestic market supplied with basic commodities and to maintain stable prices for the benefit of consumer and farmer; it also guarantees certain crop prices.[16]

---

[14] Bank of Mexico Circular 1420 of May 1, 1961.

[15] Bank of Mexico Circulars 1414 of June 22, 1960, and 1419 of October 31, 1960.

[16] Bank of Mexico Circulars 1336 of April 10, 1957, and 1386 of May 18, 1959. As of December, 1960, the share of private banks in this financing reached approximately 604 million pesos.

9. Trust Funds to Refinance Production Credits. The government has set up several trust funds to facilitate the financing of certain production activities. The principal ones are: Guarantee and Development Fund for Medium and Small Industry,[17] administered by Nacional Financiera; Guarantee and Development Fund for Tourism, also administered by Nacional Financiera; and Guarantee and Development Fund for Agriculture and Livestock and Poultry Raising,[18] administered by the trust department of the Bank of Mexico.

These investment trust funds, unlike official credit institutions, do not deal directly with the borrower. Their operations, carried out through private *financieras* and deposit banks, have made cheap, long-term credit available to many economic activities. Furthermore, these funds, within certain limits, give technical aid and carefully supervise the use actually made of the resources they have granted.[19]

The fund administered by the Bank of Mexico has under study the possibility of broadening its financing of agricultural and other activities that supply the most urgent needs of the people.

[17] By the end of June, 1962, the loanable resources of the Guarantee and Development Fund for Medium and Small Industry reached 151 million pesos (120 million pesos from the government and 31 million pesos in profits earned during its operation, which began in April, 1954). By June 30, 1962, the fund had authorized 3,959 loans amounting to 709 million pesos. These loans have been granted to 2,294 enterprises located throughout the country in such industrial zones as Mexico City, Monterrey, León, Guadalajara, Puebla, Oaxaca, and Morelia. The fund's operations have been shared by 47 deposit banks, 67 *financieras*, and 3 credit institutions of other types. Most of the loans extended by the fund are for less than 100,000 pesos, with an average of 52,632 pesos, running twenty-four months; and they are mainly to industries producing iron and steel products, food, yarn and textiles, clothing, and leather and hides (information from Nacional Financiera).

[18] In 1962, the loanable resources of the Guarantee and Development Fund for Agriculture and Livestock and Poultry Raising reached 308.8 million pesos, of which 183.7 million derive from the sale of bonds for livestock development. Since 1956, this fund has refinanced a total of 493 lines of credit, amounting to 824.6 million pesos, with 408.5 million going to agriculture, 392.5 million to livestock raising, and 13.5 million to poultry raising.

[19] For further information, see the Law of December 18, 1953, which created the Guarantee and Development Fund for Small and Medium Industry; the Law of November 14, 1956, which created the Guarantee and Development Fund for Tourism; the Law of December 31, 1954, which created the Guarantee and Development Fund for Agriculture and Livestock and Poultry Raising; and the Regulation of April 21, 1955, and descriptive pamphlets.

10. Special Compulsory-Deposit Mechanism for Maintaining a Constant Flow of Credit. In 1958, the central bank established a special mechanism in the compulsory-deposit system for deposit banks, in order to maintain a constant flow of credit from these institutions and even to guarantee a regular increase in their loan operations. This seeks to prevent seasonal or regional declines in the resources held by the private banking system, declines which could affect the normal rate of credit growth and, thereby, the general trend of economic expansion.

Through this mechanism, deposit banks whose rate of growth has fallen in relation to a comparable period in the past are authorized to continue expanding their credit with resources from the central bank. This support is limited to a growth of not more than 6 per cent per year, the rate considered normal for the banking system as a whole. This mechanism does not operate for banks that did not grow during a comparable period in the past, because its purpose is not to stimulate an artificial growth but to anticipate briefly the increment that normally could be expected.

This measure involves only a moderate and temporary expansion of central-bank credit. Banks benefiting from this mechanism are required to return the funds they have received to the central bank, once they have augmented their own resources.

By maintaining liquidity, this new instrument of monetary policy has protected the financial needs of economic development from transitory and abnormal circumstances and has preserved the credit discipline that is essential to Mexico's policy of stability.[20]

11. Rediscount Operations to Support Banks in Emergency Situations. The Bank of Mexico's practice has been to grant rediscounts at low interest to deposit banks that are in difficulties either because of an exceptional decrease in their deposits, or because of a general standstill in their portfolios due to adverse conditions throughout a region. This policy has had two functions. In the first case, it has enabled commercial banks to use funds furnished by the central bank to meet unexpected demands on their deposits, thereby maintaining both the individual stability of the institution faced with a sudden run on its accounts and the prestige of the banking system in general. The Bank of Mexico's support has reinforced public confidence in banks, because these measures, among others, have

---

[20] Bank of Mexico Circulars 1372 of September 12, 1958; 1378 of February 16, 1959; 1384 of March 13, 1959; and 1450 of May 21, 1962.

helped prevent bank failures. The certainty that deposits can be withdrawn at any time has made the public increasingly willing to deal with banks, and made it unnecessary to establish a deposit-insurance corporation similar to those existing in other countries, to cover this type of risk. In the second case, where there is a generalized freezing of credit caused by, for example, a flood or a drought that prevents farmers from repaying their bank loans, it has supplied central-bank resources to commercial banks so that they can finance, on reasonable terms, new crops and thus sustain the economic activity of the region.

12. Control of Operations between Domestic Credit Institutions and Foreign Banks. For more than ten years, the monetary authorities have provided that the central bank must approve all rediscount operations between domestic and foreign credit institutions, as well as loans made by the latter to the former and guarantees by Mexican banks of credits extended to Mexican individuals or enterprises by foreign banks.

The Bank of Mexico determines whether or not to authorize such operations on the basis of the country's capacity to pay, as well as the term of maturity, amount, and other conditions of the credit. It also gives its authorization in the following cases: *(a)* Loans to finance imports of capital goods not produced in Mexico when 50 per cent of the loan is to be amortized at the end of not less than three years, so that the credit will be, as far as possible, self-liquidating. *(b)* Loans to finance exports (mainly agricultural) when secured by the product in question ready for export.[21]

13. Control of Mortgage Financing. Since 1956 the Bank of Mexico has imposed certain regulations on the issue of mortgage bonds, which is supervised by the National Banking Commission, in order to limit increases in this type of security and to channel their proceeds into selected investments.

Mortgage bonds, and specifically *cédulas,* as stated before, are fixed-interest securities that have long been popular among investors in Mexico. Therefore the monetary authorities are especially

---

[21] Excepted from these rules are commercial credits running less than ninety days, which do not require approval of the central bank (Bank of Mexico Circulars 1164 of February 21, 1951; 1220 of February 20, 1953; and 1227 of May 20, 1953). Also related to the financing of Mexican exports is the allowance for manufactured products established by Circulars 1403 and 1404 of April 21, 1960.

concerned with achieving a safe and stable market for such securities. The Bank of Mexico uses its regulations to channel financing derived from mortgage securities, in an effort to distribute such credits more equitably and, furthermore, to direct them primarily toward definite objectives like the construction, expansion, and repair of low-cost housing and rental properties, and into purely production activities like agriculture, poultry raising, beekeeping, livestock raising, and industry in general. The regulations stipulate not only the proportions of small loans that mortgage credit companies must grant before being authorized to extend large loans[22] but also the operations that must be covered by each category of credits.

14. Regulating the Issue of *Financiera* Bonds. The regulations imposed on the issue of *financiera* bonds should be mentioned as another of the measures aimed at channeling credit into production activities. The issue of such bonds is regulated by the General Law on Credit Institutions and Auxiliary Organizations, by which the National Banking Commission is empowered to approve issues, on the advice of the Bank of Mexico.[23]

These bonds must be secured by a specific guarantee consisting of either credits or securities. Thanks to their close coordination, the National Banking Commission and the Bank of Mexico have agreed on a rule that instructs *financieras* to cover their requirements with *avío, refaccionario,* or industrial mortgage loans to enterprises whose activities are included among the industries designated by the Ministry of Finance and Public Credit.[24]

VI. THE CENTRAL BANK AND ECONOMIC DEVELOPMENT

As can be seen from the foregoing account, the Bank of Mexico in particular and Mexico's monetary authorities in general have not

22 The proportions are as follows: *(a)* not less than 55 per cent of the securities outstanding must be in issues and credits of up to 100,000 pesos each; *(b)* not more than 25 per cent of those securities in issues and credits of between 100,000 and 500,000 pesos; and *(c)* not more than 20 per cent of those securities in issues and credits of more than 500,000 pesos.

23 Arts. 29, 31, and 123 bis.

24 Moreover, Article 31 of the General Law requires *financieras* to maintain a special liquidity fund amounting to the equivalent of at least 10 per cent of the value of their bonds outstanding. A minimum 25 per cent of this must be invested in cash, or in demand deposits in other credit institutions, or in public securities designated by, and deposited in, the Bank of Mexico.

been as entirely orthodox in their operations as are traditional central banks. In fact, they have adopted somewhat revolutionary methods designed to convert the central bank indirectly into an instrument of economic development. This means that the Bank of Mexico, without sponsoring an inflationary credit policy or a deliberate deficit financing of the public sector (and it should be recognized that monetary and fiscal policies are being combined more consistently), always has been conscious of promoting economic development. Mexico's central bank certainly has striven to create confidence in the peso in order to prevent the flight of capital, to encourage the formation of domestic savings and its investment, to support and expand the securities market, and in brief, to ensure monetary stability as a stimulus to the country's growth. At no time has it claimed that stability is an end in itself, but only an efficient instrument to create a climate suitable for the development of public and private investment. The government, given its broad objectives and its store of information, is in an especially favorable situation to determine which credit needs must be met to achieve the goals that contribute to development. On the one hand, it operates through its own official banking institutions and, on the other, it carries out a very generalized selective credit control to channel part of the country's still-limited savings capacity into the investment fields most likely to further development. At the same time, it opens the door to a series of activities that otherwise never would have had access to the banking system.

No economist is unaware that monetary and credit policy, though very important, is only a cog in the complicated machinery that drives economic development. Therefore, the central bank can no more be given sole credit for rapid economic growth than it can be entirely blamed when the rate of development falters.

STRUCTURE AND BASIC OPERATIONS
OF THE PRIVATE BANKING SYSTEM IN MEXICO

SYSTEM OF SPECIALIZATION

The General Law on Credit Institutions and Auxiliary Organizations, which regulates the structure and operations of the Mexican banking system, and specifically private banks, establishes a system of specialization based on the different means by which banking institutions recruit resources and also a system of credit control based on the nature of the loanable resources at their disposal.

Under this law, there are seven different types of credit institutions: deposit banks; savings banks; *financieras;* mortgage credit companies; capitalization companies; trust companies; and savings-and-loan banks for family housing. Savings, deposit, and trust operations may be carried out in separate departments by any of these institutions, but none of the remaining operations can be combined.[1]

In addition to the seven types of strictly credit institutions, the law designates four classes of auxiliary organizations, which by their very nature cannot be considered as purely banking institutions. These are the general-deposit warehouses, clearing houses, stock exchanges, and credit unions.

From the outset, Mexico adopted a system of specialized banks, which it precisely defined in the banking law of 1932. Subsequent regulations have followed this pattern. Nevertheless, it should be made clear that the law itself provides that the specialization shall not be carried to extremes. Experience has shown that specialization carried to extremes is inadvisable because several kinds of institutions may be controlled by a single financial group and because of other reasons peculiar to Mexico's economic structure. Actually, its instruments of varying degrees of liquidity, maturity, and yield have permitted private banking great flexibility in attracting

[1] The latest amendments to the General Law on Credit Institutions, published in *Diario Oficial* of December 31, 1962, permit capitalization companies to be operated in conjunction with savings-and-loan banks for family housing, though in separate departments.

an increasing amount of domestic savings from many different sectors of the economy.

In principle, the present law differentiates banks as such—that is, deposit banks—from investment companies or institutions. Deposit banks are basically supposed to handle deposits of the general public and make short-term loans, whereas investment institutions are supposed to handle savings and medium- and long-term loans, as well as to help place issues of different enterprises among the private sector.

OUTLINE OF THE GENERAL LAW ON CREDIT INSTITUTIONS

The General Law on Credit Institutions and Auxiliary Organizations, which as a federal law applies throughout Mexico, regulates enterprises that normally exercise banking and loan functions, with the exception of the Bank of Mexico and official credit institutions, for which there are special laws.

The government department in charge of banking and credit matters is the Ministry of Finance and Public Credit, without whose authorization banking and credit business cannot be legally engaged in.

The law permits foreign banks to establish branches in Mexico, but to operate only as deposit banks. The policy followed by Mexico's banking authorities has tended to discourage the establishment of such branches and, at present, only The First National City Bank of New York has a branch in Mexico.

The law fixes certain requirements for the organization and operation of credit institutions, in addition to the above-mentioned administrative authorization. For example, it requires that banking enterprises be organized as joint-stock companies; it determines the minimum capital that must be fully subscribed and paid in; it sets special conditions to be met by the capital; it requires the appointment of a board of not less than five directors; it establishes special rules for stockholders' meetings; it stipulates that at least 10 per cent of the profits shall be allocated to a capital-reserve fund; it governs the liquidation of banking companies, etc. No bank can modify its charter without the approval of the Ministry of Finance.

The law deals in separate chapters with the seven different types of credit institutions and the auxiliary organizations, according to the system of specialization. Each chapter contains specific regulations for a given institution, but there are certain general rules that apply to all of them.

The types of transactions that may be undertaken by the institution are enumerated in the chapter devoted to that particular institution. Nevertheless, certain institutions (deposit, savings, *financieras*) are also authorized to engage in "operations that are analogous, related, or favorable to the fulfillment of their functions," thereby diluting the strict application of the rules and weakening the principle of specialization by permitting operations to be carried out conjointly.

Furthermore, the law lays down a series of rules that govern the activities of credit institutions and auxiliary organizations: liquidity ratios; guidelines for transactions in securities and foreign exchange, etc.; minimum-reserve requirements in the central bank; minimum or maximum limits on certain kinds of investments; and, especially, limits on investments in equipment, property, rights on real property, and legal expenses of installation.

The law also regulates the issue and conditions of banking securities, and it provides for certain types of credit operations to be carried out by banking enterprises. In some cases, it stipulates terms of maturity and even rates of interest on savings and loans. It also establishes rules designed to prevent the concentration of credit by limiting the percentage of loans or investments that may be granted to an institution controlled by a single person or enterprise, as well as limiting transactions with board members, executive officials, and majority shareholders of the institution.

Finally, each chapter contains prohibitions which must be observed by the institutions and which reinforce certain rules of operation and prevent the institutions from deviating from their normal functions.

THE CREDIT INSTITUTIONS

Deposit Banks

In Mexico, banking is traditionally conceived of in terms of the structure and operations of deposit banking. This type of banking has been the pioneer and backbone of the present banking system and today still constitutes its most important sector.

Deposit banks gather resources through deposits of money, most of them in checking accounts. The volume of resources in checking accounts has become very substantial and in 1961 it represented 62.5 per cent of Mexico's money supply and 39 per cent of total liabilities in the private banking system.

Deposit banks are also authorized to gather resources through time deposits. For obvious reasons, banking authorities have tried to encourage banks to attract funds into this type of deposit.

Credit transactions of deposit banks chiefly consist of cash or short-term loans to provide their clients with working capital. These loans may take the form of discounts, direct loans, *reportos* (the borrowing of securities which are then paid for and title transferred; at the expiration of an agreed term equivalent certificates are delivered to the lender and paid for at a slightly higher price), advances on securities, etc. In general, deposit-bank loans are supposed to run for not more than six months; such loans, however, can be renewed one or more times to a maximum of one year from their original date, but with certain limitations.

Nevertheless, Mexican experience has shown that a constant proportion of the funds of deposit banks, even of those accumulated in demand deposits, is genuine savings. Therefore, banking legislation has permitted these banks to grant medium-term loans on terms of from one to five years, either through investments in securities with a maturity of more than two years or through *avío* and *refaccionario* loans.[2] It should be mentioned again that *avío* loans are to finance working capital, and *refaccionario* loans to finance fixed investment. Both types of credits are supervised by the lender, who sees to it that the funds are used precisely for the purposes for which they were contracted, so that the security of the loan will take priority and be safeguarded.

Deposit banks may grant *avío* loans maturing in up to two years, and *refaccionario* loans with maturities not exceeding five years.[3] In any case, medium-term operations are limited to a given proportion of current liabilities, in the light of the liquidity of such institutions.[4]

Apart from their medium-term investments in certain kinds of securities, deposit banks may, on their own or a third party's account, engage generally in transactions in securities and keep in their portfolios securities issued by the government or by official credit institutions. The law authorizes the Ministry of Finance and Public Credit to prescribe which private securities may be purchased by the deposit banks from among those that have been approved for such transactions by the National Securities Commission.

Deposit banks, in addition to their credit-and-debit operations, may perform certain services for their clients, such as buying and selling securities, credit instruments and foreign exchange; collecting loans and making payments; handling acceptances; issuing letters of credit; carrying out the purchase and sale of gold and silver. Naturally, services and loans to clients are often combined.

[2] The amendments of December 31, 1962, raised to ten years the term of maturity permitted *refaccionario* loans.

[3] See note 2.

[4] Recent amendments consider as "medium-term credits" loans with three-year maturities made to finance the export of products manufactured in Mexico, and within the rules laid down by the Bank of Mexico, such loans can be made up to the maximum of 10 per cent of current liabilities.

In respect of current liabilities, deposit banks must maintain a minimum of 30 per cent in cash, as well as a percentage in noninterest-bearing deposits. The noninterest-bearing deposit, which originated in the need to guarantee a bank's current liquidity, has developed into Mexico's basic instrument of monetary and credit policy.

To conclude this account of deposit banks, they are the most important branch of Mexico's private banking system. Together with savings banks, they hold 56 per cent (45 per cent in deposits and 11 per cent in savings) of total banking resources, and account for 47 per cent of total financing granted by the private sector of banking. There are 106 separate deposit banks in the country, with 1,029 branches and agencies.

Savings-Deposit Operations

Savings-deposit operations may be carried out in separate departments by the principal credit institutions so authorized by the government; also, although in practice this is not the case, they may be engaged in by independent savings institutions. Actually, most deposit banks have savings departments and are referred to as commercial banks.

Savings institutions or departments may collect resources through savings deposits, stamps, and bonds. Savings-account deposits have been the main and almost the sole liability held by savings departments. In June, 1962, banking liabilities derived from savings accounts reached 3,240 million pesos, whereas liabilities derived from the issue of bonds reached only 2.7 million pesos. Deposits in savings accounts earn interest (at present, a maximum of 4.5 per cent per annum) and cannot exceed 100,000 pesos. A part of such deposits can be withdrawn on demand, depending on the regulations of the institution concerned, provided that not more than 30 per cent of the balance, or 1,000 pesos, whichever is less, is withdrawn at one time. Furthermore, a period of time must elapse between withdrawals.

Savings departments, within the limits and requirements fixed by the Law, are authorized to make loans on terms of up to one year, to invest in private and public securities, to make loans on collateral put up by the borrower or a third party on terms of up to one year, and to extend *avio* and *refaccionario* loans on terms of up to three and five years, respectively.[5]

[5] As pointed out in note 2, legal amendments of December 31, 1962, have raised the term of maturity for *refaccionario* loans to ten years. They also have assigned to savings banks important functions to promote low-cost housing. Under these amendments, savings banks may conclude special contracts with savers interested in obtaining loans for the construction of homes of "social interest," that is, family housing at a modest price. These institutions are also authorized to receive financial support from official agencies to develop special housing projects. In addition, savings banks have recently been empowered to make loans for the purchase of durable consumer goods.

It should be noted that savings departments are required to deposit a percentage of their savings liabilities with the Bank of Mexico.

The above-described practice of operating savings departments in conjunction with other kinds of banks, especially deposit banks, means that deposit and savings banks form one unit for the statistical purposes of data on resources and financing. At present, many different types of credit institutions have savings departments.

Financieras

Financieras, which under the banking law of 1932 were considered auxiliary organizations, became principal credit institutions with the reforms of 1941.

These institutions originally were introduced with two basic functions: to promote business enterprises and to make medium- and long-term loans. However, when the banking law was revised in 1950, *financieras* were authorized to accept short-term loans and credits from enterprises and individuals. This amendment enabled *financieras* to expand their short-term liabilities spectacularly.[6]

The disproportionate growth in short-term obligations of *financieras* can be attributed to several causes, among which are the restrictions imposed on deposit banks; the exemption of *financiera* obligations from the reserve requirements of the Bank of Mexico; the relative difficulty of placing long-term, low-interest securities, when short-term obligations paid a very high rate of interest; and the weakness of Mexico's securities market.

Actually, *financieras* did not draw deposits away from commercial banks, because the resources they attracted from enterprises were more in the nature of savings than of minimum operating funds—which have come to form the basis of checking accounts in deposit banks—and because when these resources were loaned by *financieras*, they were once again deposited in commercial banks. Nevertheless, the short-term transactions of *financieras* did distort the money market by raising the rate of interest and discouraging the securities market. Such considerations, together with the low degree of liquidity of *financiera* operations, convinced the monetary authorities that these institutions were not developing in a sound way.

This situation led to a legal amendment in 1957 subjecting *financiera* obligations to the legal reserve requirements of the Bank of Mexico. The Bank of Mexico later adopted measures to place a ceiling on increases in the short-term obligations of *financieras*, by requiring that all resources in excess of a specified amount be deposited in that institution. Complementing this regulation, steps have been taken to encourage *financieras* to issue

[6] The legal amendments of 1962 limit short-term borrowing by *financieras;* they can accept only loans and credits and receive deposits for periods of not less than three months.

long-term bonds as a source of long-term funds and to return to their original function of recruiting resources in the capital market.

Although there has been no change in the legal provisions requiring that bond issues be secured by a specific guarantee, in practice, the National Banking Commission and the Bank of Mexico have agreed to give prior approval to issues used for financing activities that most directly contribute to the country's development.

Financieras engage in two categories of transactions designed to accomplish their basic objectives. In order to promote enterprises, they assist in the organization and expansion of any kind of enterprise or business and, if they so desire, purchase an equity in such enterprises;[7] they subscribe to and sell obligations; they act as a common representative of bondholders; and they assume the function of cashier or treasurer for a company or enterprise.

Financing granted by *financieras* may take several forms: investments in securities; loans secured by bills deriving from installment buying and selling of merchandise; *avío* or *refaccionario* loans; loans to industry, agriculture, or livestock raising, with mortgage or trust guarantees; letters of credit for the purchase of machinery, and guarantees of bills, on the basis of loans; direct loans, with or without real security; loans for the construction or improvement of public services, etc.

Financieras may also offer certain services that do not necessarily imply the promotion or financing of enterprises, such as receiving deposits of securities and trade bills and carrying out foreign-exchange operations.

In order of importance among the country's credit institutions, *financieras* immediately follow deposit banks. In recent years, total financing by *financerias* sometimes has been, both in relative and absolute figures, greater than that granted by deposit banks.

At present, *financiera* liabilities represent 40 per cent of the total liabilities of the private banking system, and *financiera* bonds outstanding come to 1,608 million pesos. Financing by *financieras* now reaches 10,638 million pesos, which equals 48 per cent of all financing granted by the private banking system.

There are 97 of these organizations, with 32 branches, operating in Mexico.

---

[7] The legal amendments of 1962 limit the shares of *financieras* in commercial firms. They cannot acquire stock in such firms in excess of 25 per cent of the share capital. This limit can be raised to 50 per cent, in the case of new enterprises, with the approval of the Ministry of Finance and Public Credit on the advice of the Bank of Mexico. On the other hand, the new provisions limit the volume of investments by *financieras* in the stock of commercial firms to 25 per cent of the sum total of their current liabilities and their capital and capital reserves.

Mortgage Credit Companies

Another type of investment institution is the mortgage credit company, which basically undertakes to recruit long-term resources in the securities market, to issue and sell mortgage *cédulas,* and to grant long-term financing to the construction industry and, in general, to production activities.

These companies can obtain their resources by issuing mortgage bonds secured by mortgage loans or guaranteed by *cédulas* and mortgage bonds. Nevertheless, mortgage credit companies have not arrived at their present position of importance in the country's financial system by issuing mortgage bonds; rather, it has been their negotiation of the purchase and sale of *cédulas* that has permitted them to channel a significant and growing volume of savings into the institutional financing of the construction industry and other production activities. The truth of this statement is evidenced by the fact that there are at present only 241 million pesos of mortgage bonds outstanding, as against 1,816 million pesos of mortgage *cédulas.*

A *cédula* is a credit instrument issued by an individual or business enterprise and sold through a mortgage credit company on a commission basis. It is secured by real estate and jointly guaranteed by the borrower and the mortgage company.

Mortgage companies grant long-term loans (up to twenty years) principally to the construction industry, but also to production activities in general, public works, and for the payment of certain obligations (deriving from construction or from inheritance taxes).[8]

In addition to their specific functions, these institutions can keep in custody and administer the securities that they issue. At present, there are 26 mortgage credit companies, with 14 branches in Mexico.

Capitalization Companies

The capitalization companies, so called, are banks that were established to attract the savings of lower-income groups. According to a contract, regular premium payments are made to the bank in exchange for the delivery of a given amount of money after a fixed number of years.

To make this means of collecting resources more popular, banks not only pay interest on the accumulated savings—which, after the deduction of costs of administering the security, turns out to be nominal—but include in their contracts a periodic lottery awarding the winner the total value of his capitalization security. This lottery is the most effective feature of

[8] The banking amendment of 1962 assigns to mortgage companies, as well as to savings banks and savings-and-loan banks, an important role in financing the construction of low-cost housing. See Appendix II.

the capitalization system. Furthermore, the saver has the right to withdraw his savings before the end of the period agreed upon, although he suffers a considerable loss, and he may obtain loans backed by his capitalization security.

This method of gathering resources was at one time rather successful, but its prestige has fallen in recent years because simpler and more profitable savings possibilities have appeared. At present, liabilities of capitalization contracts amount to 589 million pesos, or 2.1 per cent of the total liabilities of the private banking system.

Financing carried out by capitalization companies is subject to the limits and requirements established by the law, which also regulates the system of mathematical reserves that they must maintain in order to protect their liquidity.

Capitalization companies can grant discounts and credits with six-month maturities, *avio* credits on terms of up to three years, and credits secured by securities and credits to promote low-cost housing. They may also invest in securities, and they are required to maintain 25 per cent of their current liabilities in government securities (including those issued by official institutions of credit) and 5 per cent in low-cost housing bonds issued by official credit institutions.

Financing by capitalization companies now reaches 552 million pesos, representing 2.5 per cent of total financing by the private banking system. At present, there are 13 institutions of this kind, with 22 branches.[9]

Trust Companies

Trust operations, like savings operations, may be carried out by independent institutions or by separate departments in the principal credit institutions. The latter practice prevails, and there are 110 credit institutions that have trust departments.

The trust company in Mexico is modeled after, but is not identical to, the "trust" in Anglo-Saxon law. Under Mexican law, it is defined as an operation by which a person, known as a trustor, arranges for a trust company to administer for a legal purpose certain of his properties (*afectación de un patrimonio*). A trust company must be authorized by the government to carry out its operations.

Although trust companies or departments should not be considered

[9] Capitalization companies also were affected by the 1962 legal amendments. Among other possibilities, they are authorized to operate capitalization plans for the purchase or replacement of machinery or equipment for industry, agriculture, or the development of basic activities. They also are authorized to operate capitalization plans granting the right to obtain loans for the purchase of durable consumer goods.

banks, because their function is to perform services, experience has shown that in some respects they act as banks. The banking law provides that, in addition to their trustee services, they may enter into various other activities. These include the issue of securities; the supervision of the accounts and records of business concerns; the receivership of businesses or estates, by court decision or by private agreement; the issue of participation certificates representing co-ownership of properties or securities; the receiving of deposits for administration or as a guarantee of properties, securities, etc.

The law limits the responsibilities that these companies may accept, in the light of their resources, and it regulates some of their operations, especially those related to actual financing.

Savings-and-Loan Banks for Family Housing

In 1947, legal amendments established still another kind of investment bank: the savings-and-loan bank for family housing that, as its name would indicate, is designed to meet the financial needs of a specific sector of the population. In Mexico, the problem of low-cost housing is still very serious. One of the measures taken to solve it was the creation of these institutions.

The savings-and-loan banks for family housing attract resources from the public through savings-and-loan contracts and the issue of building bonds and of savings bonds for housing.

Under the savings-and-loan contract, the borrower agrees to make regular deposits (usually monthly) and the bank obligates itself to pay interest on the accumulated savings and, once these have reached a given amount, to extend a loan to the depositor for the purchase, construction, or repair of houses or apartment houses, or for paying off encumbrances on such property.

Savings bonds for family housing are securities issued by these institutions, of which 10 per cent are covered by cash, up to 40 per cent by securities approved by the National Securities Commission, and the remainder by mortgage loans or by securities of the National Mortgage Bank. These bonds pay a maximum interest of 4.5 per cent per annum, but they may also give the holder the right to share in earnings, derived from such bonds, on investments made by the institutions.

Building bonds are securities issued by the savings-and-loan banks for family housing, which must be covered as prescribed by the Ministry of Finance. Such bonds can be issued and guaranteed through the National Mortgage Bank.

The banks under discussion may also obtain loans from the National Mortgage Bank for the financing of their specific field of activity and, within certain limits, may obtain credits guaranteed by their mortgage portfolio.

The law provides for the formation of a Building and Loan Stabilization Fund, which is held in trust by the National Mortgage Bank. This fund is contributed to by all the savings-and-loan banks and is used by them to meet any shortage of funds in making their required loans to their subscribers under their savings-and-loan contracts.

In this way, the National Mortgage Bank, with its Building and Loan Stabilization Fund, acts as a reserve bank for the savings-and-loan banks for family housing.

It should be emphasized that this type of bank can only grant loans for the purchase, construction, and repair of houses and apartment houses or for paying off encumbrances on such property.

The savings-and-loan banks for family housing are relatively unimportant, as is shown by the following data: their liabilities derived from holdings of resources amount to 113.3 million pesos, of which 89 million correspond to savings-and-loan contracts; these liabilities represent 0.4 per cent of total liabilities of the private banking system; they have extended credits totaling 121 million pesos, or 0.5 per cent of all financing by private banking; the Building and Loan Stabilization Fund has, at present, resources of 2.2 million pesos; there are only 3 banks of this type in operation.[10]

AUXILIARY ORGANIZATIONS

General-Deposit Warehouses

This auxiliary organization was created for the purpose of storage, custody, and conservation of goods and merchandise, and for the primary processing of the deposited merchandise.

The general-deposit warehouses are the only institutions authorized to

---

[10] In view of the limited development of these institutions, the amendments enacted to the banking law on December 31, 1962, reorganized the savings-and-loan banks for family housing so that they would play an important role in a massive mobilization of resources for the construction of low-cost housing. Under the new legal provisions, the savings-and-loan banks can engage in the following operations: conclude savings-and-loan contracts for family housing; obtain loans from other institutions; grant mortgage loans; purchase securities; invest in real estate and equipment for the installation of their offices and dependencies. These institutions may extend loans for the purchase, construction, enlargement, or repair of houses; purchase of land and construction of houses on that land; purchase, construction, or repair of condominium apartment houses; and the paying off of encumbrances on such property. As already pointed out, within the new legal framework, savings-and-loan banks for family housing can operate as part of institutions that simultaneously, but in separate departments, carry out capitalization operations.

issue deposit certificates and *bonos de prenda* (notes issued for loans secured by merchandise in a warehouse).

The deposit certificate credits the holder with ownership of merchandise or goods deposited in the warehouse that issues the instrument. The *bono de prenda* is evidence of the debt secured by the merchandise or goods described in the corresponding deposit certificate. Both instruments are negotiable. The law regulates the capital investment and the reserves of these institutions, as well as the basic aspects of their operations. At present, there are 29 institutions of this type.

Clearing Houses

The banking law considers clearing houses to be auxiliary credit organizations. Nevertheless, in practice, the Bank of Mexico acts as a clearing house for its member banks and, therefore, there are no autonomous agencies engaged in such operations.

Stock Exchanges

The purpose of the stock exchange is to establish suitable institutional mechanisms so that, through its members, transactions in instruments or securities can be carried out. It is considered an auxiliary credit organization because stock exchanges can actually exert considerable influence in the capital market. In Mexico, the securities market is not represented as fully as it should be on the stock exchanges, although these (there are 3, located in Mexico City, Monterrey, and Guadalajara) are gaining importance as the market becomes stronger. In fact, the development of the Mexican securities market is still far from satisfactory; whereas transactions in fixed-income securities are increasing, the market in shares remains negligible. One reason for this, among others, is that enterprises in need of money have traditionally resorted to credit, and those offering shares on the market are not always as careful of the interests of their minority shareholders as the shareholders would like.

Credit Unions

This auxiliary organization is really a principal credit institution in embryo, with some of the characteristics of the *financiera*, although its activities are limited to operations with its own members since it is organized as a cooperative.

There are five types of credit unions: agricultural, livestock, industrial, commercial, and mixed.

Among the objectives that the banking law assigns to the credit union, the following are significant: to extend loans to its members; to lend its members their guarantee or collateral security; to act as cashier or treasurer on regular deposits in money from its members; to purchase securities for its portfolio; to assume charge of, or contract for, the management or construction of projects owned by, or to be used by, its members; to promote the organization and management of industries to process and market the products of its members; to promote the organization and management of enterprises that provide its members with public services; to undertake the sale of the products of its members.

The law contains rules governing various aspects of the operations of credit unions, and, particularly, their capacity to absorb obligations, the maximum terms of their operations (five years), the composition and level of their reserve requirements in the central bank; the maximum amount they may lend a single member; their investments in securities, real estate, etc.

At present, 72 credit unions operate in the country, and they have outstanding 164.4 million pesos' worth of credits. Nevertheless, they tend to decrease in number and importance in inverse proportion to the expansion in the services of the principal credit institutions. When a credit union grows and reaches the ceiling placed on its obligations by the law, it usually becomes a credit institution, perhaps a *financiera*.

Explanatory Introduction to the Bill Presented to Congress to Amend and Expand the General Law on Credit Institutions and Auxiliary Organizations

The Chief Executive has been concerned with adjusting the existing financial mechanisms so that they may more fully and effectively contribute to the economic development of the country and to the achievement of the objectives established for the purpose of attaining the social welfare of the population.

Therefore, it is considered advisable to make various amendments to the General Law on Credit Institutions and Auxiliary Organizations, in order to expand and expedite support of production activities by the banking system, to extend credit to the consumer enabling him to purchase durable consumer goods, and to attend to the urgent needs of the broadest sectors of the population, which to date have not had access to bank loans that would permit them to purchase housing that meets minimum standards of comfort and hygiene.

Refaccionario loans, which are designed to consolidate and develop production activities, cannot be granted by a deposit bank for a period of more than five years. This prevents industrialists, agriculturalists, and livestock raisers from receiving banking support to carry out investments that require a longer term of amortization. Therefore, an amendment is proposed that permits these institutions to grant *refaccionario* credits on terms of up to ten years. In order to help national industry compete in the world market, it has been considered necessary to permit deposit institutions to grant credits of longer maturities for the export of domestically manufactured products.

In respect of *financieras,* which have expanded satisfactorily, the amendments are basically intended to ensure their solvency and orient them more definitely toward obtaining savings from the capital market, so that they can better perform their function of promoting and developing chiefly production activities.

Because the country's industrialization makes progressively larger demands on credit resources to meet growing development requirements, the Chief Executive has deemed it advisable to create within the system of capitalization companies, already adequately organized for these purposes, a new financial mechanism of specialized credit. This mechanism will permit medium and small industrialists to prepare for the purchase or replacement of their equipment by periodically depositing fixed amounts in money, thereby becoming entitled to obtain a supplementary loan sufficient to undertake investments and develop their businesses. In addition, it undoubtedly will encourage the formation of savings by gathering resources still not incorporated into the process of industrial activity.

Using a similar criterion, capitalization companies will also be authorized to grant specialized credit for the purchase of durable consumer goods, which will increase the possibilities of adding new savings to the banking system and will enable a large group of the population, particularly the medium- and lower-income sectors, to own goods made almost indispensable by modern life.

Special attention is given the problem of low-cost housing which must meet the needs of those sectors that, owing to lack of resources, have not had access to mortgage loans. Because of the rapid process of economic development and the standards of social justice inspired in the Mexican Revolution, steady progress has been made in such elements of social welfare as food and clothing. Nevertheless, housing requirements continue to mount and, although the government has devoted large and increasing amounts of funds to low-cost public housing, demographic pressure, particularly in the urban zones, has reached proportions far surpassing the possibilities of the Federal Treasury and the entire public sector.

Therefore, the Chief Executive desires to relieve this situation by establishing a housing-finance program to add resources to the public sector. The mechanisms of such a program, incorporated into the Mexican banking system, would generate substantial savings, which would be channeled precisely into the construction and purchase of housing by those sectors that lack adequate credits to do so.

In order to achieve these objectives, the mechanisms used to develop the new housing-finance program should consist of savings institutions, mortgage banks, savings-and-loan banks for family housing, as well as the capitalization companies that are authorized to operate savings-and-loan departments.

The savings institutions that have the necessary experience and have accumulated an important volume of deposits can attend to the needs of workers, artisans, or small businessmen all over the country, because they have more than a thousand offices throughout Mexico. The amendments will permit this type of institution to grant mortgage loans for low-cost housing of up to 80 per cent of the value of the guarantees, to receive deposits in special savings accounts from persons who want to receive mortgage loans, and to obtain support from other agencies constituting new sources of funds to increase mortgage operations of this kind.

Mortgage banks are to be authorized to grant loans of up to 80 per cent of the value of the guarantee in the case of low-cost housing, and to receive support from other agencies so that they too may add these funds to the resources they collect by selling mortgage bonds and *cédulas* and channel them into loans for the construction and purchase of such housing.

The rules laid down for savings-and-loan banks are intended to strengthen their financial position and promote their development. Of special significance are the amendments that provide for financing low-cost group-housing projects, which promise eventually to meet most effectively the needs of workers who belong to large unions or to large enterprises or enterprises associated for the purposes of workers' housing. These projects, supported by the government and the interested sectors, will permit expansion of housing construction, especially in regions of the country where large numbers of workers are concentrated.

These amendments are supplemented by the possibility that deposit banks and *financieras*, if circumstances so indicate, may add their resources to the housing-finance program, and by the possibility of organizing mutual funds for the sole purpose of collecting savings to be used specifically for mortgage loans for the construction or purchase of low-cost housing. The organization and function of such funds should be subject at a later date to rules and regulations governing their operations.

One of the amendments reincorporates into the banking system the general-deposit warehouses that may set up bonded storage. These warehouses will be permitted to receive imports in bond on the condition that they use such facilities for the import only of products or articles that contribute to the country's development, and not of luxury or unnecessary goods.

The Financing of Economic Development*

ALFREDO NAVARRETE R.

The Mexican Constitution of 1917, arising out of the Revolution of 1910, defines democracy as "not only a judicial structure and a political regime, *but a way of life founded in the steady economic, social, and cultural improvement of the people.*" (Italics mine.) Consequently, Mexico has an economic policy, clearly outlined by its constitution, that charges the Revolutionary governments with the economic development of the country and the equitable distribution of its results among all the sectors of the population. In this task, the evolution of financial policies and practices has played a decisive role during the last fifty years. In order to analyze this role, different periods will be contrasted: 1900–1911; 1925–1940; 1939–1950; and 1950–1959.

This analysis will show that the type and source of financing have influenced productivity by determining the allocation of resources devoted to economic and social development. For this reason, one of the initial tasks of the early governments of the Revolution was to organize private banking and create a system of national credit institutions that would channel resources into basic activities. The amount and composition of financing also affect the total cost and volume of investments that can be carried out with given resources. Furthermore, they have social implications, for they help to equalize the real burden of economic development by absorbing a part of the income of one or another of the sectors of population and, when external financing is involved, by distributing its benefits between the national economy and foreign creditors.

As noted in the conclusions of this study, one of the great accom-

* Originally published as "El financiamiento del desarrollo económico," in *La economía*, Vol. I, *México: 50 años de revolución* (México, D.F., Fondo de Cultura Económica 1960), pp. 509–535.

plishments of the Revolution has been the financing of national economic development primarily with domestic resources. This not only has meant greater independence in channeling investments and controlling means of production, but it also signifies that the Mexican economy has been capable of sustained growth, since the continuous generating of savings and their use in the formation of capital for future growth underlie the process of economic development. The appropriate channeling of national savings through the financial system has been, is, and will continue to be essential to carrying forward economic expansion, a drive that was initiated and now has been renewed by the Revolutionary governments for the benefit of all the Mexican people.

I. The Pre-Revolutionary Period: 1900–1911

Economic development is an arduous and prolonged process—better measured in decades than in years—during which the formation of capital is intensified and new techniques are introduced for the purpose of making the best possible use of the physical, human, and financial resources of a nation to raise the real income of each family and, thereby, the living standard of the people. This process was practically alien to the pre-Revolutionary economy, which could not really be considered a national economy with a drive of its own.

Mining, railroads, foreign capital, and mass poverty sum up the economy of the last epoch of the regime of Porfirio Díaz. The economic expansion of Europe and the United States required a supply of raw materials from countries then thought of as "exotic." The creditor position of the European countries, particularly Great Britain, was reflected in an abundance of capital available for investment in their colonies, as well as in the countries that had won independence from Spain. For its part, the United States, with its economy soaring, was fiercely competing with Europe for the economic penetration of Latin America. In that era, metals were the principal raw material and railroads the means of transport.

The internal economic situation of Mexico was characteristic of a feudal society. The large hacienda produced meager yields for a small group of landowners. The structure of land tenure created a subsistence economy that stood in the way of increased output, the free movement of goods and labor, and the development of a strong domestic market. Manufacturing, just emerging, consisted of a few consumer industries (cigarettes, liquors, textiles) that operated inefficiently and produced little.

Alongside this poor economy was created a large-scale economy of exports and transport, which was in the hands of foreigners. These industries, however, had almost no productive or financial effects on the rest of the economy because of their ownership and purpose.

It is estimated that in the fiscal year 1902–1903 national output at prices then current was close to 700 million pesos.[1] Primary activities—agriculture, livestock raising, forestry, and mining—generated 86 per cent of this production and the remaining activities 14 per cent. Correlatively, more than three-fifths of the labor force worked in agriculture and livestock raising. Corn and sugar cane were leading crops. In 1911, the output of steel ingots came to roughly 8o thousand tons and the installed electric-power capacity was only 165,100 kilowatts.

In order to contrast post-Revolutionary development in these basic industries, it will suffice to mention that in 1959 the output of steel ingots was 1,300,000 tons and the electric-power capacity approximated 3 million kilowatts.

With such low levels of production, most of the population received starvation incomes. The government, under the slogan "Order and Progress," spoke of an economic transformation of the country, which it did not have the means to accomplish. It made the costly mistake of believing that foreign investment by itself would bring economic prosperity. Without a change in the feudal structure and without adequate economic, political, and social bases, this policy only shifted the ownership of national wealth by turning labor, haciendas, mines, and transport over to foreigners, with slight benefit to the majority of the population.

The foregoing conditions explain why there was not enough accumulation of domestic capital.

In the last years of the regime of Porfirio Díaz, it is estimated that United States investment alone represented more than half the national wealth; that is, North Americans owned not only more

---

[1] Unpublished estimate for *Historia moderna de México*, at 1900 prices adjusted by using the index of wholesale prices published in *Estadísticas del comercio exterior de México, 1877–1911* (México, D.F., El Colegio de México, 1960) , p. 156.

than the rest of the foreigners, but more than all Mexicans together.[2]

The total value of foreign investment in the country in 1911, both
direct and indirect, was 3,400 million pesos. Direct investment accounted for 85 per cent and indirect (government bonds) 15 per
cent.

TABLE 1

Foreign Investments in Mexico, 1911

Sector	Millions of Pesos	Per Cent	Per Cent
Total	3,401	100	
Indirect (public debt)	498	15	
Direct	2,903	85	100
Transport	1,131		39
Mining	817		28
Petroleum	104		4
Trade (includes banking)	288		10
Public utilities (telephone, telegraph, electric power)	238		8
Agriculture and livestock	194		7
Industry	(131) [1]		4

[1] Presumably calculated: figure not given in original.
Source: El Colegio de México, unpublished data for *Historia moderna de México.*

The principal investments were strategically located for foreign
powers. Investments in transport (railways) made up 40 per cent
of direct foreign investment. These could be used for economic and,
potentially, military penetration, as most of the lines were extensions
of United States railways, or else connected with Mexico's main
port, Veracruz.

After railways, nonreplaceable resources—mining and petroleum—
attracted more than 30 per cent of total foreign investment; banks,
commerce, and electric energy received 18 per cent. In effect, mineral
exports, transport facilities, and finance were in the hands of foreigners.

Foreign financing of economic activities was disproportionate
simply because most activities were controlled by foreigners. The

[2] See the author's "Exchange Stability, Business Cycles and Economic Development" (doctoral dissertation, Harvard University, 1949).

government followed the liberal doctrine of nonintervention in economic matters. Nevertheless, the State did intervene to give foreign investment all manner of privileges and concessions (excessive subsidies for the construction of railway lines, mineral and petroleum concessions, unlimited customs privileges, and vast land grants).

Investments

The period 1900–1911 was one of heavy investment. For example, it is estimated that the gross total investment in the fiscal year 1902–1903 accounted for 13 per cent of that year's production, a ratio comparable to the average of 14 per cent registered in the last few decades. Nevertheless, this high level of investment in the time of Porfirio Díaz had quite a different effect on economic activity and on the welfare of the majority of the people.

On the one hand, of every peso invested in the 1901–1910 decade, roughly 66 cents was invested by foreigners. In the fiscal year 1902–1903, for example, 45 per cent of new investment was direct foreign investment, which encouraged an economy based on the export of the country's natural resources, for the benefit chiefly of the powerful industrial nations. On the other hand, almost half of new private investment (40 per cent) went into commerce and construction, 7 per cent into banks, and only 8 per cent into manufacturing.[8]

Public investment represented only 5 per cent of new investment. It should be noted in this respect that total expenditures of the federal government in the fiscal year 1902–1903 accounted for 9 per cent of the national product, a percentage very close to the present one. Nevertheless, current expenditures represented 93 per cent of the total, whereas in the 1950's they decreased to an average 65 per cent. Stated in other terms, the Revolutionary governments invest proportionately five times as much as was invested by the government under the dictatorship of Porfirio Díaz.

There existed during this period a huge bureaucracy, not to administer investment in the public interest but to safeguard the political and military stability of the regime. Moreover, in spite of its policy of liberalism, the government absorbed 11 per cent of

[8] Worksheets for *Historia moderna de México,* cited in note 1. The figures for national investment are investments made in pesos in commercial and industrial firms.

national income. In contrast, the Revolutionary governments, which have transformed the country both economically and socially, have utilized only about 9 per cent in recent years.

In the year 1902–1903, there was probably a budgetary surplus of 10 million pesos, or 15 per cent of total revenues for that year. It should be added that 50 per cent of government revenue came from foreign-trade taxes.

TABLE 2

Functional Breakdown of Public Investment
(Thousands of Pesos)

Type of Investment	Fiscal Year 1909–1910	Per Cent	Annual Average during 1950–1959 Decade	Per Cent
Total	8,549	100	4,401,370	100
Basic development	2,203	26	3,633,840	82
Agriculture and livestock	391	5	638,040	14
Manufacturing	29	......	1,334,400	30
Transport and communications	1,783	21	1,661,400	38
Land	235	3	1,517,450	35
Maritime	802	9	124,440	3
Other	746	9	19,510	......
Social	3,610	42	609,680	14
Administration and defense	2,736	32	157,850	4

Source: For 1909–1910: from unpublished data of El Colegio de México prepared for *Historia moderna de México;* for 1950–1959: from Dirección de Inversiones Públicas, Secretaría de la Presidencia.

In the composition of public investment for the fiscal year 1909–1910, the principal category was that of social overhead capital, which constituted 12 per cent. These figures referred mainly to water and drainage projects undertaken in the Valley of Mexico; investments in education and health were minimal. Only 26 per cent of investment went into basic development, as compared with an average 82 per cent for the 1950–1959 decade. There were almost no public investments in industry. On the other hand, 32 per cent of government investment was devoted to administration and defense, whereas in the 1950's this percentage fell to 4 per cent.

In contrast to the pre-Revolutionary situation, from 1950 to 1959 private domestic investment represented more than half of new investment, and private foreign investment but a small proportion. Measured by the inflow of new investment, the reinvestment of profits by foreign-owned enterprises and credits to these enterprises from their home offices abroad (although these sums did not constitute total investment made in the country by foreign capital), the foreign sector represented about 10 per cent. By comparison, the government and governmental agencies created by the Revolution accounted for 40 per cent. Therefore, public investment, a product of the Revolutionary regime, has not been at the expense of domestic private investment, but rather has displaced the dangerous volume of foreign investment of the days of "Order and Progress."

TABLE 3

Gross Fixed Investment
(Millions of Pesos)

Fiscal Period	(1) Aggregate Investment	%	(2) Public Investment	%	(3) Total	%	Private Investment (4) National	%	(5) Foreign	%
I. 1902–03	94	100	5	5	89	95	47	50	42	45
II. 1939–1950	31,779	100	12,586	40	19,193	60	17,157	54	2,036	6
III. 1950–1959	116,961	100	46,011	39	70,950	61	59,816	51	11,134	10

Sources:
I. El Colegio de México, unpublished data for *Historia moderna de México.*
II. Combined Mexican Working Party and the IBRD, *The Economic Development of Mexico* (Baltimore, The Johns Hopkins Press, 1953), and Bank of Mexico, annual report, 1959. Foreign investment includes new investment, reinvestment of earnings, and intercompany accounts.
III. Public investment: from Dirección de Inversiones Públicas, Secretaría de la Presidencia. Total private investment: from Nacional Financiera, Economic Research Department. Direct foreign investment: from the Bank of Mexico, annual reports.

The Financing of Investment

In 1902–1903, foreign capital came to 45 per cent of annual new investment, but its participation in the financing of that investment was even greater, because in addition to direct financing, it made funds available to the economy through purchases of government bonds and banking investments. By contrast, in 1950–1959, investment was 88 per cent financed with domestic savings and only 12 per cent with external resources.

During the period of Porfirio Díaz, public savings represented 15

TABLE 4

Financing of Investment
(Millions of Pesos at 1960 Prices)

Fiscal Period	Aggregate Investment	%	Internal Savings — Total	%	Public	%	Private	%	External Savings — Total	%	Direct Investment	%	Borrowing	%
I. 1902–03	94	100	45	47	14	15	31	32	49	53	42	47	7	6
II. 1939–1950	31,779	100	29,320	92	10,630	33	18,690	59	2,459	8	1,453	5	1,006	3
III. 1950–1959	116,961	100	102,513	88	32,794	28	69,719	60	14,448	12	8,337	7	6,111	5

Sources:
I. El Colegio de México, unpublished data for *Historia moderna de México.*
II. Public savings: from Combined Mexican Working Party, *The Economic Development of Mexico.* Foreign investment: from the Bank of Mexico, annual report, 1959 (excludes reinvestments). Net foreign borrowing: from Nacional Financiera, Economic Research Department (excludes changes in short-term liabilities).
III. Public savings: from Nacional Financiera, Economic Research Department. Foreign direct investment: Bank of Mexico. Foreign borrowing: Nacional Financiera, Economic Research Department.

per cent of the funds available for investment, but the government invested only 5 per cent. That is, although public savings would have permitted greater investment with internal funds, the passive attitude of the State, in the face of widespread poverty, was to maintain a cash surplus.

The inflow of foreign investment in 1902–1903 was 49 million pesos, according to the current-account balance in the balance of payments estimated by the Monetary Commission. In that year, new direct investment amounted to 42 million pesos, or 85 per cent of funds from abroad. The remaining 15 per cent included, therefore, increased foreign purchases of government bonds, in addition to changes in short-term assets, for which there are no details.

These figures show that the great majority of external savings came as direct investment. Thanks to financial changes that took place after Mexico's rebellion, in the 1950–1959 decade loans were 42 per cent of external savings, three times the fraction they represented during the Díaz period.

The Public Debt

The public debt amounted to 497 million pesos, divided into three main categories: (1) Direct external federal debt (309 million pesos), made up of bonds issued by the federal government and repayable in foreign exchange. (2) Indirect external federal debt (45 million pesos), bonds not issued but guaranteed by the federal government, also repayable in foreign exchange. (3) Internal debt, state as well as federal (143 million pesos), redeemable in domestic currency.

The direct external federal debt amounted to 309 million pesos and was used mostly to consolidate and repay other debts, with very little applied to the financing of productive investment:

a) Mexican Consolidated External Loan at 6 per cent, 1888: to refinance part of the existing debt; to reduce liabilities of the Tehuantepec Railroad; and to repay some loans to the National Bank of Mexico.

b) Debt of the Tehuantepec Railroad at 5 per cent, 1889: to finish the Isthmus Railroad.

c) External Debt at 6 per cent, 1890: for the repayment of credits extended by the railroad companies.

d) External Debt at 6 per cent, 1893: to consolidate the floating debt contracted because of an unbalanced budget resulting from crop failures and a decline in the price of silver.

e) Consolidated External Gold Debt at 5 per cent, 1899: to refinance all previous debts in order to consolidate the debt and reduce the rate of interest.

f) External Debt of Mexico City at 5 per cent, 1899–1903: for municipal works.

g) Treasury Bonds at 4.5 per cent, 1903–1904 (short term): to pay for subsidies and public works.

h) Gold Debt at 4 per cent, 1904: a loan of U.S. $40 million for the redemption of Treasury Bonds at 4.5 per cent, 1903–1904; for debts in silver pesos; for the redemption of certificates; and for various public works.

i) Mexican External Gold Debt at 4 per cent, 1910: to convert the consolidated foreign debt of 1899 into a new debt at only 4 per cent annually. Eleven million pounds sterling was received under this loan.

As can be seen from the foregoing, the external federal debt was contracted largely to redeem or convert prior debts.

The indirect federal debt consisted of railroad bonds and the Loan Fund for Irrigation Works and Agricultural Development. The internal debt, though payable in pesos, was held almost entirely by foreigners.

The principal characteristic of the public debt was that all of it was in the hands of foreigners, and it was in great part nonproductive. In contrast, in 1960 the majority of government bonds was held by Mexican nationals, and most of the funds had been used for productive pursuits. With regard to debt servicing, 78 per cent was for interest payments and the rest for amortization, whereas in 1959, interest payments represented 13 per cent of total service, and payments of principal 87 per cent.

In brief, internal financial resources were very small at the beginning of the century, since there were no savings banks or financing companies, nor was there a stock exchange. Almost all of the important banks and some of the lesser ones were largely owned by foreign interests. The lack of domestic capital and the requirements of public finance facilitated foreign investments in banks. At the end of the Díaz period, the National Bank of Mexico, for example, had a paid-up capital of 32 million pesos, of which 70 per cent was French and the remaining 30 per cent was divided between German and United States capital. This bank took care of the short-term needs of the Treasury for debt redemption. The Bank of London and Mexico had 47 per cent French capital and substantial amounts of United States capital in the remaining 53 per cent.

During this period, long-term capital was almost unavailable domestically. Close to 80 per cent of bank credit was on a short-term basis and at high rates of interest. Therefore, the little domestic capital that existed went into speculation rather than productive investment.

The poverty and ignorance of the population, the exploitation of Mexico's land and labor by foreigners, as well as the political regime, exploded in a rebellion that resounded throughout the world as an expression of the Mexican people's yearning for material and spiritual progress. Investments and the form and character of their financing are essential to the attainment of collective welfare and dignity.

II. THE POST-REVOLUTIONARY PERIOD: 1925-1940

After the armed revolt, the Revolution entered into its constructive stage, having as its goal the transformation of the economic and social structure of the country for the benefit of the Mexican people. The Constitution of 1917 entrusted national monetary and credit policy exclusively to the federal government; Article 73, Section X, gives it power to legislate on credit institutions and to establish and, under the provisions of Article 28, control the sole bank of issue. Under this mandate, a series of agencies were created that were indispensable to the achievement of the economic objectives. In this way were established the first public credit institutions to aid the government in its program of public works and general economic development. Foremost among these were the Bank of Mexico in 1925, the National Bank of Agricultural Credit in 1926, the National Urban Mortgage and Public Works Bank in 1933, and the Nacional Financiera, a government instrument for industrialization, in 1934.

The financial policy of the Revolution can be understood only as part of the greater economic and social policy of the nation. There was a natural concern, once warfare had ceased, to put the finances of the country in order, to control the issue of currency, and to halt the growth of the public debt incurred by the Revolutionary movement. At the beginning, the Bank of Mexico and the National Banking Commission, using fairly orthodox procedures, concentrated their efforts on limiting the expansion of the money supply by private banks, on lowering the interest rate on bank credit, and on reducing speculation in foreign exchange. Public financial policy was directed toward balancing the budget. But after the monetary and banking reform of 1931-1932, which reinforced the position of the central bank, and after the abandonment of the gold standard, which facilitated the use of paper money, and after confidence and a degree of liquidity in the monetary system had been restored, fiscal policy began to take shape as an instrument of economic development.

The primary preoccupation was no longer a balanced budget with a cash surplus. Public spending was channeled not only to stimulate economic activity, which had begun to recover from the great world depression, but also to carry out investments to raise the productive capacity of the country and to transform the economic and social structure, now that the government had begun to participate actively in the process of economic growth.

Economic development also required the creation of a truly national economy with rural and urban activities integrated, uniting the country geographically and culturally, orienting production to satisfy internal demand, and fostering progress through the efforts of the Mexicans themselves. A radical change in the role of foreign financing was necessary.

From 1926, when direct foreign investment was estimated at an aggregate of 3,500 million pesos, it began to diminish, influenced in part by the financial collapse of 1929. But the steady decline of the 1930's was due principally to the emigration of the oil companies to Venezuela in search of better fields, and to the oil expropriation in 1938, which, incidentally, converted those direct investments into public debt.

In 1939, direct foreign investment in Mexico was estimated at 2,572 million pesos, with 52 per cent in public utilities and transport and 40 per cent in mining.

Moreover, it was not to be expected that new loans would flow in from abroad. Since 1924, all servicing of the external debt had been suspended because of the country's economic inability to comply with the onerous terms of the De La Huerta–Lamont Agreement of 1922.

In view of the general conditions of the period, marked by intense socio-political mobility, private productive investment was probably only a small part of new domestic investment.

On the other hand, a vast program of public works had been under way since 1935; it is estimated that investment by the federal government during the period 1935–1940 was 1,018 million pesos. The six-year plan established that budgeted expenditures should no longer be a simple accounting exercise, but should become a genuine expression of the social and economic development that the government proposed to carry out. Actually, during the six-year period, 15 per cent of expenditures was allocated to communications and public works, 14 per cent to education, 8 per cent to agriculture and development, and 10.5 per cent to service the public debt.

Public investment during the six-year period from 1934 to 1940 was financed solely with internal resources. In addition to tax revenues, which were insufficient, the government resorted to a budgetary deficit, with overdrafts on the central bank, and, especially in the final two years, to the issue of government bonds which were taken up by the Bank of Mexico. The accumulated deficit from 1936 to 1938 amounted to 119 million pesos. Even so, this deficit was steadily reduced in relative terms; in 1939, 39 per cent of investment by the public sector (the federal government plus the autonomous public agencies) was derived from tax revenues; 36 per cent from current earnings of the agencies themselves; and 25 per cent from loans from the official banking system.

Because economic activity was at a low level, with existing productive factors not fully utilized, deficit financing was able initially to generate increases in production and employment without raising prices too much. The indices of the period show that, as compared with 1929, production had gone up 58 per cent in 1938, and employment 11 per cent. But more significantly, important infrastructural investments were made that increased the productive capacity of the economy and that, together with an intensified agrarian reform and the nationalization of basic sectors, stimulated the development of productive forces.

In the 1930's, there were two devaluations, which fundamentally cannot be attributed to financial policy. The devaluation of 1933 (when parity was fixed at 3.60 pesos to the dollar) was considerably influenced by several years of declining exports, as a result of the economic crisis in the United States. The rate of exchange was forced down in 1938 by the flight of capital, owing to the labor disputes in, and the subsequent expropriation of, the petroleum industry, as well as the 1937 depression in the United States; the negative trade balance was also affected by the relative rise of Mexican prices. (The new rate was pegged at 4.85 pesos to the dollar at the end of 1940.)

During the period under discussion, the financing of domestic investment shifted from external to predominantly internal sources. In external savings, direct foreign investment was reduced from the excessive proportions of the past and was replaced by public debt. By 1939, external savings financed only 15 per cent of total investment and internal savings 85 per cent, with public savings accounting for 39 per cent, and private savings for 46 per cent.

III. PERIOD OF RAPID DEVELOPMENT: 1939–1950

Although the construction of public works began in Mexico around 1925 and the modernization of agriculture some ten years later, industrialization began in earnest in 1940, giving new impetus to economic development.

The period of most rapid growth was from 1939 to 1950, when the annual rate of increase in real product was 6.6 per cent and in population 2.8 per cent, with per capita product gaining an average 3.8 per cent. This trend was supported by a sharp rise in total investment, which in real terms increased at an average annual rate of 10.5 per cent. Public investment was the prime mover of this development; its rate of growth was 12.3 per cent, while that of private investment was 9.3 per cent. Public investment during this period was very substantial, representing 40 per cent of total investment.

In general, although the proportion of product devoted to investment was only 12.8 per cent, there was a high return on investment, since during the Second World War the capacity of installed plants was fully utilized.

It should be pointed out that in this period, when capital formation was most rapid, investment was mainly financed with internal savings. In fact, internal savings financed, on the average, 92 per cent of total annual investment, and external resources only 8 per cent.

Structural changes also took place in the composition of internal and external savings. Within internal savings, public resources became an important component of financing, inasmuch as they rose to as much as 33 per cent of total investment; private savings represented an average 59 per cent. With regard to external savings, foreign investment in the form of loans, which previously had been insignificant, climbed to 42 per cent of external resources.

During this period of rapid development, a progressively larger share of the increase in national income was saved, thereby raising the ratio of savings to national income. The propensity to save went up from approximately 9 per cent in 1939 to about 12 per cent in the early 1950's. At the same time, the steady growth in real national product permitted an absolute increase in aggregate and per capita consumption, although higher prices limited the demand of the lower-income sectors.

There was also an impressive development of the financial system: in the resources of credit institutions, which increased eightfold over the decade; in savings deposits and in financing companies; in the amount of fixed-interest securities outstanding; and in stock-market operations.

During this period, under its new Organic Law of December, 1940, Nacional Financiera began large-scale promotion of industrialization, started developing the stock market and long-term credit, and supported the government in the issue of public securities. Certificates of participation in Nacional Financiera were introduced in 1941, which reinforced the stock market. The National Securities Commission was created in 1946, the National Insurance Commission in 1946, and the National Savings Board in 1949.

Financing Public Investment

The fiscal resources of the federal government are the main source of financing not only investments of the government but of the growing sector of decentralized agencies and state-participation enterprises. The latter sector depended on current fiscal revenues for 22 per cent of its investment and on its own operating surplus for 56 per cent. Government revenues furnished more than half the funds for financing the investment of the entire public sector. These funds, added to the 26 per cent derived from the earnings of the agencies and enterprises, left a gap of 23 per cent to be covered by internal and external financing.

If the magnitude of the effort and the composition and productivity of public investment, with its decisive effect on the rate of development, are taken into account, the inflationary component in its financing—the 14 per cent accounted for by an increase in internal debt—cannot be considered excessive, and it compares favorably with the experience of other countries rapidly developing an unplanned economy. Furthermore, total internal debt rose to only between 6 and 7 per cent of national income.

The inflationary pressures, which adversely affected income distribution and monetary stability, originated chiefly in external factors and were intensified by the structural limitations of the economy. It should be remembered that the 1948 devaluation, with the new parity of 8.65 pesos to the dollar, came at a time of economic recession abroad and of postwar adjustment, when many other countries also devalued.

The increase in domestic debt, primarily through the issue of Treasury certificates (which were withdrawn after 1950) and of long-term securities, furnished financing at a modest cost. These measures were taken in order to finance necessary works that were not attractive to the private sector; and by the end of the decade 75 per cent of the internal debt consisted of bonds issued for the construction of roads and public works and for expansion of the electric-power industry.

It was possible to carry out this financing at moderate cost through the Bank of Mexico, Nacional Financiera, and other national credit institutions that absorbed the issues, and on a reduced scale, through the investments of insurance companies, private banks, and individual investors. Nacional Financiera was instrumental in obtaining large amounts of noninflationary resources by placing its certificates of participation outside the banking system, and these funds were in turn invested principally in government securities in the years immediately following the issue of the certificates.

During the period under consideration, the public sector was provided with a new source of financing—development loans from abroad, which contributed 9 per cent of public investment.

After service on the old foreign debt had been suspended for fifteen years, the Mexican government signed the Agreement of November, 1941, with the United States government, under which debts resulting from general claims derived largely from the armed rebellion were consolidated. The acknowledgment and initial payment of this debt prepared the ground for negotiations, through Nacional Financiera, of the first loans from the Export-Import Bank.

In November, 1942, Mexico signed a new agreement with the International Committee of Bankers, consolidating the debts of the Agreement of 1922 on favorable conditions that fixed Mexico's obligations at the rate of one peso to the dollar, when the rate of exchange was 4.85 pesos to the dollar.

Under the Agreement of 1946, the railroad debt assumed by the government was also settled, and in 1947 obligations to the oil companies were formally recognized. The payment of capital and interest on these debts has been kept up since 1941 (by 1960, almost all the old debt had been redeemed), and the renewal of service in that year marked the beginning of a new policy in the use of external loans. From 1942 to 1950, credits—principally from the Export-Import Bank and the International Bank for Reconstruction and Development—were used for roads, railways, electric power, and other industries. They were low-interest loans, with terms of maturity that took into account the productive duration of the project and the time required to make them self-liquidating. Because these funds came from reputable banking institutions, they have not been used for stock-market or other types of speculation, nor have they burdened Mexico's national sovereignty with guarantees of specific taxes or mortgages, as was the case with the loans before the Revolution.

Financing Private Investment

Although the private sector as a whole saved more than it invested, like the public sector it utilized resources of other sectors. Private investors resorted primarily to credit from banks and other financial institutions, and less so to the issue of fixed-interest securities. These credits were probably less inflationary than the public securities purchased by the central bank, since most of the funds came from private institutions with less overall capacity to increase the money supply.

Private-investment capital was mainly derived from its high rate of earnings, which was favored by the rise in prices, by the low cost of transport and energy supplied by the government, and by low taxes or, in the case of new enterprises, generous tax exemptions.

Considering, on the one hand, that half of all public investment was financed with fiscal revenues collected through a not-very-progressive tax system and, on the other hand, that prices and earnings moved upward, it may be concluded that there was a very large burden on low-income groups to make possible the exceptional growth of national investment during the 1939-1950 period.

Foreign private capital also participated actively in the form of direct investment. Its net contribution was 7.5 per cent of the financing of private investment, but actually it contributed more, since foreign firms reinvested their profits and obtained local financing.

Direct foreign investment increased very little during 1941-1943, rising in cumulative value from 2,260 million to 2,460 million pesos. But after 1944, with the sole exception of 1946, the flow of investment grew substantially, reaching an estimated cumulative value in 1950 of 4,900 million pesos, or double the 1943 level.[4]

Nevertheless, at the end of this period, the composition of these investments had changed significantly. Mining dropped to 20 per cent of total foreign investment, even though almost all investment in this branch continued to be external. Transport accounted for only 13 per cent and commerce 12 per cent. All these reductions were offset by a sharp rise in investment in the manufacturing industry, which by 1959 represented 26 per cent of the total, and electric power, gas, and water, 24 per cent.

IV. THE DECADE 1950–1959

The period 1950-1959 is characterized by a structural change in industrial production. The output of production goods increased more rapidly than that of consumer goods. Whereas the value of capital invested in the manufacture of production goods accounted for 37 per cent of the total invested in manufacturing in 1950, it rose to 50 per cent by the end of the decade. This structural change was due to gains made in the chemical, paper, iron and steel, and transport machinery and equipment industries. It should be mentioned that all these basic industries have been helped or stimulated, directly or indirectly, by Nacional Financiera. In 1959, industry already came to 25 per cent of the gross national product. The growth of the economy has been balanced, even taking into account

4 Data from the *Annual Report* of the Bank of Mexico, 1955.

the period from 1939 to 1959. In fact, agricultural product increased 223 per cent, while industrial output rose 225 per cent.

In spite of external and internal difficulties, from 1950 to 1959 the national economy achieved an annual rate of growth of 4.8 per cent, while population expanded at a rate of 3.0 per cent. That is, the increase in real per capita product was an average 1.8 per cent per annum.

The rate of growth was appreciably less than in 1939-1950. There were two economic recessions in the United States that, together with internal factors (weather conditions affecting agriculture, and changes in administration), caused a reduction in output in 1953. Later, the Mexican economy suffered from the 1958-1959 economic recession in the United States.

One of the fundamental causes, apart from the external ones, for this lag in development was the declining rate of growth of investment: whereas, in the 1939–1950 period it increased at an annual rate of 10.5 per cent, in the following decade it went up at a rate of only 5.6 per cent.

The decline originated chiefly in the severe drop in the rate of growth of public investment, which fell from 12.3 per cent per annum of 4.0 per cent, at the same time that private investment decreased from 9.2 to 6.0 per cent.

The share of national product going into investment was 14.8 per cent, a substantially greater proportion than in the preceding period, when it was 12.8 per cent. Nevertheless, the capital-output ratio rose to 3.08, which slowed down growth. This ratio was undoubtedly affected by public investment, which in general yields results only in the long run, and by the larger volume of capital in production of investment goods in both the public and the private sectors.

Even with real production and money income at their highest levels, the propensity to save was maintained. Although it is estimated that external resources financed a higher proportion of total investment during the period 1950–1959 than during that of 1939–1950, such resources corresponded to long-term funds and did not include the flow of short-term credits, for which figures are less reliable. Taking into account the increase in foreign-exchange reserves and in private credits that have accompanied the sizable rise in Mexico's international transactions, the net contribution of external resources has actually been reduced. Furthermore, the larger volume of interest and profit remittances abroad should be considered.

On the other hand, it is possible that a greater part of internal savings has been used for accumulating liquid assets and inventories instead of for real investment. This situation indicates the importance of monetary stability in economic development for adequately channeling domestic savings, as well as of a fiscal policy that will furnish more noninflationary resources for public investment.

Financing Public Investment

From 1950 to 1959, public investment was 49 per cent financed out of fiscal revenues. The proportion derived from current surpluses of government agencies and enterprises was likewise reduced, and the gap between the savings and the investment of this sector widened.

The inflationary component of public financing—increases in the internal debt—diminished from the 14 per cent in the preceding period to 10 per cent, and changes in holdings of this debt also lowered its inflationary content. On the other hand, external credits climbed to 14 per cent of total public investment. The increase took place in the sector of government agencies and enterprises, which was 30 per cent financed from this source.

The public sector experienced an overall deficit—largely a reflection of the deficit in the sector of government agencies and enterprises—of 13,200 million pesos during all the 1950-1959 period; half of this was incurred from 1957 to 1959 (during the 1939–1950 period, the deficit was close to 2,000 million pesos), and can be attributed to various causes.

In the first place, fiscal revenues represented only 8 per cent of the national product. After 1935, this ratio, which was then 8.5 per cent, declined to 7.5 per cent in 1959. Again this indicates the need for a revision of the fiscal machinery, so that the government, the driving force behind economic development, can count on greater amounts of noninflationary resources for public investments.

On the other hand, in recent years current expenditures of the government increased from 5.3 per cent of the national product in 1955 to 6.0 per cent in 1958. Increases in salaries and subsidies of basic foodstuffs were important factors. Therefore, government savings diminished, especially after 1955, from 2,658 million pesos to

1,999 million pesos in 1958. Nevertheless, in 1959 they recovered, reaching 2,702 million pesos.

The decentralized agencies and state-participation enterprises, although expanding rapidly, did not succeed in augmenting their own resources in equal proportion, a failure which points to the need to lower operation costs and to gradually raise some prices.

By 1959, however, the government had already reduced its deficit by close to 1,000 million pesos, thanks to the improved financial position of the principal autonomous public agencies and to the elimination of some subsidies, which lowered the government's current expenses. This decrease in the deficit was at higher levels of public investment.

The heavy deficit of the final years of this period (1957-1959) did not cause the money supply to expand excessively, because through credit policy the availability of resources to other sectors was restricted. Impact on prices was also lessened by increased financing with external savings, together with an increase in liquidity.

Furthermore, the rising long-term government debt was absorbed more and more by the private banking system, through the deposit requirements administered since 1949 by the Bank of Mexico to channel private funds into long-term credits and investments considered necessary to economic development. At the end of 1959, only 30 per cent of the public debt and 15 per cent of the securities of public agencies were in the hands of the Bank of Mexico. The rest was in portfolios of private credit institutions with limited capacity to increase the money supply.

The country has a financing machinery that is much more flexible than is commonly believed, although it operates in a restricted sector of the economy. The foregoing statement is borne out by the striking growth of specialized institutions, such as *financieras* and mortgage companies, investment houses, and consumer credit companies, as well as the devices founded by *financieras* and investors for managing their funds, sometimes for the purpose of evading the credit regulations of the central bank. Examples are the use of trusts, the operations of commercial and industrial firms to gather funds from the public, and the activity of private groups in the organization and capitalization of new firms. Furthermore, there is a rapidly growing middle class that can be educated to invest in securities.

However, rather than an inelastic demand for securities, it is the cheap financing needed by the public and industrial sectors that makes securities unattractive, for they pay lower interest rates than those prevailing in the market. In this situation, it is evident that various measures should be taken. For one thing, extending the central bank's portfolio requirements to nonbanking institutions would help recruit a larger part of the savings of the financial system for low-cost public financing. Also, easily negotiable securities paying higher interest could be offered to the investing public insofar as the funds could be profitably invested and the securities supported on the market by the central bank. The ready acceptance of the certificates issued in 1960 by Nacional Financiera, placed largely among new savers, is very encouraging.

Additional resources from abroad would still be desirable to help meet the foreign-exchange requirements of the economy. The use of development credits is mainly limited by the capacity of the economy to employ profitably the funds and to generate the foreign exchange needed for future payment. To the extent that funds can be obtained through long-term, low-interest loans, the capacity to service such loans with a given amount of exchange is enhanced. Therefore it is important to keep a balance between the different external sources of financing (official institutions, private banks, credit institutions, and nonbanking investors), in order to maintain a favorable relation of indebtedness on short, medium, and long-term bases.

By changing the form and origin of external financing, its cost has been appreciably reduced. In recent years, development loans, primarily for investment by the public sector, have predominated, and they offer not only greater flexibility in their allocation but also control over the new productive capacity.

Financing Private Investment

In the sector of private investment, internal savings furnished nearly 88 per cent of financing in the period 1950-1959. Almost all external resources were derived from direct investment, with a minor part in the form of medium- and long-term loans.

Cumulative direct foreign investment was worth 17,407 million pesos by the end of 1959. Its structure had undergone profound changes already begun in the 1939-1950 period. Whereas transport represented almost 40 per cent of total foreign investment in 1911, it amounted to only 2 per cent in 1959. Mining dropped from 28 per cent to 15 per cent. By contrast, investment in industry mounted from 4 to 44 per cent, in commerce from 10 to 16 per cent, and in public utilities from 8 to 18 per cent.

Direct foreign investment represents but a small part of total investment and is mainly in manufacturing, leaving the strategic activities—railways, oil, electric power—in Mexican hands.

The emergence of the progressive Mexican entrepreneur means more competition, which will be reflected in better-quality products at lower prices, with a view to the potential domestic market. It is also to be hoped that these businesses will depend less on bank credit, often limited to closed groups, and will resort more to the sale of shares to the public, a procedure which offers broader and financially sounder opportunities.

The maximum capacity of economic growth is not fixed, nor is the total volume of financial resources available for productive investment. The principal aim of financial policy is to obtain the maximum effect of available financial resources on economic development, making sure that its burden and benefits are equitably shared by the community.

V. CONCLUSIONS

The basic conclusion to be drawn from the analysis of the most significant changes that have taken place over the last fifty years in the financing of Mexico's economic development is that the rapid economic, political, and social progress of the Mexican people in this half century would not have been possible under the systems prevailing during the regime of Porfirio Díaz; and that this progress is founded on the structural changes that the Revolutionary governments have introduced.

The foregoing conclusion is supported by the following considerations:

First. The economic structure of the country during the regime of Porfirio Díaz was oriented toward the exterior. The Revolution sought to organize the national economy to satisfy internal needs. In effect, economic development, which before the Revolution was based on mining and railroads, signified the export of the country's nonreplaceable natural resources, such as raw materials to supply foreign industry. The railways were simply a means of sending raw

materials abroad and of introducing manufactured products. With
the Revolution, an effort was made to integrate agriculture, industry, transport, commerce, and finance, in order to improve the
real standard of living of laborers and farmers.

Second. During the regime of Porfirio Díaz, more than half of
each peso of new investment was of external origin. This affected
the use of Mexico's resources and made the foreigner the real bene-
ficiary of such investment. The savings generated in Mexico soon
left the country as interest and profit remittances to foreign investors. It signified, furthermore, that confronted with any world
depression, the country could not sustain the disproportionate service of such investments and had to fall into default, moratorium,
or restrictions on external payments. Under the governments of the
Revolution, 90 per cent of new investment has been financed with
funds of internal origin, and there have been only supplementary
direct investments and loans from abroad. Therefore the government has been able to orient national investment toward fields that
permit an accelerated improvement in the Mexican standard of
living. National entrepreneurs who wish to operate in new fields
acquire, through management contracts, industrial techniques and
experience; or they form an association, keeping the majority, with
foreign investors. These methods make it possible for Mexican enterprises to follow price and investment policies in keeping with the
needs of the Mexican market.

Third. The action of the Revolutionary governments has not
been at the expense of private Mexican investment. On the contrary, the participation of private savings in national economic
activity has doubled. In fact, public investment has filled the va-
cancy left by the massive foreign investment of the regime of Porfirio
Díaz.

Fourth. The Revolutionary governments have been responsible
for a drastic change in the composition of capital from abroad. For
the direct investments (89 per cent) preferred in the epoch of
Porfirio Díaz they have substituted productive development loans,
which keep property in the hands of Mexicans and which, in recent
years, have outstripped direct investments.

Fifth. During the regime of Porfirio Díaz, the public debt was
entirely financed out of foreign funds. Since then, the financing has
been mainly with Mexican funds. This domestic financing of the
public debt has gone through various stages. During the initial peri-

od of armed conflict, unlimited paper money was issued. Afterwards, overdrafts were made on the central bank. Subsequently, they changed to short-term Treasury certificates, and finally, to the issue of long-term bonds. These issues, at the beginning, were primarily absorbed by the central bank; a short time later, they constituted the principal part of the common funds of Nacional Financiera. At present, most of these public securities are held by private banks and investors. The Revolutionary governments have created and fostered an important national-securities market.

In the future, the revolution will continue to advance, inevitably making further changes in the systems of financing the economic and social development of the Mexican people.

In fifty years of revolution, Mexico has learned to be on guard against political dogmas and practices relating to its financial experience. It has passed through different stages demanding different approaches and techniques, and it expects that future stages will also demand new emphasis.

For example, the policy of forced savings through inflation should not be condemned as inappropriate or "inefficient" during the first stages of the development of a backward economy, because it must be judged in the light of real and possible alternatives under the historical circumstances. At the outset of its economic development, Mexico could not easily have resorted to a modern system of voluntary savings or an efficient tax system. For the same reason, inflation cannot now be considered the best method of promoting Mexico's economic development. National savings are being generated in satisfactory amounts and can be collected by existing mechanisms that should be improved (taxes, securities market, and profits of state enterprises). It is necessary to encourage their growth and to channel them into productive investments. Mexico's permanent task is essentially to develop more and more rapidly, ensuring direct benefits to urban and rural workers. It must safeguard its economic independence by financing its development with mainly national resources. To achieve this objective, Mexico will have to undertake a serious revision of its fiscal policy, reinforce its securities markets, and improve the financial structure of the agencies and enterprises of the public sector. This basic problem must be resolved in the coming decade. For its solution, Mexicans are heir to their Revolutionary convictions, education, and technical preparation. With these tools they can forge a solid and just economy that will be an example to the world of what can be accomplished by continuing the Revolutionary ideals of a people who seek the source of their progress and welfare in their own labor.

The accomplishments of the Mexican Revolution in its fifty years of existence may be summed up as political stability, greater social well-being, and an impressive expansion and diversification of the productive capacity of the country. At the same time, the constant and patient Mexicanization of national wealth and sources of employment is found at the core of this creative process—yesterday in violent and forceful stages, today in a more subdued and quiet manner, but always with the firm and unswerving purpose of attaining a prosperous Mexico for the Mexican people.

III. PROBLEMS AND PROSPECTS

Income Distribution in Mexico

BY IFIGENIA M. DE NAVARRETE

Fundamental Problems of the Mexican Economy

BY VICTOR L. URQUIDI

Income Distribution in Mexico*

IFIGENIA M. DE NAVARRETE

The available estimates of national-income distribution by production factors in Mexico have consistently caused a great deal of controversy, not always of a constructive nature. The statistics used annually to calculate the national product do not furnish an adequate basis for estimating the payments received by the factors of production and, consequently, for drawing up a system of national accounts. Annually, the Bank of Mexico derives from census data a breakdown of the national product by the main sectors of industry; changes between census years are approximated by means of production and price indices. The main weakness of these estimates is considered to lie in the commercial sector, for which the most recent data was compiled in 1944 since there was no census of trade and services in 1950.

I. DISTRIBUTION OF INCOME AMONG PRODUCTION FACTORS

Taking into account the foregoing deficiencies, this study made use only of those figures on national-income distribution by productive sectors corresponding to census years 1940 and 1950, as shown in Table 1.

The estimates for 1940 and the unrevised estimate of 1950 were taken from the Report of the Combined Mexican Working Party.[1]

* This paper is a translation of Chapters III and IV of Ifigenia M. de Navarrete's *La distribución del ingreso y el desarrollo económico de México* (México, D.F., Instituto de Investigaciones Económicas, Escuela Nacional de Economía, 1960).

[1] *The Economic Development of Mexico,* Report of the Combined Mexican Working Party, published for the International Bank for Reconstruction and Development (Baltimore, The Johns Hopkins Press, 1953).

TABLE 1

Factoral Income Distribution, 1940 and 1950
(Millions of Pesos; in Percentages)

	1940	% of Total	Unrevised Calculation		Revised Calculation	
			1950	% of Total	1950	% of Total
Wages and salaries[1]	1,841	29.7	9,040	23.9	10,198[5]	29.6
Net agricultural income	1,288	20.7	7,490	19.8	8,991[6]	26.1
Nonagricultural mixed income[2]	912	14.7	3,580	9.5	3,580[7]	10.4
Property income	2,184	35.2	17,792	47.0	11,597	33.7
Profits[3]	1,674	27.0	15,508	41.0	9,190	26.7
Interest	94	1.5	625	1.6	367	1.1
Rent	416	6.7	1,659	4.4	2,040	5.9
Income from government property	n.d.	n.d.	n.d.	n.d.	198	0.6
Less: adjustments[4]	— 18	— 0.3	— 86	— 0.2	— 150	— 0.4
Total: Net national product (income) at factor cost	6,207	100.0	37,816	100.0	34,414	100.0

[1] Includes social benefits.

[2] Includes income of self-employed.

[3] Excludes net income transferred abroad (mainly dividends on foreign investments) : 135 million pesos in 1940 and 261 million in 1950.

[4] For 1940 and 1950, nondeducted indirect taxes; in the revised calculation, interest on the public debt.

[5] Excludes 1,050 million pesos of agricultural wages.

[6] Net agricultural product: 9,090 million pesos less 99 million of indirect taxes (of the remaining 8,991 million, 7,941 are mixed incomes and 1,050 are wages and salaries).

[7] Estimate of the Combined Working Party.

Sources: For figures for 1940 and for unrevised calculation for 1950: Report of the Combined Mexican Working Party, *The Economic Development of Mexico*, Table 2. For revised calculation for 1950: Banco de México, Nacional Financiera, y otros, *Estructura y proyección de la economía de México* (processed), Table IV, pp. 182–189; for net agricultural product: *ibid.*, p. 23.

The revised estimate for 1950 was based on a system of national accounts derived from an input-output table for that year. All available statistics were used for the 1950 revised estimate, including data from the 1950 census, which had already been finished at the time of the revision. Thus the 1950 revision was deemed an improvement over the estimates of the Combined Mexican Working Party, which are less accurate because those estimates had to draw on preliminary and incomplete data of the 1950 census. On the other hand, the revised calculation undervalues profits to the extent that trade volume is underestimated.

As shown in Table 1, the national income by factor distribution exhibits the following characteristics:

1. The wages-and-salaries category comprised 30 per cent of the national income in 1940, and maintained its relative importance in the revised calculation of 1950.

This proportion, apparently very low if compared with corresponding proportions of other countries, is closely related to the number of nonagricultural wage earners in the labor force, which is also very low—33 per cent in 1950—as can be seen in Table 2.[2]

TABLE 2

Gainfully Employed Labor Force
(Thousands)

	1940	% of Total	1950	% of Total	% of Change
Wage earners	3,069	56.0	3,831	52.5	24.8
Agricultural	1,913	34.9	1,431	19.6	— 25.2
Nonagricultural	1,156	21.1	2,400	32.9	107.6
Enterpreneurs[1]	2,411	44.0	3,467	47.5	43.8
Agricultural	1,726	31.5	2,536	34.7	46.9
Nonagricultural	685	12.5	931	12.8	35.9
Total gainfully employed	5,480	100.0	7,298	100.0	33.2

[1] Includes self-employed workers.
Source: Population censuses of 1940 and 1950.

In the unrevised estimate, wages and salaries declined to 24 per

[2] As pointed out by Mr. Eliel Vargas, Banco de México, there is in Mexico, as in other countries, a close relationship between the proportion of wages and salaries and the proportion of wage earners in the labor force. That is, in countries where the number of wage earners is large, the proportion of wages and salaries is high, and vice versa.

cent; to the extent that industrial development continues, the number of these workers will keep on rising.

The aggregate labor force increased 33 per cent; the number of entrepreneurs and self-employed workers, 44 per cent; and wage earners, 25 per cent. Nevertheless, wage earners did not expand their share in the national income, partly because the increment in the labor force in relation to the increase in the supply of capital goods tends to keep wages low, especially among unskilled and semiskilled groups.

Another reason that accounts for the small share of wages and salaries of the wage-earning class is its low educational and technical level; in other countries, where the level of elementary education is much higher, part of the pay received by salaried employees is in a sense a return on capital invested in them (education, training).[3]

2. Owing to the difficulty of breaking down mixed incomes, net agricultural income, which includes wages, profits, rents, interest, and other items, was recorded separately. In 1940, net agricultural income represented 21 per cent of national income and, according to the estimates of the Combined Mexican Working Party, it was 20 per cent in 1950. The revised calculation brings it up to 26 per cent, a gain that is explained primarily by the increase in cattle raising, which underwent upward revision when the Agricultural and Livestock Census data became available.

3. The category designated as "nonagricultural mixed income" largely comprises independent producers who work for themselves, sometimes with very little capital. For this reason, many researchers consider the income of this group as equivalent to wages. Agricultural income was separated from this category, and the figures of the Combined Mexican Working Party were relied upon for the rest of the mixed-income groups. Owing to the smaller aggregate figure for national income in the revised estimate, nonagricultural mixed incomes slightly increased their relative share.

4. The category designated "profits" is a residual. It can also be compensation to a factor of production—the "entrepreneur." For the sum total of the enterprises, profits are the difference between (*a*) the sales proceeds of consumer goods and services plus the value of

---

[3] In Mexico, according to the 1950 census data, the adult population had received an average of two years' of education, whereas in the United States the average was eleven years.

investment—including net change in inventories—and *(b)* payments to factors of production, excluding payments received by those who can make use of the residual, whom we call "entrepreneurs."

In Mexican statistics, the foregoing concept includes the net income of all enterprises, not only those explicitly organized as incorporated capital enterprises, but also those that operate under individual proprietors. In other countries and in the United Nations manuals, the term "profits" is reserved for the net income of corporate enterprises. Profits, as they are very broadly defined in Mexico, were 27 per cent of the income in 1940. The Combined Working Party estimated that their share had risen to 41 per cent by 1950, whereas in the revised calculation they remained at the same level as in 1940, a reflection in part of the downward adjustment in the commerce component. On that evidence, many researchers stated that the inequity of income distribution became more acute and highly adverse to labor, although the Combined Working Party itself recognized that

the standards of living for industrial workers and for agricultural workers in the new agricultural regions are well above those in the older unimproved farming areas. Improvements in the standard of living occurred for workers when they moved from the old agricultural lands into the new and expanding agricultural regions or into commerce and industry. These changes helped to raise the overall standard of living in Mexico. However, no significant improvement was discernible in the real income of farmers in the old areas or in that of industrial workers as a group, although, of course, the number of workers that improved their standard of living increased considerably.[4]

In spite of the estimates revision of the calculations, then, the statements made by the Combined Working Party continue to be valid, as will be seen if the figures are arranged somewhat differently—as in Table 3—following the method used by Mr. Flores Márquez in his study of the distribution of income.[5] That is to say, during the 1940–1950 period the benefits of Mexico's economic development were distributed equitably and were absorbed almost entirely by a growing group of the population that could derive its income

[4] Report of the Combined Mexican Working Party, *Economic Development of Mexico*, p. 11.

[5] Miguel Flores Márquez, "La distribución del ingreso en México" (mimeographed thesis, National School of Economics [Escuela Nacional de Economía], Mexico, 1958).

TABLE 3

Factoral Income Distribution
(Millions of Pesos at 1950 Prices; in Percentages)

Sector	Gainfully Employed[1] (Thousands)		Aggregate Income			Income per Worker (at 1950 Prices)			% Change in Income per Worker	
	1940	1950	1940[2]	1950[2]	1950 Adjusted[3]	1940[2]	1950	1950 Adjusted[3]	1950/40[2]	1950/40[3]
All sectors	5,480	7,298	17,612	37,816	34,414	3,214	5,182	4,716	61.2	46.7
Entrepreneurs	2,411	3,467	10,548	27,399	22,649	4,375	7,903	6,533	80.6	49.3
Wage earners	3,069	3,831	7,064	10,417	11,765	2,302	2,719	3,071	18.1	33.4
Agriculture	3,639	3,967	3,655	7,490	8,991	1,004	1,888	2,266	88.0	125.7
Entrepreneurs	1,726	2,536	2,086	6,630	7,941	1,209	2,614	3,131	116.2	159.0
Wage earners	1,913	1,431	1,569	860	1,050	820	601	734	— 26.7	— 10.5
Nonagricultural	1,841	3,331	13,957	30,826	25,423	7,581	9,104	7,632	20.1	0.7
Entrepreneurs	685	931	8,462	20,769	14,708	12,353	22,308	15,798	80.6	27.9
Wage earners[4]	1,156	2,400	5,495	9,557	10,715	4,753	3,982	4,465	— 16.2	6.1

1 Population censuses of 1940 and 1950.
2 Miguel Flores Márquez, "La distribución del ingreso en México," Tables 4 and 6. Income of self-employed proprietors in the amount of 460 million pesos in 1940 and 1,922 million in 1950 (Combined Working Party, *The Economic Development of Mexico*, Table 2) was deducted from Flores Márquez' estimate of nonagricultural wages.
3 See Table 1.
4 Included for 1950, 517 million pesos of capital income received by wage earners, according to the census; on this basis, the income of wage earners for 1940 includes 272 million pesos of capital income—at 1950 prices—or 96 million pesos at 1940 prices—that is, 4.4 per cent of property incomes. See Table 1.

from profits. The inflation of that decade favored those who were in a position to buy and sell.

Flores Márquez divides the labor force into two groups: *(a)* wage earners and *(b)* "entrepreneurs," the latter group covering all the rest, including those who are self-employed both in the farm sector *(ejidatarios)* and in urban areas. He divides the economy into two sectors: agricultural and nonagricultural. He uses the figures of the Combined Working Party, supplemented by figures taken directly from the census. In addition, his study makes use of the revised figures of the input-output table for 1950. As shown in Table 3, the results point exactly in the same direction to a lesser—but no less spectacular—degree.

The following analysis refers only to the revised figures. Before going on, it should be noted that income at factor cost reflects only the probable payment to factors, not the income actually received; that is, they are not personal-income figures. To arrive at that level, it would be necessary to deduct, among other items, business taxes, undistributed business profits, and public-enterprise profits. Nevertheless, in the case of Mexico, such adjustments can be dispensed with without invalidating the results. On the one hand, undistributed profits, although they are usually reinvested and do not go into the pockets of capitalists, do increase the capitalists' wealth and command over capital goods; on the other hand, taxes on business were fairly moderate during the forties.[6]

During the 1940-1950 period, real income per working person went up 47 per cent, although this increase was very unevenly distributed. Relatively speaking, the sector that benefited the most was agriculture. Its 126-per-cent rise in average income was entirely attributable to a 159-per-cent increase in the income of "entrepreneurs," since the average income of the wage-earner group fell 11 per cent, whereas their numbers decreased 30 per cent as a result

[6] Furthermore, it is debatable whether taxes on exports and the production of minerals should be included as direct taxes on the assumption that, because the price of primary products is determined in the international markets, they are paid out of profits and not passed on to the consumer; or whether they are passed back to and borne by the wage earners, in which case they should not be considered direct taxes on business. These taxes amounted to 73 million pesos in 1940 and 728 million in 1950. (*Sources:* for 1940: Report of the Combined Mexican Working Party, *Economic Development of Mexico,* Table 118; for 1950: Secretaría de Hacienda y Credito Público for the year 1950.)

of the shift to urban occupations and probably also of the emigration of *braceros*. The increase in the total average income of the
"industrial" sector was barely 1 per cent. This rise was altogether
concentrated in the entrepreneur sector—where average income rose
28 per cent—whereas in the wage-earner sector it declined 6 per
cent. Nevertheless, owing to the differences in average income between agriculture and other sectors, the real income of wage earners
taken as a group went up 33 per cent despite the fall in each of
the two sectors taken separately.

In other words, wage earners can lose ground in each sector and
still advance as a group, because the disparity between urban and
rural productivity and between different branches of the economy
(see Fig. 1) permits shifts to better-paid jobs even though real wages
may be declining.[7]

TABLE 4

Ratio of Nonagricultural to Agricultural Average Incomes
(Ratios at 1950 Prices)

	1940	*1950*
Total average income	7.5	3.37
Nonagricultural entrepreneurs	10.22	5.05
Nonagricultural wage earners	5.80	6.08

Source: Table 3.

As can be observed, in 1940 the average income per working
person in nonagricultural activities was eight times higher than in
agricultural activities. On the average, a nonagricultural entrepreneur earned ten times more than an agricultural entrepreneur, and
an industrial wage earner six times more than an agricultural day
laborer.[8] In 1950, the disparity in average income between the nonagricultural and the agricultural entrepreneurs was impressively re-

[7] Diego López Rosada and Juan Noyola Vásquez, in their article "Los
salarios reales en México" (*El Trimestre Económico* [April-June, 1951], p. 207)
reached the conclusion that "the average real wage of all the economically
active population has increased, although it has decreased in almost every
given category of work."

[8] The 1950 figure for the income of nonagricultural entrepreneurs is low
if it is remembered that the commerce and profits components are probably
undervalued in the estimate of the national product derived from the input-
output table.

duced. On the other hand, the average income of a nonagricultural wage earner continued to be six times that of an agricultural wage earner.

If the average income of the entrepreneur is compared with that of the wage earner, it becomes clear that from 1940 to 1950 the gap between these average incomes increased spectacularly in the agricultural sector and to a lesser degree in the nonagricultural sector.

TABLE 5

Ratio of Entrepreneur to Wage-earner Average Incomes
(Ratios at 1950 Prices)

	1940	*1950*
Average income of all entrepreneurs	1.90	2.13
Agricultural entrepreneurs	1.47	4.27
Nonagricultural entrepreneurs	2.60	3.54

These figures do not necessarily mean that the improvement in the living standard of the entrepreneurs was proportional to their growing share of the income, for the larger part of their income was reinvested or paid in taxes—although at still very low levels.

Keynes's well-known postulate can be applied here: during an expansionary period, given the organization, equipment, and techniques, money wages increase; but real wages move in the opposite direction, because effective demand expands more rapidly than output and, therefore, prices outstrip wages.[9] This situation will not induce investment directly related to wage earners' consumption, but to other investments and to the consumption of those groups that derive income from profits. The level of employment, stimulated by low wages, will expand to the point where the decline in real consumption exceeds the increase in effective demand for investment goods and luxury articles (allowing for the import leakage). This circumstance may explain in part Mexico's internal depression of 1952-1953, although external causes such as the decrease in the capacity to import also contributed.

A grouping of all entrepreneurs on one side and all wage earners on the other will furnish an idea of the variations in the structure of demand.

[9] John Maynard Keynes, *The General Theory of Employment, Interest and Money* (London, MacMillan and Co., 1936), Chap. 19, p. 10.

TABLE 6

Structure of Demand, 1940–1950
(Millions of Pesos at 1950 Prices)

	1940	% of Total	1950	% of Total	% of Change 1950/1940
Aggregate income:	17,612	100.0	34,414	100.0	95.4
Entrepreneurs	10,548	59.9	22,649	65.8	114.7
Wage earners	7,064	40.1	11,765	34.2	66.5
Agricultural sector:	3,655	20.8	8,991	26.1	146.0
Entrepreneurs	2,086	11.9	7,941	23.1	280.7
Wage earners	1,569	8.9	1,050	3.0	− 33.1
Nonagricultural sector:	13,957	79.2	25,423	73.9	82.2
Entrepreneurs	8,462	48.0	14,708	42.8	73.8
Wage earners	5,495	31.2	10,715	31.1	95.0

Source: Table 3.

As may be seen from Table 6, in 1940 entrepreneurs received 60 per cent of the income, and wage earners 40 per cent; by 1950, entrepreneurs had augmented their purchasing power to 66 per cent of the total income, whereas wage earners had decreased theirs to 34 per cent of total income.

Therefore, those researchers who protested the unfair distribution of income were right, but so were those who claimed that there had been a general rise in the standard of living. An analysis of the data shows that these statements are not contradictory. Actually, the decade registers both trends:

First. In real terms there was a gain of 95 per cent in aggregate income and of 47 per cent in average income per worker (entrepreneurs and wage earners combined—Table 3) .

Second. There was a very uneven distribution of the increase in income. Least benefited were the wage earners, whose aggregate income went up 66 per cent; but since their number expanded 25 per cent, their average income rose 33 per cent. The most favored were the entrepreneurs, whose total income increased 115 per cent, whose number grew 44 per cent, and whose average income rose 49 per cent.

Third. The economic development of the decade widened the gap between the average incomes of entrepreneur and wage earner, especially in the agricultural sector. The unequal distribution of the increase in income is intensified when it is taken into account that the entrepreneur sector embraces income levels that vary from the humble *ejidatario* and artisan to the prosperous merchant and industrialist. The same reasoning is not equally applicable to the wage earners, because the dispersion of their wages is much less than that of mixed incomes and profits.[10]

Fourth. The most desperate economic conditions were those of agricultural wage earners. Their total income decreased 33 per cent, but since their numbers fell 25 per cent, their average income diminished only 11 per cent. This situation reveals that large rural groups remain in a critical state of backwardness and poverty.

Fifth. There was a rise in the average standard of living of workers who could shift from activities of very low productivity—chiefly rural—to more remunerative employment; and there was a drop in the standard of living of those who remained in the same occupational category, where the loss in their real wages was not offset by an increase in their supply of work.

Sixth. There was a greater increase in the relative productivity of agriculture, an increase that was partly a reflection of its very low starting point.

II. PERSONAL-INCOME DISTRIBUTION

The total absence of data on the distribution of personal income in Mexico has up to now prevented even a superficial analysis of this question.

Income tax is schedular[11] and, since there is no tax on aggregate personal income, this basic source of information for personal-income statistics is lacking. Moreover, there is no regular and continuous tabulation of social-security data. The social-security system still has not been extended to all of Mexico and, at present, covers only 25 per cent of the wage-earning population. Nor, until recently, were there any surveys of family incomes.

In October, 1956, a nationwide sampling survey was made of the incomes and expenditures of the population.[12] Five thousand ques-

[10] In 1956, wage earners with incomes of more than 1,000 pesos a month represented barely 9 per cent of all wage earners in Mexico (see Table 10).

[11] Income tax is based on schedules—legislated for each type of business organization, for the professions, etc.; it is not a personal-income tax working across the board.

[12] In 1954, the Sampling Department (Departamento de Muestra) had carried out the same survey for the Federal District alone.

tionnaires were used, with the family as the sampling unit. Mexico was divided into five zones, plus the Federal District, in which a special sampling was made by sections. The survey's basic data on the incomes of a universe of 5,779,426 families is in Table 7A, which includes Federal District data that had not been published before.

Even though the survey was less comprehensive than studies of this type should be, it was decided to make use of it because it constituted the first source of overall information about a problem crucial to the country's economy and politics. The form in which it is here presented is believed to reflect—if not accurately, with reasonable approximation—the situation that prevails in Mexico as regards the distribution of personal income by family as well as by geographic zones.

The survey was based on official population estimates and adopted the family as the unit, considered to be made up on the average of 5.6 members. The families were grouped according to money-income level and not size. Individuals who lived alone or independently were not considered separately. As the survey was conducted in the month of October (of 1956) it probably reflects seasonal factors, principally the seasonal employment of manual laborers.

The data of the sample was adjusted in order to make it coincide with total personal income calculated on the basis of the national-income aggregate, taking into account what is called in the sampling survey "expenditures in kind," which are at the same time "income in kind"; the latter term refers to consumption items received in kind, as a supplement to money income, such as housing, electricity, foodstuffs. The methods and assumptions used to effect the adjustment are set forth in Tables 11 and 11A and on page 158 of this essay.

Comparisons between zones were made only on the basis of the reported money income, because it was believed that it was better to work with the data in its purest form and that, in any case, the difference in regional incomes would stand out. On the one hand, incomes in kind, which are of primary importance to families in the lowest income brackets, were excluded. On the other hand, no adjustment was made for the "omitted" income not declared by high-income families. In spite of these limitations, the figures do indicate the degree of income disparity by geographic zones and of income concentration as *between* zones, but they are less reliable regarding the concentration of income *within* each zone.

The degree of income concentration by geographic zones is shown in Figure 1. The Y-axis measures the cumulative percentage of families and the X-axis that of incomes. The rightmost line represents equality—that is, 10 per cent of the families receive 10 per cent of the income, 20 per cent receive 20 per cent, etc. This presentation, originated by Corrado Gini, is most useful in pointing out the higher-income groups. The more a zone line moves to the left, the higher the income concentration in that zone. In Mexico, the most inequitable is found in the Federal District and the least inequitable in the North Pacific Zone. Figure 1 shows that the highest 10-per-cent income group received almost 40 per cent of the total income in the Federal District and 30 per cent of the income in the North Pacific Zone. Furthermore, the highest 3-per-cent income group received 21 per cent of aggregate income in the Federal District, 19 per cent in the North Zone, 18 per cent in the Gulf of Mexico Zone, and 15 per cent in the North Pacific Zone.

According to the unadjusted figures derived from the sample, the greater part of family income was concentrated in the Federal District (25 per cent), in the Central Zone (24 per cent), and in the North Zone (20 per cent). These regions are, at the same time, the most densely populated, comprising 14 per cent, 35 per cent, and 20 per cent, respectively, of the total population (see Table 7). The average money-income per family for all of Mexico was 693 pesos per month. The highest incomes correspond to the Federal District (1,282 pesos per month per family) and the North Pacific Zone (1,189 pesos per month per family). These two regions had an average income 1.8 times the average for the Republic. Bearing in mind, however, that the cost of living is higher in these regions, real income is smaller than it appears to be.[18]

The Gulf of Mexico and the North Zones are most representative of the economic condition of the average Mexican family. But while the Gulf states are quite homogeneous in their degree of economic development, those in the North Zone are very dissimilar. Taking as an index states' expenditures per inhabitant, the Gulf states—Tabasco, Yucatán, Campeche, and Veracruz—spent 43, 44, 50, and

[18] The following is an indication—certainly not a wholly adequate one—of the differences in the cost of living: the minimum wage was 11 pesos and 9.50 pesos for city and countryside, respectively, in the Federal District; 11 pesos in the North Pacific Zone; 9 and 7 pesos in the Gulf of Mexico Zone; 8 and 6 pesos in the North Zone, 7 and 6 pesos in the Central Zone; and 5 and 4 pesos in the South Pacific Zone.

TABLE 7

Family-Income Distribution by Income Classes and Geographic Zones in Order of Average Monthly Income Levels, 1956

Geographic Zones[1]	Total Monthly Income of Zone (Millions of Pesos)	(% of Total)	Number of Families (Thousands)	(% of Total)	Monthly Income per Family (Pesos)	(% of Total)	Number of Families with Reported Incomes — Less than 300 Pesos	From 300 to 500 Pesos	From 500 to 1,000 Pesos	From 1,000 to 3,000	More than 3,000
Republic of Mexico	4,004.0	100.0	5,779.4	100.0	693	1.00	2,009	1,245	1,592	799	135
Federal District	997.1	24.9	777.4	13.5	1,282	1.85	51	140	307	223	55
North Pacific	483.7	12.1	406.8	7.0	1,189	1.72	62	54	114	151	26
Gulf of Mexico	464.7	11.6	665.8	11.5	689	0.99	198	164	192	97	16
North	790.6	19.7	1,171.2	20.3	675	0.97	372	255	375	145	2
Central	940.3	23.5	2,025.0	35.0	464	0.67	964	459	452	141	10
South Pacific	327.6	8.2	733.2	12.7	447	0.65	362	173	152	42	3

1 States in these zones are:
North Pacific: Baja California, Nayarit, Sinaloa, Sonora.
Gulf of Mexico: Campeche, Tabasco, Veracruz, Yucatán.
North: Chihuahua, Coahuila, Durango, Nuevo León, San Luis Potosí, Tamaulipas, Zacatecas.
Central: Aguascalientes, Guanajuato, Hidalgo, Jalisco, México, Michoacán, Morelos, Puebla, Querétaro, Tlaxcala.
South Pacific: Colima, Chiapas, Guerrero, Oaxaca.
Source: Table 7A.

TABLE 7A

Distribution of Monthly Family Income in Mexico, 1956

Zones[1] and Income Classes	Number of Families	Percentage of Total	Average Income (Pesos)	Class Income Thousands of Pesos	Class Income Percentage of Total	Increasing Cumulative No. of Families (%)	Increasing Cumulative Income by Class (%)	Decreasing Cumulative No. of Families (%)	Decreasing Cumulative Income by Class (%)
North Pacific	406,773	100.0	1,189.10	483,693	100.0				
Less than 100	2,372	0.6	55.00	130	0.0	0.6	0.0	100.0	100.0
From 101 to 200	23,718	5.8	166.85	3,975	0.8	6.4	0.8	99.4	100.0
From 201 to 300	35,578	8.8	270.95		2.0	15.2	2.8	93.6	99.2
From 301 to 400	18,975	4.7	355.28		1.4	19.9	4.2	84.8	97.0
From 401 to 500	35,578	8.7	472.87		3.5	26.6	7.7	80.2	95.8
From 501 to 750	71,156	17.5	649.15		9.5	46.1	17.2	71.4	92.3
From 751 to 1,000	42,693	10.5	892.82		7.9	56.6	25.1	53.9	82.7
From 1,001 - 2,000	120,965	29.7	1,448.40		36.2	86.3	61.3	43.4	74.9
From 2,001 - 3,000	29,648	7.3	2,488.57		15.3	93.6	76.6	13.7	38.6
More than 3,000	26,090	6.4	4,335.23	113,106	23.4	100.0	100.0	6.4	23.4
North	1,171,181	100.0	675.00	790,558	100.0				
Less than 100	34,815	3.0	70.91		0.3	3.0	0.3	100.0	100.0
From 101 to 200	151,794	12.9	156.58		3.0	15.9	3.3	97.0	99.7
From 201 to 300	185,217	15.8	265.63	49,199	6.2	31.7	9.5	84.1	96.7
From 301 to 400	137,868	11.8	358.99	49,493	6.3	43.5	15.8	68.3	90.5
From 401 to 500	116,979	10.0	451.81	52,852	6.7	53.5	22.5	56.5	84.2
From 501 to 750	243,706	20.8	628.14		19.4	74.3	41.9	46.5	77.5
From 751 to 1,000	130,905	11.2	871.56		14.4	85.5	53.3	25.7	58.1
From 1,001 to 2,000	125,394	10.7	1,438.72		22.8	96.2	79.1	14.5	43.7
From 2,001 to 3,000	19,496	1.7	2,490.21		6.1	97.9	85.2	3.8	20.9
More than 3,000	25,067	2.1	4,656.89	116,734	14.8	100.0	100.0	2.1	14.8

[1] The states included in each zone and the variance ratios are as follows:
North Pacific: Baja California, Nayarit, Sinaloa, Sonora (C.V. = + 10.1%).
North: Chihuahua, Coahuila, Durango, Nuevo León, San Luis Potosí, Tamaulipas, Zacatecas (C.V. = ± 6.7%).
Central: Aguascalientes, Guanajuato, Hidalgo, Jalisco, México, Michoacán, Morelos, Puebla, Querétaro, Tlaxcala (C.V. = ± 5.2%).
Gulf of Mexico: Campeche, Tabasco, Veracruz, Yucatán (C.V. = ± 4.8%).
South Pacific: Colima, Chiapas, Guerrero, Oaxaca (C.V. = ± 4.3%).
Federal District (C.V. = ± 7.5%).
Source: General Bureau of Statistics, Department of Sampling (Dirección General de Estadística, Departamento de Muestra), survey conducted in October, 1956.

TABLE 7A (Continued)

Zones1 and Income Classes	Number of Families	Percentage of Total	Average Income (Pesos)	Class Income Thousands of Pesos	Class Income Percentage of Total	Increasing Cumulative No. of Families (%)	Increasing Cumulative Income by Class (%)	Decreasing Cumulative No. of Families (%)	Decreasing Cumulative Income by Class (%)
Central	2,024,998	100.0	464.32	940,254					
Less than 100	118,990	5.9	73.30	8,722	0.9	5.9	0.9	100.0	100.0
From 101 to 200	448,918	22.2	155.38	69,753	7.4	28.1	8.3	94.1	99.1
From 201 to 300	395,913	19.5	260.06	102,961	11.0	47.6	19.3	71.9	91.7
From 301 to 400	250,961	12.4	359.24	90,155	9.6	60.0	28.9	52.4	80.7
From 401 to 500	207,692	10.3	459.10	95,351	10.1	70.3	39.0	40.0	71.1
From 501 to 750	311,538	15.4	626.12	195,060	20.7	85.7	59.7	29.7	61.0
From 751 to 1,000	140,625	6.9	858.22	120,678	12.8	92.6	72.5	14.3	40.2
From 1,001 to 2,000	117,909	5.8	1,391.62	164,084	17.5	98.4	90.0	7.4	27.4
From 2,001 to 3,000	22,716	1.1	2,466.43	56,027	6.0	99.5	96.0	1.6	9.9
More than 3,000	9,736	0.5	3,846.95	37,454	4.0	100.0	100.0	0.5	4.0
Gulf of Mexico	665,808	100.0	697.87	464,653					
Less than 100	6,814	1.0	65.00	443	0.1	1.0	0.1	100.0	100.0
From 101 to 200	79,819	12.0	167.34	13,357	2.9	13.0	3.0	99.0	99.9
From 201 to 300	110,968	16.7	264.73	29,377	6.3	29.7	9.3	87.0	97.0
From 301 to 400	87,606	13.2	359.22	31,470	6.8	42.9	16.1	70.3	90.7
From 401 to 500	75,925	11.4	458.61	34,820	7.5	54.3	23.6	57.1	83.9
From 501 to 750	121,676	18.3	627.45	76,346	16.4	72.6	40.0	45.7	76.4
From 751 to 1,000	70,085	10.5	862.37	60,439	13.0	83.1	53.0	27.4	60.1
From 1,001 to 2,000	77,872	11.7	1,357.85	105,738	22.8	94.8	75.8	16.9	47.0
From 2,001 to 3,000	19,468	2.9	2,507.68	48,820	10.5	97.7	86.3	5.2	24.2
More than 3,000	15,575	2.3	4,099.06	63,843	13.7	100.0	100.0	2.3	13.7
South Pacific	733,229	100.0	446.60	327,463	100.0				
Less than 100	56,640	7.7	65.00	3,682	1.1	7.7	1.1	100.0	100.0
From 101 to 200	156,640	21.4	158.38	24,792	7.6	29.1	8.7	92.3	98.9
From 201 to 300	149,323	20.4	263.33	39,321	12.0	49.5	20.7	70.9	91.3
From 301 to 400	93,713	12.8	370.88	34,756	10.6	62.3	31.3	50.5	79.3
From 401 to 500	79,296	10.8	458.33	36,344	11.1	73.1	42.4	37.7	68.7
From 501 to 750	101,952	13.9	623.85	63,603	19.4	87.0	61.8	26.9	57.6
From 751 to 1,000	50,461	6.9	878.98	44,354	13.6	93.9	75.4	13.0	38.2

Size class (hectares)									
From 1,001 to 2,000	36,044	4.9	1,464.55	52,788	16.1	98.8	91.5	6.1	24.6
From 2,001 to 3,000	6,179	0.8	2,313.89	14,298	4.4	96.6	95.9	1.2	8.5
More than 3,000	3,089	0.4	4,378.33	13,525	4.1	100.0	100.0	0.4	4.1
Federal District	777,437	100.0	1,282.46		100.0				
Less than 100	3,780	0.5	81.38	307	0.0	0.5	0.0	100.0	100.0
From 101 to 200	8,821	1.1	180.00		0.2	1.6	0.2	99.5	100.0
From 201 to 300	39,061	5.0	275.32	10,754	1.1	6.6	1.3	198.4	99.8
From 301 to 400	66,781	8.6	369.61	24,683	2.5	15.2	3.8	93.0	98.7
From 401 to 500	73,082	9.4	468.46	34,236	3.4	24.6	7.2	84.8	96.2
From 501 to 750	199,084	25.6	633.42	126,104	12.6	50.2	19.8	75.4	92.8
From 751 to 1,000	108,362	14.0	880.99	95,466	9.6	64.2	29.4	49.8	80.2
From 1,001 to 2,000	168,844	21.7	1,450.81	244,961	24.6	85.9	54.0	35.8	70.6
From 2,001 to 3,000	54,181	7.0	2,577.26	139,640	14.0	92.9	68.0	14.1	46.0
More than 3,000	55,441	7.1	5,759.20	319,296	32.0	100.0	100.0	7.1	32.0
Total in Mexico	5,779,426	100.0	692.80	4,004,035	100.0	100.0	100.0	100.0	100.0
Less than 100	223,411	3.9	72.20	16,132	0.4	3.9	0.4	100.0	100.0
From 101 to 200	869,602	15.0	157.79	137,215	3.4	18.9	3.8	96.1	99.6
From 201 to 300	916,060	15.9	263.35	241,252	6.0	34.8	9.8	81.1	96.2
From 301 to 400	655,904	11.3	361.78	237,298	5.9	46.1	15.7	65.2	90.2
From 401 to 500	588,552	10.2	459.47	270,427	6.8	56.3	22.5	53.9	84.3
From 501 to 750	1,049,112	18.2	629.47	660,386	16.5	74.5	39.0	43.7	77.5
From 751 to 1,000	543,131	9.4	871.16	473,155	11.8	83.9	50.8	25.5	61.0
From 1,001 to 2,000	646,968	11.2	1,426.80	923,097	23.1	95.1	73.9	16.1	49.2
From 2,001 to 3,000	151,688	2.6	2,512.49	381,115	9.5	97.7	83.4	4.9	26.1
More than 3,000	134,998	2.3	4,918.28	663,958	16.6	100.0	100.0	2.3	16.6

1 The states included in each zone and the variance ratios are as follows:
North Pacific: Baja California, Nayarit, Sinaloa, Sonora (C.V. = + 10.1%).
North: Chihuahua, Coahuila, Durango, Nuevo León, San Luis Potosí, Tamaulipas, Zacatecas (C.V. = ± 6.7%).
Central: Aguascalientes, Guanajuato, Hidalgo, Jalisco, México, Michoacán, Morelos, Puebla, Querétaro, Tlaxcala (C.V. = ± 5.2%).
Gulf of Mexico: Campeche, Tabasco, Veracruz, Yucatán (C.V. = ± 4.8%).
South Pacific: Colima, Chiapas, Guerrero, Oaxaca (C.V. = ± 4.3%).
Federal District (C.V. = ±7.5%).

Source: General Bureau of Statistics, Department of Sampling (Dirección General de Estadística, Departamento de Muestra), survey conducted in October, 1956.

FIGURE 1

*Percentage Distribution of Total Family Income
by Regions, October, 1956*

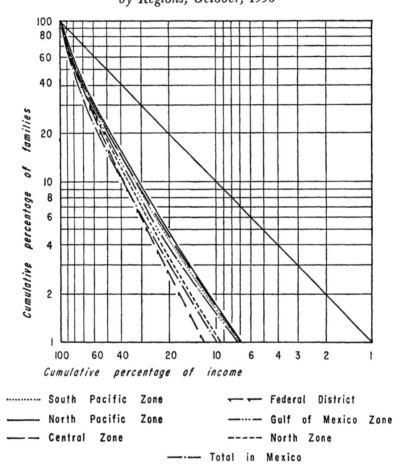

············· South Pacific Zone   ▸— ▸— Federal District

———— North Pacific Zone   —···— Gulf of Mexico Zone

— — Central Zone   ----- North Zone

—·— Total in Mexico

34 pesos per year, respectively, in 1955–1956. On the other hand, states in the North Zone are very uneven, ranging from those as developed as Chihuahua and Nuevo León to others as poor as Zacatecas and San Luis Potosí; in 1955–1956, the state governments disbursed 90 and 60 pesos per person yearly in the former, and 26 and 25 in the latter.

Notwithstanding these variations, the poorest regions are clearly the Central and South Pacific Zones. These zones are also made up of rather homogeneous states, with the possible exception of Colima, which is relatively better off. In these zones, where income per family was 66 per cent of the average income in Mexico, was concentrated 50 per cent of the total population, including the majority of families with monthly incomes of less than 300 and 500 pesos. Moreover, the number of families earning more than 1,000 pesos per month is very small (see Table 7) .

FIGURE 2

Distribution of Average Family Income by Regions

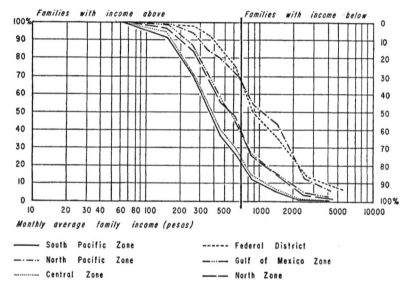

Figure 2 indicates on the *Y*-axis the percentage of families and on the *X*-axis the percentage in pesos, of the monthly family income in each zone. The uppermost and rightmost lines denote the highest average incomes. If it is roughly assumed that the 700-peso average family income for Mexico as a whole was barely sufficient to provide minimum food, clothing, housing, and amusement, Figure 2 leads to the conclusion that in November, 1956, the following lacked economic capability:

(1) 33 per cent of the families in the Federal District and North Pacific Zone; (2) 60 per cent of the families in the Gulf of Mexico and the North Zones; (3) 80 per cent of the families in the Central and South Pacific Zones.

TABLE 8

Number of Workers by Wage Classes and Zones, 1956

	Federal District		Central		North	
	Number	% of Total	Number	% of Total	Number	% of Total
Wage earners by wage classes						
Totals	1,078,030	100.0	1,260,191	100.0	831,222	100.0
Less than 100	36,250	3.4	215,608	17.1	68,539	8.2
From 101 to 200	69,347	6.4	327,129	26.0	167,703	20.2
From 201 to 300	154,455	14.3	255,260	20.2	195,410	23.5
From 301 to 400	215,921	20.0	138,782	11.0	116,663	14.0
From 401 to 500	171,791	15.9	102,848	8.2	77,289	9.3
From 501 to 750	200,161	18.6	123,913	9.8	113,746	13.7
From 751 to 1,000	104,020	9.7	53,282	4.2	43,748	5.3
From 1,001 to 2,000	78,803	7.3	37,174	3.0	34,999	4.2
From 2,001 to 3,000	26,793	2.5	3,717	0.3	10,208	1.2
More than 3,000	20,489	1.9	2,478	0.2	2,917	0.4
Totals						
Labor force	1,530,361	100.0	3,369,182	100.0	1,927,852	100.0
Wage earners	1,078,030	70.4	1,260,191	37.4	831,222	43.1
Others	452,331	29.6	2,108,991	62.6	1,096,630	56.9

TABLE 8 (Continued)

	Gulf of Mexico		North Pacific		South Pacific		All Mexico	
	Number	% of Total	Number	% of Total	Number	% of Total	Number	% of Total
Wage earners by wage classes								
Totals	422,378	100.0	385,711	100.0	305,637	100.0	4,283,169	100.0
Less than 100	14,147	3.4	13,217	3.4	37,156	12.2	384,917	9.0
From 101 to 200	44,461	10.5	49,265	12.8	79,106	25.9	737,011	17.2
From 201 to 300	57,597	13.6	43,257	11.2	64,723	21.2	770,702	18.0
From 301 to 400	48,503	11.5	42,056	11.0	38,354	12.5	600,279	14.0
From 401 to 500	35,367	8.4	45,660	11.8	23,972	7.8	456,927	10.7
From 501 to 750	83,869	19.9	82,919	21.5	32,361	10.5	636,960	14.9
From 751 to 1,000	46,482	11.0	48,064	12.5	20,376	6.7	315,972	7.4
From 1,001 to 2,000	60,628	14.3	54,072	14.0	5,993	2.0	271,669	6.3
From 2,000 to 3,000	18,188	4.3	3,605	0.9	3,596	1.2	66,107	1.5
More than 3,000	13,136	3.1	3,605	0.9	....	....	42,625	1.0
Totals								
Labor force	1,112,532	100.0	681,303	100.0	1,239,327	100.0	9,860,557	100.0
Wage earners	422,378	38.0	385,711	56.6	305,637	24.7	4,283,169	43.4
Others	690,154	62.0	295,592	43.4	933,690	75.3	5,577,388	56.6

Source: General Bureau of Statistics, Department of Sampling (Dirección General de Estadística, Departamento de Muestra), *Ingresos y egresos de la población de México* (México, D.F., 1958).

It may be stated that in all Mexico approximately two out of three families lacked economic capability, in the sense that their incomes were below the already-low average income.[14]

The principal cause of the inequality of income levels by regions lies in their different degrees of regional industrialization.

First. If the percentage of wage earners in the labor force is taken as an index of industrialization, it proves to be directly proportional to the level of income. The percentages were 70 per cent in the Federal District; 57 per cent in the North Pacific Zone; 43 per cent in the North Zone; 38 per cent in the Gulf of Mexico Zone; 37 per cent in the Central Zone; and 25 per cent in the poorest region, the South Pacific Zone (see Tables 8 and 9). The lowest-paid workers were concentrated in the last two zones. In the Central and the South Pacific Zones 60 per cent of the population had money incomes of less than 300 pesos a month, whereas in the Federal District, 24 per cent received under 300 pesos.

Second. If the occupational structure of Mexico is examined (Table 9), there is an inverse correlation between the level of average income and the proportion of the labor force employed in agriculture; that is, in the poorest zones, the agrarian population prevails.

Third. There is a direct correlation, although not so striking as in the first-mentioned, between the level of average income and the number of office workers and sales clerks—43 per cent in the Federal District; 22 per cent in the Gulf states and the North Zone; and 15 per cent in the South Pacific Zone. Owing to faulty classification, the number of industrial and manual workers does not clearly indicate the degree of regional development, because in this group were included all kinds of manual workers, whereas it would have been advisable to separate artisans and the self-employed from wage earners.

Fourth. Highly skilled manpower such as proprietors, professionals, technicians, and business or government officials also showed a very pronounced direct correlation with the level of average income in the zone: 10 per cent of the total labor force in the Federal District; 7 per cent in the North Pacific Zone; 5 per cent in the Gulf

14 The economic levels of families could be measured with greater accuracy by taking into account the number of members per family by income level, but this data is lacking.

TABLE 9

Workers by Wage Classes, Zones, and Occupation, 1956
(Percentage Distribution)

	Federal District	North Pacific	Gulf of Mexico	North	Central	South Pacific	All Mexico
Monthly wage (pesos)							
Less than 300	24.1	27.4	27.5	51.9	63.3	59.3	44.2
From 300 to 500	25.9	22.8	19.9	23.3	19.2	20.3	34.7
From 500 to 1,000	28.3	34.0	30.9	19.0	14.0	17.2	22.3
More than 1,000	11.7	15.8	21.7	5.8	3.5	3.2	8.8
Totals	100.0	100.0	100.0	100.0	100.0	100.0	100.0
Average family income (pesos)	1,282	1,189	698	675	464	447	693
Percentage of wage earners in the labor force	70.4	56.6	38.0	43.1	37.4	24.7	43.4
Total employment	100.0	100.0	100.0	100.0	100.0	100.0	100.0
Professional, technical, managerial, etc.	10.0	6.8	4.5	5.1	2.9	3.1	5.0
Office workers, sales clerks	43.0	24.4	22.3	22.2	17.5	15.1	23.1
Farmers	1.1	27.2	42.0	36.5	47.2	48.2	36.1
Factory workers and artisans	35.1	29.2	21.5	25.7	22.2	22.0	25.3
Service employees and others	10.8	12.4	9.7	10.5	10.2	11.3	10.5

source: Table 8 and Table 9A.

TABLE 9A

Distribution of the Labor Force by Occupation and by Zones, 1956

Types of Occupation	Federal District	% of Total	Central Zone	% of Total	North Zone	% of Total
Professional and technical	124,510	8.1	87,978	2.6	87,497	4.5
Business managers and officials	28,368	1.9	11,157	0.3	11,667	0.6
Office workers	368,800	24.1	146,217	4.3	182,285	9.5
Sales clerks	288,420	18.9	433,607	13.2	244,992	12.7
Farmers, ranchers, etc.	17,337	1.1	1,588,558	47.2	704,351	36.5
Factory workers, artisans, miners, etc.	537,499	35.1	748,482	22.2	495,818	25.7
Service employees	127,661	8.3	288,716	8.6	193,951	10.1
Unspecified	37,826	2.5	54,522	1.6	7,291	0.4
Total Population	4,073,770		10,610,988		6,136,995	
Percentage of labor force and total population	37.6		31.8		31.4	
Number of families	777,437		2,024,998		1,171,181	
Workers per family	1.97		1.66		1.65	

TABLE 9A (Continued)

Distribution of the Labor Force by Occupation and by Zones, 1956

Types of Occupation	Gulf of Mexico	% of Total	North Pacific	% of Total	South Pacific	% of Total	All of Mexico	% of Total
Professional and technical	35,367	3.2	43,257	6.3	33,560	2.7	412,169	4.2
Business managers and officials	14,147	1.3	3,605	0.5	8,390	0.7	77,329	0.8
Office workers	85,890	7.7	57,695	8.5	64,723	5.2	905,590	9.2
Sales clerks	162,686	14.6	108,144	15.9	122,255	9.9	1,370,104	13.9
Farmers, ranchers, etc.	466,839	42.0	185,046	27.2	596,891	48.2	3,559,022	36.1
Factory workers, artisans,	240,493	21.5	199,462	29.2	273,275	22.0	2,494,919	25.3
Service employees	103,068	9.3	79,306	11.7	136,637	11.0	929,339	9.4
Unspecified	4,042	0.4	4,808	00.7	3,596	0.3	112,085	1.1
Total Population	3,488,835		2,131,489		3,842,120		30,284,197	
Percentage of labor force and total population	31.9		32.0		32.2		32.6	
Number of families	665,808		406,773		783,229		5,779,426	
Workers per family	1.67		1.67		1.69		1.71	

Source: General Bureau of Statistics, Department of Sampling (Dirección General de Estadística, Departamento de Muestro), Ingresos y egresos de la población de México (México, D.F., 1958).

states and the North Zone; and 3 per cent in the Central and the South Pacific Zones.

Fifth. The number of workers engaged in other service activities is quite uniform throughout the Republic (about 10 per cent).

This data differs somewhat from the occupational estimates of the labor force because of the exclusion of unpaid workers and inadequacies in the sample.

The distribution of family income in 1950 was estimated on the basis of information on income in the 1950 Population Census, and of the calculation of personal income carried out in connection with the input-output study (Table 10). The census information refers to the money income of 5,105,000 families with an aggregate annual income of 23,637 million pesos, or an average monthly income of 386 pesos per family. This data was adjusted to a total of 32,808 million pesos for personal income as derived from the national accounts. The income not accounted for was calculated according to the following procedure:

a) On the basis of the data of the 1956 survey (Table 11A), an index was drawn up of the "income in kind" received by families earning less than 400 pesos a month.

b) The distribution of the difference of 5,830 million pesos among families with incomes above 400 pesos a month was determined according to the relative importance of the average income of each group. That is, it is assumed that there is a deliberate underreporting of incomes, proportionate to income levels. Under this assumption, 60 per cent of the difference was assigned to the top level and 40 per cent was divided among the four next-highest groups.

For the distribution of personal income in 1957, the data of the survey was used, adding to money income the income in kind received by families. Although the addition of monetary incomes to incomes in kind is not arithmetically sound—the former are average of aggregates, whereas the latter are only average of incomes for families that in each level declared such incomes—in practice the error is minimal, for 85 per cent of all families reported income in kind. These are more important for families with low incomes (see Table 11A), all of whom are assumed to have received some income in kind: imputed rent, consumption of homemade farm products. For families with incomes above 500 pesos a month, a specific estimate of income in kind was less important, since the amount of un-

TABLE 10

Distribution of Personal Income in Mexico, 1950

Limit of Monthly Average Incomes (pesos)	Total Income[1]				Adjustments			Aggregate Income[5] (Millions of Pesos) (8)	Average Income	
	Number of Families (Thousands) (1)	Monthly (Millions of Pesos) (2)	Annual (Millions of Pesos) (3)	Average Monthly Income (Pesos) (4)	% of Income in Kind[2] (5)	% of the Total[3] (6)	Applied to Difference[4] (Pesos) (7)		Annual (Pesos) (9)	Monthly (Pesos) (10)
Up to 75	191	9.6	115	50	257			296	1,550	129
Up to 150	1,320	149.2	1,790	113	161			2,882	2,184	182
Up to 200	993	173.8	2,086	175	140			2,920	2,940	245
Up to 300	887	221.8	2,662	250	127			3,381	3,812	318
Up to 400	557	195.0	2,340	350	122			2,855	5,123	427
Up to 600	550	275.0	3,300	500		4.1	239	3,539	6,435	536
Up to 1,000	363	290.4	3,485	800		6.6	385	3,780	10,661	888
Up to 1,500	123	153.8	1,846	1,250		10.4	606	2,452	19,935	1,661
Up to 3,000	76	171.0	2,052	2,250		18.5	1,079	3,131	41,198	3,433
More than 3,000	45	330.1	3,961	7,336		60.4	3,521	7,482	166,267	13,856
Totals	5,105	1,969.7	23,637	386		100.0	5,830	32,808	6,427	536

[1] Data compiled by the Population Census of 1950, special section (Censo de Población, 1950, *parte especial*).

[2] Income in kind is important for money incomes up to 400 pesos per month, and it was estimated on the basis of the Survey of Incomes and Expenditures referred to in Table 11A.

[3] The sum of the average monthly incomes of more than 350 pesos is 12,136 pesos (column 4).

[4] Refers to the difference between personal income derived from the census (23,637 million pesos plus 3,341 million pesos in income in kind) and personal income derived from the national accounts for 1950 ((32,808 million pesos).

[5] Column 3 times column 5 for the first five income groups; from there up, column 3 plus column 7.

TABLE 11

Personal-Income Distribution in Mexico, 1957

Monthly Money-Income Classes (Pesos)	Income Calculated by Sampling[1]			Adjustments			Average Income		
	Monthly (Millions of Pesos) (1)	Annual (Millions of Pesos) (2)	Average Monthly (Pesos) (3)	% of the Sum of Income above 500 Applied to Income Difference[3] (4)	Pesos per Month[2] (Millions of Pesos) (5)	Adjusted Annual Income (2) + (5) (Millions of Pesos) (6)	Number of Families (7)	Annual (Pesos) (8)	Monthly (Pesos) (9)
Less than 100	41.3	496	185	....	....	496	223,411	2,220	185
From 101 to 200	221.7	2,660	255	....	....	2,660	869,602	3,059	255
From 201 to 300	336.6	4,039	367	....	....	4,039	916,060	4,409	367
From 301 to 400	301.8	3,622	460	....	....	3,622	655,904	5,522	460
From 401 to 500	331.2	3,974	563	....	....	3,974	588,552	6,752	563
From 501 to 750	780.8	9,370	744	6.4	1,336	10,706	1,049,112	10,205	850
From 751 to 1,000	560.2	6,722	1,031	8.7	1,816	8,538	543,131	15,720	1,310
From 1,001 to 2,000	1,053.3	12,640	1,628	14.0	2,922	15,562	646,968	24,054	2,004
From 2,001 to 3,000	413.8	4,966	2,728	23.6	4,927	9,893	151,688	65,219	5,435
More than 3,000	742.0	8,904	5,496	47.3	9,874	18,778	134,998	139,098	11,592
Totals	4,782.7	57,393	828	100.0	20,875	78,268	5,779,426	13,542	1,128

1 General Bureau of Statistics, Department of Sampling (Dirección General de Estadística, Departamento de Muestra), survey of October, 1956. Includes money income and income in kind. Income in kind is estimated only for money-income classes below 501 pesos.

2 The sum of average incomes above 500 pesos per month—which are assumed to be undervalued—is 11,627 million pesos.

3 The difference between personal income estimated on the basis of the sampling survey and the national income calculated by the Bank of Mexico, less taxes on business, undistributed business profits, and net earnings of government enterprises.

TABLE 11A

Average Money Incomes and Expenditures, Deficit, and Income in Kind by Income Groups in Mexico, 1956

Monthly Income (Pesos)	Number of Families	Average Income	Average Expenditures	Difference	Average Money Income in Kind	Incomes plus Money Income in Kind	Income in Kind as Percent of Money Income
Less than 100	223,411	72.20	94.69	− 22.49	113	185	151
From 101 to 200	869,602	157.79	184.88	− 27.09	97	255	61
From 201 to 300	916,060	263.35	287.11	− 23.76	104	367	40
From 301 to 400	655,904	361.78	369.33	− 7.55	98	460	27
From 401 to 500	588,552	459.47	444.98	+ 14.49	103	562	22
From 501 to 750	1,049,112	629.47	574.44	+ 55.03	115	744	18
From 751 to 1,000	543,131	871.16	769.63	+ 101.53	160	1,031	18
From 1,001 to 2,000	646,968	1,426.80	1,182.72	+ 244.08	201	1,628	14
From 2,001 to 3,000	151,688	2,512.49	1,804.09	+ 708.40	216	2,728	9
More than 3,000	134,998	4,918.28	3,044.13	+1,874.15	578	5,496	11
Totals	5,779,426	692.80	591.68	101.12	135	828	19

Source: General Bureau of Statistics, Department of Sampling (Dirección General de Estadística, Departamento de Muestra).

accounted-for income allocated to them was sufficient to cover income in kind. The aggregate annual income (money and in kind) derived from the survey was 57,393 million pesos, as shown in Table 11. The difference between the aggregate family income derived from the sample and the aggregate family income in the Bank of Mexico's national-income account was determined as shown in Table 12.

TABLE 12

Adjustments for the Calculation of Personal Income in 1957
(Millions of Pesos)

National Income (Bank of Mexico)		$92,000
Less: Overestimate (9%) [1]		8,280
		$83,720
Taxes on business[2]	$2,178	
Undistributed profits[3]	2,000	
Net income of government enterprises[4]	1,274	5,452
(I) Personal income (from national-income accounts)		78,268
(II) Personal income (from sampling survey)		57,393
(III) Difference between (I) and (II)		$20,875

[1] According to input-output table for 1950.
[2] Income tax, Schedules I, II, III, VI, VII, and excess profits.
[3] Estimate based on statistics compiled by the Ministry of Finance for 1953.
[4] Data of National Investments Bureau (Dirección Nacional de Inversiones).

As in 1950, the difference between the two calculations was divided among incomes averaging more than 500 pesos a month, according to their relative importance; it is assumed that underreporting of incomes occurs only above this level (see Table 11).

The percentage comparison between the 1950 and 1957 distributions of income appears in Table 13 and is represented in the form of a Lorenz Curve in Figure 3.

In both 1950 and 1957, the results indicate an extremely high concentration of incomes. In 1950, 3,948,000 families (77 per cent) had an income of less than 500 pesos a month and accounted for 38 per cent of the income. On the other hand, 121,000 families (2.4 per cent of the total) had incomes of more than 3,000 pesos a month and enjoyed 32 per cent of the total income.

In 1957, 2,665,000 families (46 per cent of the total) had incomes below 500 pesos a month and received barely 14 per cent of the total income. On the other hand, 286,686 families (5 per cent of the total) had an income of over 3,000 pesos a month and held 37 per cent of the total income.

TABLE 13

Percentage Distribution of Personal Income in Mexico, 1950 and 1957

Average Monthly Income (in Pesos)		Percentage of the Total				Cumulative Percentages			
		1950		1957		1950		1957	
1950	1957	Families	Incomes	Families	Incomes	Families	Incomes	Families	Incomes
129	185	3.7	0.9	3.9	0.6	3.7	0.9	3.9	0.6
182	255	25.8	8.8	15.0	3.4	29.5	9.7	18.9	4.0
245	367	19.5	8.9	15.9	5.2	49.0	18.6	34.8	9.2
318	460	17.4	10.3	11.3	4.6	66.4	28.9	46.1	13.8
427	563	10.9	8.7	10.2	5.1	77.3	37.6	56.3	18.9
536	850	10.8	10.8	18.2	13.7	88.1	48.4	74.5	32.6
888	1,310	7.1	11.8	9.4	10.9	95.2	60.2	83.9	43.5
1,661	2,004	2.4	7.5	11.2	19.9	97.6	67.7	95.1	63.4
3,433	5,435	1.5	9.5	2.6	12.6	99.1	77.2	97.7	76.0
13,856	11,592	0.9	22.8	2.3	24.0	100.0	100.0	100.0	100.0
Totals:									
536	1,128	100.0	100.0	100.0	100.0				

Source: Tables 10 and 11.

Before continuing, it would be helpful to keep in mind the following considerations:

1. The distribution of personal income, as here apportioned, is rather conservative. It must be remembered that the figures used for national income are 9 per cent lower than the estimate published by the Bank of Mexico. The difference between the estimate of the Bank of Mexico and the one adopted here is essentially due to the extent that the undervaluation is excessive, profits will be greater, especially those that correspond to wholesale and retail business operated on a large scale by the most prosperous entrepreneurs.

2. No deduction was made for the income of nonprofit institutions such as churches, clubs, unions, schools, and for individuals living on the incomes of private institutions.

3. The calculation of personal income in the national accounts does not include transfer payments—government and business subsidies to private individuals.

Considerations 2 and 3 would tend to improve the distribution of income. Nevertheless, since Consideration 1 is more important, it is reasonable to assume that the distribution of income appearing in this study conservatively reflects actual conditions in both 1950 and 1957.

To gain a more precise idea of the changes that occurred between 1950 and 1957 in families belonging to different levels of income, the total number of families was divided into ten equal percentage groups in order of income levels. In other words, the population was distributed by deciles, following Newton's numerical method of divided differences[15] and based on the information in Table 13. In order to compare family conditions in real terms, 1950 incomes were adjusted to reflect the 1957 price level (see Table 14). It must be kept in mind that this data does not necessarily reflect changes in the position of a given family, but only compares the economic conditions of family units located in a certain relative position in 1950, with the conditions of other units in the same position in 1957. Actually, families shift to better or worse positions; some are incorporated for the first time as units and others disappear.

Furthermore, we must keep in mind that the conversion of in-

---

[15] F. B. Hildebrand, *Introduction to Numerical Analysis* (New York, McGraw-Hill, 1956), p. 43.

TABLE 14

Personal-Income Distribution in Mexico by Deciles of Families, 1950 and 1957

Deciles	% of Families 1950	% of Families 1957	Average Monthly Income at 1957 Prices1 (Pesos) 1950	Average Monthly Income at 1957 Prices1 (Pesos) 1957	1950 % of Total Income	1950 Cumulative Income	1957 % of Total Income	1957 Cumulative Income
I	10.0	10.0	247	192	2.7	2.7	1.7	1.7
II	10.0	10.0	311	304	3.4	6.1	2.7	4.4
III	10.0	10.0	348	350	3.8	9.9	3.1	7.5
IV	10.0	10.0	403	429	4.4	14.3	3.8	11.3
V	10.0	10.0	440	485	4.8	19.1	4.3	15.6
VI	10.0	10.0	504	632	5.5	24.6	5.6	21.2
VII	10.0	10.0	641	835	7.0	31.6	7.4	28.6
VIII	10.0	10.0	788	1,128	8.6	40.2	10.0	38.6
IX	10.0	10.0	989	1,658	10.8	51.0	14.7	53.3
X	5.2	5.1	1,621	2,233	9.2	60.2	10.1	63.4
	2.4	2.6	2,858	5,460	7.5	67.7	12.6	76.0
	2.4	2.3	12,329	11,765	32.3	100.0	24.0	100.0
Totals	100.00	100.0			100.0		100.0	
Averages			916	1,128				

1 Based on the wholesale-price index of the Bank of Mexico.
Source: Table 13.

comes to constant prices using a single price index, irrespective of its inherent defects, does not take into account the possibility that prices to consumers may change differently for different income groups.

With all these qualifications, the results presented in Table 14 once again point out the fact that the increase in the country's income was very inequitably distributed:

1. Average family income in Mexico as a whole rose—at 1957 prices—from 916 pesos a month in 1950 to 1,128 pesos a month in 1957, a rise representing an increase in real terms of 23 per cent in seven years.[16]

2. The income of the lowest 20 per cent of the population worsened in both relative and absolute terms. In this period, the poorest people not only did not benefit but were actually hurt.

3. In a rising scale of incomes, the next 30 per cent of the families became relatively worse off, but gained in real terms.

4. The families in the sixth decile from the bottom maintained their relative position, and improved their situation in real terms.

5. The 37.6 per cent of the families that occupy Deciles VII to X (excluding the top 2.4 per cent in the income scale) proved to be the ones who really profited most, because they substantially improved their relative and absolute positions.

6. The 2.4 per cent of the population at the top of the income scale slipped relatively and suffered a slight loss in real income. Nevertheless, it must be borne in mind that this group, given its economic importance, is not sufficiently subdivided; it is possible, therefore, that one part of the families may have bettered its situation and only the top-income group may have seen its wedge of the pie reduced from 1950 to 1957. Moreover, it must not be forgotten that these are figures of income and not of wealth. If ownership of assets were examined, a different picture might result, for those who receive the highest incomes are, generally, those who benefit from the accumulation of material possessions.

The extreme concentration of income in Mexico was paralleled

---

[16] In this period, the gross national product went up 48 per cent in real terms, and industrial production expanded 72 per cent; the latter increase was divided between a 44-per-cent increase in consumer-goods industries and a 216-per-cent increase in producer-goods industries, so that consumption rose less than investment.

in other countries during their periods of the rapid emergence of an industrial and financial middle class; and it is still found in countries with a colonial status where a large part of the population lives from subsistence agriculture.

TABLE 15

Percentage of Total Income Distributed among Families in the Top-Income Scale

Countries	Years	% of Families	% of Total Personal Incomes
United States	1929[2]	5	30
	1935/36[2]	5	27
	1944[3]	5	21
	1950[3]	5	21
United Kingdom[1]	1880	5	46
	1910	5	43
	1929	5	33
	1938	5	31
	1947	5	24
Mexico	1950	5	40
	1957	5	37
Southern Rhodesia[4]	1946	5	65
Kenya[4]	1949	3	51
Northern Rhodesia[4]	1946	1.4	45
Italy[5]	1948	10	34
Puerto Rico[5]	1948	10	41
India[1]	1950	20	55
Ceylon[1]	1950	20	50
Mexico	1950	10	49
		20	60
	1957	10	47
		20	61

[1] Simon Kuznets, "Economic Growth and Income Inequality," *American Economic Review*, Vol. 45, No. 1 (March 1955), p. 4.

[2] Selma Goldsmith, George Jaszi, *et al.*, "Size Distribution of Income Since the Mid-Thirties," *Review of Economics and Statistics*, Vol. XXXVI, No. 1 (February, 1954), Table 2, p. 4.

[3] U.S. Department of Commerce, Office of Business Economics, *Income Distribution in the United States* (n.d.), p. 15.

[4] United Nations, *National Income and Its Distribution in Underdeveloped Countries*, Statistical Papers, Series E, No. 3 (1951), Table 12, p. 19.

[5] *Ibid.*, Table 26, p. 29.

FIGURE 3
Percentage Distribution of Personal Income

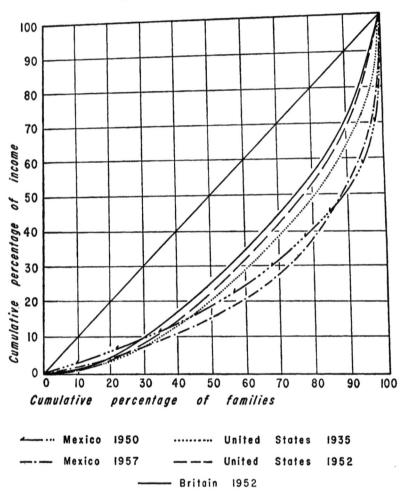

Furthermore, reference was made to the distribution of personal income in the United States in 1935 and 1952, and in the United Kingdom in 1952, both of which are represented in the Lorenz Curve in Figure 3. For all the given countries and years, the best income distribution was found in the United Kingdom and the worst in Mexico, followed by the United States in 1935.

TABLE 16

Personal-Income Distribution in the United States (1935 and 1952) and Great Britain (1952)

Income Classes (Dollars)	United States, 1935–36				United States and Great Britain, 1952					
	% of Total		Cumulative Percentages		Percentage of Families	Percentages of Incomes		Cumulative % of Families	Cumulative % of Incomes	
	Families	Incomes	Families	Incomes		U.S.	Great Britain		U.S.	Great Britain
Up to 250	5.4	0.5	5.4	0.5	10	1	2	10	1	2
Up to 500	11.6	3.0	17.0	3.5	10	3	3	20	4	5
Up to 750	14.6	6.1	31.6	9.6	10	5	5	30	9	10
Up to 1,000	14.9	8.7	46.5	18.3	10	6	7	40	15	17
Up to 1,500	22.2	18.0	68.7	36.3	10	8	8	50	23	25
Up to 2,000	13.2	15.0	81.9	51.3	10	9	9	60	32	34
Up to 3,000	11.2	17.9	93.1	69.2	10	10	10	70	42	44
Up to 5,000	4.6	11.1	97.7	80.3	10	12	12	80	54	56
Up to 10,000	1.5	6.9	99.2	87.2	10	15	14	90	69	70
More than 10,000	0.8	12.8	100.0	100.0	10	31	30	100	100	100

Sources: Mary Jane Bowman, "A Graphical Analysis of Personal Income Distribution in the United States," American Economic Review, Vol. XXXV, No. 4 (September, 1945), pp. 607–628, with data of the U.S. National Resources Committee, Consumer Finances in the United States, 1935–1936; and Harold Lydall and John B. Lansing, "A Comparison of the Distribution of Personal Income and Wealth in the U.S. and Great Britain," American Economic Review, Vol. XLIX, No. 1 (March, 1959), Table 2, p. 48.

The figures shown in Tables 14 and 16 were used to divide the families into economic classes (Table 17) that were defined in this manner: the middle class is taken as that group of the population whose share of income is in proportion to its size, so that 1 per cent of the population receives 1 per cent of the income or an income equal to the average; the lower class receives a share of income less than its percentage of the population; and the upper class receives a share of income greater than its percentage of the population. Therefore, this definition varies according to the degree of development and the real resources in each economy.

TABLE 17

Distribution of Families and Incomes
by Socio-economic Class
(Percentages)

Socio-economic Class	Mexico 1950		Mexico 1957		United States 1935		United States 1952		Great Britain 1952	
	F.	I.	F.	I.	F.	I.	F.	I.	F.	I.
Lower class	70	31	65	25	47	18	40	15	40	17
Middle class	18	17	19	18	35	33	40	39	40	39
Well-to-do class	7	12	11	20	11	18	10	15	10	14
Wealthy class	5	40	5	37	7	31	10	31	10	30
Totals	100	100	100	100	100	100	100	100	100	100

NOTE: F. = Families; I. = Incomes.

The figures in Table 17 call for the following observations:

In Mexico, the lower class comprised a higher percentage of the population than in the United States and England, and it was 5 per cent higher in 1950 than in 1957. Although it received a relatively higher share of total income, the difference in income levels places it in a situation of much more acute poverty.

The percentage of the Mexican middle class was a great deal smaller than that of the United States or Great Britian.

The well-to-do class was relatively equal in proportion, but received a higher share of the income in Mexico than in the United States or England.

The percentage of the wealthy class (with a share in the income at least three times its proportional number) was smaller in Mexico, but this class received a greater portion of the income than did its counterpart in the United States or England.

It may be concluded that, owing to its low level of national income, Mexico has extended the benefits of economic development only to that portion of the population receiving an income equal or superior to the average income; this portion comprised 30 per cent of the total population in 1950 and 35 per cent in 1957.

Fundamental Problems of the Mexican Economy*

VICTOR L. URQUIDI

This essay incorporates some of my views on the fundamental problems of the Mexican economy. Space does not permit me to cover a great deal of ground or go into the subject very deeply. Moreover, in order to present the central ideas more clearly and to give unity to the exposition as a whole, I have left out many figures and specific data, trusting that this omission will not weaken my argument.[1] After an introduction referring to the recent progress of the Mexican economy, I go on to consider the following points: the influence of the world economy on that of Mexico; the Mexican view of agricultural development; and the nature of Mexico's industrial development. Then I discuss the significance of the public sector, the distribution of income, and the monetary and financial strategy of development, concluding with a brief overall evaluation.

INTRODUCTION: RECENT ECONOMIC PROGRESS IN MEXICO

Unquestionably the Mexican economy is undergoing a process of growth and transformation. This can be observed simply by comparing present facts with the recent past, and it is confirmed by the indices and figures that economists use to chart the rate of growth, even allowing for possible inaccuracies in these figures.

* Based on two lectures given at the Colegio Nacional on November 14 and 17, 1960; published in *Cuadernos Americanos*, Vol. CXIV, No. 1 (1961).

1 Appendix I, at the end of this essay, presents some significant indices and lists the principal sources of the data used in the tables and cited in the text. (Since this was written, many of the figures—notably the national-product series—have been revised; accordingly, the tables have been corrected through 1960, with corresponding changes in text where necessary. No attempt has been made to bring this essay up to date to cover events beyond 1960.)

The Mexican economy in general has tripled in the last twenty years. It is estimated that real income has increased during this period at a compound rate of about 6.3 per cent annually; given a population rate of growth of 2.9 per cent, this means that there has been a per capita increase in income of 3.3 per cent. Production has expanded more or less evenly: except for mining, and to some extent agriculture, all of the principal sectors or branches of economic activity have developed at a similar pace. In real terms, industrial output, as well as transportation and other services, is today from three to four times higher than in 1940; and the agricultural product is two and a half times greater. The average productivity of capital—of equipment and other tangible assets—has risen. There has been an overall improvement in production techniques. There also has been rapid growth in the means of communication, electric-power capacity, land under irrigation, and many other installations that represent large investment efforts in the past and increased yields in the present and future. This expansion and interaction of the basic economic structure undoubtedly has benefited all branches of activity and has contributed to raising both productivity and income.

The progress of the Mexican economy since 1940 can, of course, be traced back to the preceding period: the post-Revolution years and the thirties, when many of the public works that have helped so much to integrate the national market and increase production were initiated. At that time, some industrial expansion was already evident. However, the Mexican economy as a whole, because of slow internal changes and particularly unfavorable external factors, was almost stagnant in the twenty years before 1940. Since agricultural production was apparently quite rigid, it may barely have kept pace with the rise in population. The "miracle" of Mexico's economic development has been brought about for the most part in the last two decades.

The demographic structure of Mexico has also changed in a way that is typical of growing economies. The percentage of the total population engaged in productive work is higher today than it was twenty years ago. Moreover, in the 15-to-64 age group, the proportion of people gainfully employed is much greater than it was in 1940: 62 per cent as compared with 52 per cent. This difference indicates to what extent the country's potential labor force has been absorbed into income-generating activities; in particular, there has been a very rapid increase in the number of female wage earners. From the standpoint of occupation, there has been a decrease in the proportion of the economically active population engaged in agriculture and related activities. In other words, economic development has been characterized by a greater flow of labor into industry, transportation, commerce, services, and government than into agriculture and livestock raising. Today nonagricultural activities employ almost half the active population, compared with just over a third two decades ago and even less before then; on the other hand, the country's agricultural labor force has risen by more than a million persons in the last ten years. Mexico's population increase, more rapid since 1940, continues to be high despite urban growth and the effect that urbanization may have on the birth rate.

TABLE 1

Population and Labor Force
(Thousands of Inhabitants)

Years	Total Population[1]	Economically Active Population					Population in 15-to-64 Age Group
		Total	Male	Female	Agricultural[3]	Non-Agricultural	
1940	19,654	5,858	5,426	432	3,831	2,027	10,966
1945	22,514	6,992	....	....	4,299	2,693	
1950	25,791	8,345	7,207	1,138	4,824	3,521	14,124
1955	30,012	9,753	....	....	5,445	4,308	
1960	34,923	11,332	9,297	2,035	6,145	5,187	18,161

[1] Annual average rates of growth: 1931–1940, 1.7 per cent; 1941–1950, 2.8 per cent; 1951–1960, 3.1 per cent.
[2] The share of agriculturally occupied population in the total economically active population was 65.4 per cent in 1940, 57.8 per cent in 1950, and 54.2 in 1960.
Source: For the principal sources of data used in this table and those that follow, see Appendix I.

The nature of Mexico's industrial development in the last twenty years also indicates that the country is establishing a solid base for an improved standard of living. Steel-production capacity, negligible two decades ago, has increased sevenfold in only the last fifteen years. Electric-power capacity is four times greater than it was in 1940. The chemical industry can now produce several times more than scarcely a decade ago. The output of petroleum derivatives has risen steadily. The manufacture of equipment and machinery

TABLE 2

Gross Domestic Product

	1940	1945	1950	1955	1960
Gross domestic product					
Millions of pesos at 1960 prices	41,112	57,359	77,015	103,622	140,168
(Index, 1940 = 100)	100	140	187	252	341
By activity:					
(Indices, 1940 = 100)					
Agricultural and livestock output	100	112	170	222	256
Manufacturing	100	163	217	298	440
Mining	100	106	103	119	136
Electric energy	100	122	175	278	426
Petroleum	100	118	177	242	368
Construction	100	184	164	224	331
Transport	100	143	204	293	374
Distribution and trade	100	147	200	265	357
Government	100	150	194	225	297
Other	100	139	188	265	386

has expanded to an extent that is not yet adequately recorded by statistics. The first steps have been taken toward the production of vehicles. The variety of consumer goods now made in Mexico is impressive. In addition, all of this has strengthened the country's international-payments position by reducing, often radically, the ratio of imports to domestic consumption, thus making available increasing amounts of foreign exchange to pay for the high-priority capital and semiprocessed goods that still must come from abroad.

Growth and transformation have been accompanied by broader education and by better sanitation, reflected in lower mortality rates. Social services also have been widely extended and have given the worker more security in his job and income. Undeniably, Mexico has made great strides both culturally and socially.

Mexico's progress in so many different areas meets, in a general way, the current definition of an integrated economic and social development. More than an increase in a given statistic, it has meant a change in the structure of production and of social relationships, together with a rise to new cultural, technical, and moral levels.

Economic progress in Mexico, however, has not overcome a number of serious difficulties, many of which are obscured by the aggregate figures and the overall picture. Some of these problems and obstacles have a long history and can be expected to continue into the future. By recognizing and defining them, Mexico can profit by past experience, and the principles of a more effective policy of economic development can be laid down. Mexico has reached its present standard of living after fifty years of drastic social and political changes under a constitution that altered the system and concept of private property and the role of the State. It now must decide whether the achievements and present trends of its economy are satisfactory, or whether the economic goals still before it require a reappraisal of social relationships and of the ways of administering and utilizing the country's resources and potential productivity.

The following discussion will attempt only to open the way to a fuller understanding of the present state of the Mexican economy and how it may be expected to develop in the future.

THE INFLUENCE OF THE WORLD ECONOMY

Many of Mexico's problems derive from its position within the world economy, since its progress is largely financed by its export earnings and it receives additional resources from abroad in aid of its development.

The world economy has not always maintained a high rate of growth, but even when it has been generally dynamic it has not necessarily benefited Mexico's foreign trade. The first countries to industrialize initially needed raw materials and food from other parts of the world, and, during the last quarter of the nineteenth century and the first decade of the present, Mexico was certainly one of the countries that most actively participated in the expanding trade between the less-developed regions and the industrial areas of the United States, Canada, and northwestern Europe. The following example will suffice to demonstrate: during this period, world imports of primary products grew at an average annual rate of 3.3 per cent (in the United States and Canada at 4.7 per cent and in northwestern Europe, except Great Britain, at 3.6 per cent). During roughly the same period leading up to the First World War, total Mexican exports, consisting principally of primary products, increased at a compound rate of 7.2 per cent annually. At that time, the progress of the economically advanced nations was more closely linked to the external trade of the underdeveloped areas than it is today; and the increase in the share of Mexico's raw-materials exports in the world market of that period was probably not equaled by the other nations of Latin America or even of other regions.

At present, especially since the Second World War, the picture is different. Industrial countries have become more self-sufficient and have perfected their techniques to a degree that has enabled them to replace some primary products by domestically produced articles. Moreover, the potential output of raw materials has multiplied throughout the world and purchases previously made from a given country are now often made from others. This explains in part the stagnation in Mexico's mineral exports and the precarious situation of coffee and other products. The same highly developed countries, notably the United States, have become competitors in the export market for certain commodities such as cotton, which until a few years ago was the fastest-growing source of Mexico's foreign-exchange earnings.

With all its complexity, international trade in primary products clearly reveals that markets have weakened noticeably in the last several years and that, except for mineral products, prospective long-run trends in world consumption are not very promising. It is not that industrial output in the most advanced countries has slackened. According to a recent study by the United Nations, output increased between 1938 and 1958 at the rate of 4.5 per cent annually in a group of industrialized countries of Western Europe, North America, and Oceania, and output per worker also rose; in the postwar years of 1948–1953, the increase reached 6.3 per cent a year. But the volume of world imports of primary products in much the same period hardly expanded; until 1953, its rate of increase was less than 0.5 per cent yearly. Industrialized countries require for their own growth less and less of the traditionally staple exports of countries like Mexico. An additional cause of concern is the industrial lethargy in some countries in the last five to eight years, above all, as of 1960, in the United States, Mexico's major market.

These phenomena are, of course, important, because exports have in a certain sense been the driving force behind Mexico's accelerated economic development in the last twenty years. External demand was a direct incentive to agricultural production, with an attendant increase in the volume of employment; the income thus created strengthened the domestic market, which in turn encouraged the investment of savings in industrialization; and greater tax revenues enabled the government to expand the nation's productive capacity. Notwithstanding Mexico's tremendous internal effort, exports have played an incalculable role in the country's development. Therefore it is disquieting that since 1955, largely because of declining world prices, exports have leveled off, a loss giving rise to a situation that has been alleviated only in part by increased tourist expenditures in Mexico. Under recent conditions of the world economy, Mexico's growth, even with tourism, has lost some of its momentum.

TABLE 3

Foreign Trade and Tourism
(Indices Based on Value at 1960 Prices; 1940 = 100)

	1940	1945	1950	1955	1960
Exports	100	115	136	185	208
Terms of trade	100	133	158	145	108
Capacity to import generated					
by exports	100	152	216	269	225
Tourism and border visitors	100	91	246	372	415
Imports	100	204	250	328	378
For consumption	100	186	164	210	191
For investment	100	236	315	406	469
Imports of raw materials	100	186	233	288	397
Metallic	100	167	218	283	357
Nonmetallic	100	194	240	290	413
Fuels and lubricants	100	206	389	972	582

It should not be concluded that this prospect is inevitable. The industrial economy of the more advanced countries could regain a more rapid pace, and effective international measures could be taken to stabilize prices. Mexico, on the other hand, can further diversify its exports to win new markets; it can promote tourism more intensively; and it can take advantage of the Latin American Free Trade Area to increase its exports of manufactures. Nevertheless, Mexico cannot ignore the influence of economic trends abroad on its general economic development and the adverse effect these trends may have on its domestic economy.

THE MEXICAN VIEW OF
AGRICULTURAL DEVELOPMENT

Economic development requires, as is well known, that an increasing share of the national income be devoted to creating new productive capacity so that more goods and services will be available to improve living conditions. But the composition of annual investment is as important as its sum total; how much goes into the agricultural sector; how much into transport; how much into the installation of factories and machinery; how much into the construction of dwellings, schools, hospitals, etc.

For the purpose of a general analysis, it is enough to consider two vast sectors: agriculture and industry. In an underdeveloped country agriculture is, except in certain export crops, the poorer and less productive sector; and industry, if it exists to a significant degree, faces serious limitations of market, technology, supply of qualified personnel and management, and other disadvantages, although its output per worker is usually greater than that of agriculture. The industrial sector purchases foodstuffs and raw materials from the agricultural sector, which in turn consumes some of the former's products. Although they are interrelated and act upon one another, they are both linked to the world economy. Part of the market for agricultural and livestock products is abroad, and the necessary agricultural equipment and some materials for agriculture have to be imported. The industrial sector also creates a demand for imported materials and equipment and, indirectly, a demand for many classes of consumer goods that cannot be satisfied by domestic industry.

In the economy of the second half of the nineteenth century, production and investment in a country such as Mexico were determined by so-called "market forces." If external demand for certain agricultural and livestock products grew, output increased and attracted capital investment; on the other hand, the narrow domestic market for other products, owing to the social and economic conditions of the population, did not encourage investments for the purpose of expanding or modernizing the production of basic commodities. Investment in industry was inhibited by the competition of imported manufactures and the very low purchasing power of the rural population. So long as exports grew rapidly, the demand for imports of consumer goods could be satisfied without any foreign-exchange difficulties. But when exports began to fall, the government found it necessary to take positive measures to stimulate the industrial development of the country.

This process had already begun in Mexico when the Revolution broke out. The Revolution modified the structure of the internal market, gave mobility to manpower, changed the land-tenure system, and aroused intense industrial nationalism. The criterion of "natural" economic forces was replaced in part by a social criterion that would later be called an economic-development policy. The government assumed the responsibility of directly and indirectly orienting much of the investment in agriculture, industry, and other activities so that it would serve the public interest and—within the limitations imposed by international trade conditions—generate a process of uninterrupted national growth.

The Mexican Revolution produced a mixed economy that, except for its agrarian system, was similar to other mixed economies that developed after the First World War. At the outset, however, it operated with notorious disregard for the fundamental interrelation between agriculture and industry that is essential to a balanced and rapid growth. Whether or not there was an understanding of the problem, the fact remains that immediately after the Revolution important efforts were made to develop industry, whereas agricultural production advanced much less than it should have. Until the beginning of the Second World War, agricultural output in Mexico rose annually scarcely 1.5 to 2 per cent. The total harvested area apparently increased, on an average, no more than 1 per cent a year. Only gains in irrigated land—in 1940 still a small acreage—denoted a significant qualitative change during that early period. Foodstuffs had to be imported to take care of the basic necessities of the population.

TABLE 4

Agricultural Development

	1940	1945	1950	1955	1960
Agricultural and livestock output					
(Index, 1940 = 100)	100	112	170	222	256
Agricultural output	100	131	220	308	336
Mainly for domestic consumption	100	126	243	303	371
Mainly for export	100	138	257	420	437
Livestock production	100	98	129	154	198
Harvested-crop area					
Thousands of hectares	5,904	6,413	8,576	10,516	11,868
(Index, 1940 = 100)	100	109	145	178	201
Area of irrigation districts					
Thousands of hectares	267	624	1,187	1,889	2,296
(Index, 1940 = 100)	100	234	445	707	860

During and especially just after the war, the general situation in agriculture changed considerably. Since 1945 an average annual increase in agricultural output of 6.5 per cent has been recorded. But an analysis of this figure reveals that production for export markets,

TABLE 5

Crop Yields

	1940–1944 Average	1945–1949 Average	1950–1954 Average	1955–1959 Average
Yield per hectare (Indices, 1940–1944 = 100)				
Cotton	100	113	132	184
Sugar cane	100	100	101	109
Corn	100	119	129	139
Beans	100	109	129	168
Wheat	100	111	127	180

primarily of cotton and coffee, increased more rapidly than output for domestic markets, even including wheat in the latter. In view of the already-weakened international market for farm commodities, the general development of Mexican agriculture will increasingly depend on the possibility of augmenting cereal and livestock production. Corn and meat, in particular, continue to be a fundamental problem in Mexico, where they could contribute substantially to rural income.

In the last twenty years, agricultural yields have undoubtedly risen, although less in corn than in wheat or cotton. The cultivated area has been extended, and irrigation, used largely for export crops, has had very positive effects. One-third of the total farm land is irrigated. Flood control in the tropics has been another significant factor. Techniques have improved, better seeds are being used, and agricultural services have been expanded. Cattle raising has recovered from the scourge of hoof-and-mouth disease. Social, cultural, and political conditions of rural life have favored the progress of agriculture. The peasant has been given his rightful place in society, and he not only has possession of land, but he can avail himself of government aid and bank credit to organize his activities. Nevertheless, there is still considerable rigidity in the supply of agricultural products for the domestic market.

As industry and other sectors absorb progressively more manpower, and the income of the industrial worker and urban dweller continues to mount, it may be foreseen that a greater supply of foodstuffs will be needed; and if this demand cannot be satisfied by domestic production, it will have to be met by imports. From the point of view of foreign-trade prospects, however, most of the proceeds from exports and tourism should be used for purchasing imports that can be less easily replaced. It is essential that Mexico build up as speedily as possible a productive, flexible, well-oriented and prosperous agriculture that will respond to the growing demand for its products generated by industrialization and urbanization; that will constitute a widespread and stable market for the industries manufacturing consumer and other goods; and that ultimately will improve income distribution, another of Mexico's great problems.

This undertaking, after being studied in detail by experts, should be carried out by the government, which can provide the necessary conditions and inducements and direct its own investments and credit resources to the main areas requiring intensified effort: rural education and instruction in agricultural methods; the organization of *ejidatarios*[2] and small private farmers along cooperative lines in order to remedy the disadvantages of excessively small holdings or, in the case of sufficiently large farm units, to raise output; technical advice on crops and market conditions; the diffusion and expansion of bank credit and the improvement of marketing and transport services; the creation of associated activities to enable the rural family to supplement its income and employ its time productively during slack seasons. All this presupposes, moreover, greater stimulus to research and experimentation, as well as the training of technical and specialized personnel and the improvement of government services. It involves national planning in which agricultural projections are coordinated with those of industry and others. In such a general framework, public investments in agriculture, whether in irrigation and flood control, land clearance, or mechanization, would be guided by rational development criteria.

THE TERMS OF INDUSTRIAL DEVELOPMENT

Industrialization as such does not need to be justified today; it is the only means of attaining a permanent rise in the standard of living. Although some theoreticians still engage in Byzantine speculations on the international division of labor, all underdeveloped countries owe most of their progress in late years to industrial expansion. Furthermore, a recent United Nations study indicates that the average annual rate of growth of industrial output, except dur-

[2] Holders of a parcel of land granted by the government under the land-reform program.

ing the Second World War and postwar periods, has been greater in the underdeveloped countries than in the more industrialized countries with a higher per capita income.

On the other hand, proper subjects for inquiry are the frequent lack of harmony between industrial and agricultural development and the kind, or more specifically the structural content, of industrialization. It should be remembered that, historically, the underdeveloped countries began to industrialize according to classical precepts. Factories were established with little or no State intervention, for the purpose of transforming a resource or raw material into either a semiprocessed commodity for export or a manufactured article for domestic consumption. It was generally conceded that articles for domestic consumption could be accorded temporary tariff protection and some measure of credit facilities. But if an industry required longer-lasting and higher protection, had to import its raw materials, or depended excessively on government aid, it was considered uneconomic; its products were to be imported from abroad, while the country specialized in producing and exporting primary products.

Events such as the two great wars and the world depression of the thirties as well as an overall consideration of economic development permit a new, less fatalistic, approach to the question of industrialization. World demand for primary products is generally not very elastic; it increases slowly, partly because industrial growth in the more advanced countries has slackened and partly because of substitutions and technical innovations, which also have an adverse effect on the exporters of primary products. However, underdeveloped countries, where the demand for all kinds of manufactured goods is as a rule highly income-elastic, can pay for their imports of such goods only with the proceeds from their uncertain or weakened exports of primary products. It is therefore advisable, in the interest of external equilibrium, to avoid the importation of certain manufactured articles so that foreign exchange can be used mainly to purchase commodities that cannot be replaced by domestic output or that, like equipment and machinery, involve difficult techniques. Industrialization thus becomes a means of maintaining the balance of payments between the country and the rest of the world.

Another decisive function of industrialization is to give more productive employment to that part of the rural population displaced by the mechanization of agriculture, in addition to the farm-workers who emigrate to cities for other reasons. Unless this manpower is absorbed by industry, it joins the ranks of the underemployed, who make no contribution to productivity and constitute a social and economic burden.

Industrialization is the most effective instrument available to raise the value of farm production and to speed up the transition from a subsistence economy to a commercial and technical one. Industry not only generates a permanent demand for agricultural products, but it also supplies agriculture with the implements and materials necessary to meet that demand.

Without enumerating all the effects of industrialization on general development, there can remain no doubt that only an industrial society can create the spirit of technical modernization and scientific advance that today characterizes the highest cultural levels.

It should be emphasized that if the underdeveloped countries have embarked on industrialization with an intensity and on a scale not foreseen in the classical theories of political economy, it is because a careful examination of two fundamental phenomena in their economies—the disparity between their import requirements and their export possibilities, and their surplus rural population—has left them no choice. These problems of preventing external disequilibrium and underemployment are, from an economic point of view, the most valid explanations of the process of industrialization. They are present to varying degrees in any underdeveloped country and, of course, exist in Mexico.

Industrialization in Mexico has been rapid and relatively recent. Before 1940, according to some indices, industrial output rose at an average annual rate of about 5 per cent, although it started from very low levels in the initial post-Revolutionary period. To give but one example, by 1940 Mexico's steel capacity was only 180,000 metric tons. Manufacturing output diversified and expanded, thanks to the war and some internal stimulus provided by the government, which gradually developed a firmer and broader policy of industrial promotion. Furthermore, the cotton and coffee booms of the postwar period, together with other gains in agriculture, generated private savings that were invested in industry. And the government saw to it that there were adequate supplies of electric power and fuel. The process of import replacement was initiated and the absorption of manpower into industry was begun.

TABLE 6

Industrial Development

	1940	1945	1950	1955	1960
Manufacturing output					
(Index, 1940 = 100)	100	163	217	298	440
Steel					
Capacity					
Thousands of tons	180	275	450	850	1,915
(Index, 1940 = 100)	100	153	250	472	1,064
Output					
Thousands of tons	149	230	390	725	1,540
(Index, 1940 = 100)	100	156	265	493	1,048
Caustic soda					
Capacity					
Thousands of tons	––	––	11	25	85
(Index, 1950 = 100)	––	––	100	227	773
Output					
Thousands of tons	––	––	8	23	66
(Index, 1950 = 100)	––	––	100	288	825
Fertilizers					
Output					
Thousands of tons	––	––	67	194	389
(Index, 1950 = 100)	––	––	100	290	581
Petroleum refining					
Daily capacity					
Thousands of barrels	118[1]	––	224	266	293
(Index, 1938 = 100)	100	––	190	225	248
Electric energy					
Installed capacity					
Thousands of KW	681	720	1,235	1,930	3,021
(Index, 1940 = 100)	100	106	181	284	444

[1] 1938.

Industrial output in the last fifteen years has increased at a compound annual rate of roughly 7 per cent, which is higher than the rate of growth of aggregate income. Nevertheless, it is not certain that industrialization is sufficiently rapid to satisfy the two requirements: the employment of surplus rural population and the replacement of imports quickly enough to maintain external balance. It is possible and even probable that Mexico's industrialization may still be too slow.

If this is true, it gives rise to various other problems. First, the lag may be partly due to the low purchasing power of the great majority of the population, especially the rural. If average rural income was raised substantially, many industries that produce consumer goods could operate at full capacity and, since the raw materials used in the textile, shoe and clothing, processed food, and other industries are chiefly domestically produced, output of manufactures could be increased without appreciably adding to the volume of imports. It is also likely that production costs in these industries would be reduced. Moreover, a wider market would make possible the local manufacture of industrial parts and even of the equipment necessary for future expansion. Generalized agricultural progress also would encourage the establishment of industries to produce farm machinery and equipment for processing primary materials; and it would have a positive effect on the building-materials industries. Unless income distribution is improved, consumer-goods industries will gradually saturate their limited, and at times luxury, urban markets, where competition from imports is strongest, and they will continue to grow at a rate only slightly above that of the population, namely, around 4 per cent per annum. This is not the way to take advantage of the country's consumption potential or to meet the needs of the population.

There are other sectors of industry where the problems are of a different order. The manufacture of durable consumer goods—household equipment, furniture, television sets, etc.—has the advantage of an income-elastic market; but since it has not been integrated nationally, it requires imports of parts and materials that add to Mexico's total purchases abroad. In these cases, expansion must be vertical in order to increase employment and eliminate imports, and horizontal in order to achieve economically the benefits of modern technology. This sector clearly should be subject to planning, with provisions made for the impact of a new industry on those already existing. In this way, industries could make optimum use of equipment and processes for which the capital-labor ratio is high and could produce low-cost, standardized articles within the reach of the lower-income consumer. Mexico has made some progress in this direction, but the task ahead is still enormous. Of greatest complexity and magnitude is the manufacture of automobiles, which, until recently, was in the highly disorganized and uneconomical stage of mere assembly of imported parts.

The problem of capital goods is similar. These goods include transport equipment (closely associated with the automobile industry), for which demand can be projected with reasonable accuracy; and machinery for industry, agriculture, construction, etc., for which the demand of its heterogeneous market is hard to forecast. Imports of the latter type are difficult to replace in the short run because their production requires long experience, a heavy investment in technology, fairly large markets, and ample financial resources. Generally, an underdeveloped country reserves its foreign exchange, insofar as is possible, for the purchase of machinery and equipment abroad. Nevertheless, if it has a steel industry, it should try to advance to the manufacture of machines and their parts. Mexico is entering this phase and, for the moment, has vast possibilities of expansion.

The most vulnerable and unstable sector of producer goods is that of intermediate products—the raw or semiprocessed materials that are used in the manufacture of other goods, both for producers and consumers. Modern industrialization does not need to have all its primary materials locally supplied. On economic grounds it is possible to justify the use of imported materials to initiate the manufacture of an article. But eventually a way must be found to substitute domestic output for these materials, which otherwise will rapidly swell their share of total imports and absorb a considerable proportion of the available foreign exchange. For example, in Mexico in the past twenty years the volume of imports of metallic raw materials has grown at a compound annual rate of 7 per cent, and that of nonmetallic materials, including chemical products, at 7.4 per cent annually (see Table 3). Raw and semiprocessed materials constitute more than 40 per cent of Mexico's imports and in recent years have outstripped every other group of imports, with the exception of fuels (since 1956 undergoing a high rate of import replacement) and industrial machinery. In the interest of external equilibrium and higher employment, they should be obtained or processed within the country.

Import replacement of semiprocessed goods has made advances in chemicals, steel, and other activities where production expands swiftly. Nevertheless, it is necessary to further promote the intermediate-product industries in order to supply a growing share of the future foreseeable market. This is a difficult undertaking because it must be carried out in constant competition with the imported article, which as a rule cannot be dispensed with until domestic output meets internal demand, and because technology progresses rapidly in such industries. A different and cheaper chemical product may tomorrow replace one considered adequate today and thereby render existing factory installations obsolete. Moreover, the prospective internal market may not justify for some time a sufficiently large scale of production; such is the case of certain metallic products, chemicals, and others. The manufacture of intermediate products, even though a major part may be in the hands of private enterprise, requires continual coordination, supervised by the government, so that it will fit into the national program of industrialization and economic growth. Mexico has not yet reached this stage of coordinated development.

There are three more aspects of industrialization that should be mentioned, however briefly. Because of the technical nature of industrial processes, the different branches of industry are closely dependent upon one another. Therefore, industrial development has to be generalized throughout all sectors, in order to employ productive capacity to the utmost, take advantage of by-products, and, by creating a diversified demand, spur new industrial development. This is a powerful complementary argument for adequate planning of industrial growth.

Another important aspect of an industrial-development policy is an expanded training program for skilled workers, supervisors, technicians, engineers, and administrative and management personnel. Mexico, despite the great effort already made, cannot invest too much in human resources.

Finally, technological innovations in industry engender problems that must be given serious consideration. The experience gained in setting up two or three small research institutes, which still operate with very limited funds, has yet to have an appreciable effect on industry. Mexico's position of technological inferiority can have grave economic consequences. In the first place, Mexico does not efficiently exploit its own natural resources for industrial purposes. Furthermore, it supplies a low-income market with consumer goods and machinery manufactured on the basis of industrial techniques designed for high-income countries. On the other hand, payment for processes and technical services from abroad, as well as royalties on patents, is an additional drain on its foreign-exchange reserves. This situation can be remedied only over a long period of time, but intensified technological and scientific research supported by both government and industry would be a step in that direction.

The foregoing observations on the problems of industry are, of course, only a summary of what should go into a policy of industrial development in Mexico. Unfortunately, despite the encouraging

progress of recent years, Mexico still lacks a well-defined industrial
policy.

SIGNIFICANCE OF THE PUBLIC SECTOR

Since 1917, when Mexico's present constitution was established, the
government has been the principal promoter of economic development and the guardian of national wealth. Within a mixed economy the government plays an important role in production and
investment, which it may carry out on its own account or in conjunction with private enterprise. The concept of almost unrestricted
private property under pre-Revolution liberalism has been modified to fit the special circumstances of various sectors, especially the
agrarian, and provisions have been enacted to grant the government
a monopoly of some industrial branches. An extensive and varied
public regulation of private economic activity is practiced in Mexico.

TABLE 7

Public Revenues

Years	Federal Government	Federal District	States and Territories	Munic- ipalities	Total[1]
	Millions of pesos				
1957	8,037	810	1,285	376	10,508
1958	8,610	937	1,387	433	11,367
1959	9,053	1,021	1,557	466	12,097
1960	10,967	1,346	1,856	576	14,745
	Percentage of gross domestic product (at 1960 prices)				
1957	7.5	0.8	1.2	0.4	9.8
1958	7.4	0.8	1.2	0.4	9.8
1959	7.3	0.8	1.3	0.4	9.7
1960	7.8	1.0	1.3	0.4	10.5

[1] Includes small percentage of double-counting due to intrapublic sector
transfers.

When examining the problems of economic development it should
be specified that the "public sector" of the Mexican economy embraces not only the federal, state, and municipal governments that
collect taxes and expend public funds, but also the autonomous
agencies and the industrial, commercial, financial, and other corporations partially or wholly owned by the government. Most of
these agencies and enterprises carry out directly or through others

investments in activities that are essential to the economic growth and social improvement of the country. At the same time, they act as producers of part of the national income.

Unfortunately, despite the importance of this expanded public sector, its quantitative extent is not known. Statistics in Mexico are still not sufficiently advanced to represent in a system of national accounts the overall share of government activity. Data are available only for budgetary revenues and expenditures of the federal and Federal District governments and of the state and municipal governments (the latter are approximate estimates), but not globally for current revenues and expenditures of government-owned and autonomous public enterprises. Therefore, it is possible to calculate the fiscal burden of the public sector on the private economy and the public sector's contribution to the private economy in the form of government services, but not the contribution of government-owned and autonomous public enterprises to the national income or to such portions of it as industry, agriculture, petroleum, and transport.

As regards taxation in Mexico, the government collects just over 10 per cent of the gross national product, a ratio that is unusually low in comparison with those of other countries; it suggests that the fiscal burden in Mexico is light on the whole and that ranges or types of income amounting to a substantial sum avoid or evade taxation. Total current expenditures are even lower than tax revenues, inasmuch as part of the latter is used to finance public investment. In other words, the government, by not extending its current expenditures to the limit of its tax collections—and, incidentally, not providing the country with sufficient services—effects a public saving that it invests in expanding national productive capacity. In Mexico, contrary to what is generally assumed, the government actually does a great deal with very little.

The surplus of tax revenues over current expenditures, though important, is not the only source of public-investment financing. In the immediate postwar period, when borrowing abroad had barely been initiated, it constituted more than 70 per cent; at present, it covers about one-third. Equally important today is the reinvestment of the net income of the autonomous government agencies and the government-owned corporations. Private savings, part of which the government absorbs through bond issues, are one of the least significant sources. On the other hand, medium and long-term external

Mexico's Recent Economic Growth

borrowings are increasing in relative importance. Mexico is using all these resources to carry out a volume of gross public investment that varies between 4 and 6 per cent of the national product. This means that the public sector of the economy, even with the aid of foreign credit, still has a relatively small impact on aggregate expenditure.

TABLE 8

Gross Fixed Investment, Public and Private
(Indices Based on Values at 1960 Prices; 1940 = 100)

	1940	1945	1950	1955	1960
Total gross fixed investment	100	213	272	314	409
Public	100	202	303	284	388
Private[1]	100	221	246	338	426

[1] Excludes increase in stock of cattle.

An examination of private investment will reinforce the foregoing observation. According to some estimates, since the postwar period private investment has increased in volume much more rapidly than public investment and now makes up close to two-thirds of the annual total, compared with 60 per cent or less ten years ago. Nevertheless, private investment cannot be said to signify a very intense effort at capital formation, in view of the fact that perhaps more than one-fifth of it is in private housing, which, even were it all medium and low-cost, would raise only indirectly the productive capacity of the country. It would appear, therefore, that the joint action of private and public investment, the latter in declining proportion, is somewhat weak. An aggregate gross investment ratio of from 13 to 15 per cent of aggregate output cannot and should not be considered satisfactory. An increase to 18 or 20 per cent is needed to assure a more rapid rate of growth in overall production.

A higher investment ratio poses two questions: whether to expand private investment or public investment, or both; and how to augment the average productivity of investment. To rely on private investment alone to accelerate the rate of growth would risk, on the one hand, nonfulfillment of the desired goals and, on the other hand, investments that would not contribute to the general development of the country. Private investment might not accomplish the desired goals for many reasons, but primarily because it is either excluded from, or not likely to be attracted to, sectors such as agriculture, transport, energy, and fuel. As for its social utility, private investment would have little value—to take an extreme example—if it resulted only in the expanded construction of luxurious beach resorts.

Consequently, a sound program of economic development would require an increase in public investment not only to raise productive capacity in those sectors that might not attract private capital, but also to build up a solid public infrastructure that would encourage and facilitate large-scale private investments in industry. The pattern of the Mexican economy is such that, despite everything that has been done up to now, if the government does not continue expanding means of communication, electric-power capacity, areas under irrigation, water supplies, and other general utilities, private investment cannot prosper. Far from conflicting with public investment, private investment is dependent upon it.

But public investment should probably broaden its scope, even in the field of industry. For example, the government has established industrial enterprises (sometimes of questionable efficiency) in order to initiate new import-replacing activities. A development policy aimed at maintaining industrial growth at a rate high enough to assure external equilibrium and to absorb surplus rural population can be slowed down or blocked by lack of initiative or drive on the part of private enterprise. When this happens the government should not hesitate to set up the necessary industrial installations, provided, of course, that they are operated with maximum efficiency.

In brief, a better standard of living depends on a development of the agricultural, electrical, transport, and even industrial sectors that cannot conceivably be accomplished unless the public sector participates more intensively in investment activity. Furthermore, low-cost housing, school construction, drinking water, and hospital and social services every year lag farther behind the country's mounting needs.

If there remains any question of entrusting private enterprise with the immense task of enlarging the country's productive capacity, it should be resolved in the light of the urgencies of development. These must not be sacrificed to a mere theoretical possibility. The free play of private economic forces, no matter how wise the individual motives for investment may be, cannot result in a volume of investment that, in amount and composition, will meet the demands of growth. The public economy will have to assume the main responsibility and open up paths of development that can be followed by the rest of the national economy.

Nevertheless, the Mexican public sector is poor in resources, slow and complicated in procedure, uncoordinated in operation, and frequently inefficient in the execution of its programs. Government and administration in Mexico seem to be organized in a way more appropriate to the past—when economic development was altogether unplanned. The task of coordinating the policy of development must be carefully evaluated in economic terms; it cannot and should not be left to partial arrangements, emergencies, or the impromptu solutions of politicians or experts. At this critical stage of national evolution, Mexico can no longer excuse the deficiencies in its planning and development on the grounds that, *"a la mexicana,"* it trusts to good luck. Having realized in recent years that its problems of growth become daily more complex and difficult of solution, Mexico has not, however, sufficiently applied itself to formulating an integrated development policy expressed in attainable quantitative objectives that anyone can understand. There is certainly talk of planning, sometimes dealing with one sector of the economy, sometimes with a region. But it appears to be no more than a physical planning of projects without any clear economic content. A global concept of the country's development—one that continues beyond the presidential term of office—is still lacking, as are adequate studies on which to base it.

TABLE 9

Highways

	1940	1945	1950	1955	1960
Length of highways (terracing, gravel, and hard top)					
Kilometers	9,929	17,404	21,422	27,276	45,089
(Index, 1940=100)	100	175	216	275	454

Because available information about the public sector of the Mexican economy refers exclusively to government investment and tax resources, it obscures the fact that it is as important to adopt an economic policy as it is to carry out an investment or to collect a tax. A policy must be designed to use the administrative action of central, regional, or autonomous public agencies to attain the objectives for which the investment was originally undertaken. To give a classic example in Mexico: the completion of a dam that is not accompanied by drainage works, a rational utilization of water, an extension of agricultural services, an improvement in local transport, an adequate marketing system, information on markets, etc. may be a magnificent monument to the vision of a statesman and to the exceptional skill of Mexican engineers, but it does not necessarily contribute to national productivity. Another more recent example: the construction of fine roads leading to tourist attractions, of modern hotels and other facilities, without a clear program of the ways and means to increase tourism, may enhance the beauty of Mexico's resorts, archeological heritage, and colonial buildings, but the resources so invested will not accelerate Mexico's general economic development. In Mexico, the finished construction is too frequently taken as the solution to the problem. Planning does not consist only in carrying out public works and inducing private investment, but also in creating conditions that will permit the community to derive utmost benefit from the investment, tomorrow as well as today.

THE DISTRIBUTION OF INCOME

The fiscal weakness of the public sector is both a cause and an effect of the income distribution prevailing in Mexico, though clearly not the sole cause or the sole effect. The unequal and unfair distribution of income has many origins, some of a social and institutional nature and others related to the development process itself. One of the functions of a tax system and of the public sector in general is to help correct the unequal distribution of income, not only for moral reasons but also for sound economic reasons connected with development. If, as in Mexico, the tax system does not perform this function and the services provided by the government through current expenditures do not adequately compensate for the reduced income of the majority of the population, a vicious circle arises in which the concentration of national income and industrial and urban wealth distorts the fiscal structure in a way that probably intensifies the inequality. Inequality of income, in turn, obstructs economic development by adversely affecting external equilibrium, a situation promoting unproductive and luxury forms of consumption and investment and lowering the purchasing power of the rural and most of the urban population.

Taking into account its social revolution and the diversified nature of its economic development in the last twenty years, Mexico has a surprisingly uneven distribution of income. There are three structural elements, among many others, that help explain this: the relative rigidity of agricultural production; the high rate of demographic growth, which results in increasing numbers of unskilled workers; and the modest pace of industrialization. Consequently, the inequality of income is not so unexpected as would at first appear.

Indirect data, such as the apparent per capita consumption of food staples, indicate that the distribution of income in Mexico worsened after 1925. But the degree of inequality reached was not known until a short time ago when a revealing study, based on surveys conducted by the Mexican Bureau of Statistics and on other sources, was published by Ifigenia Navarrete. It is estimated that in 1957, 46 per cent of the Mexican family units had an average income (including services and goods in kind) of less than 500 pesos monthly and received as a group less than one-seventh of the total personal income of the country. Approximately another 38 per cent of the families, earning between 500 and 1,300 pesos a month, received under one-third of the total income. A small middle-class group with incomes of between 1,300 and 5,400 pesos monthly—constituting close to 14 per cent of the families—received another third of the income. The remaining one-fourth of the income was in the hands of families whose incomes averaged over 5,400 pesos a month and who made up barely 2.3 per cent of the total.

Comparing the above distribution with that of 1950, Mrs. Navarrete's calculations show that the lower 20 per cent of the families, with average incomes of roughly 300 pesos monthly, was better off in 1950; that half of the total number of families, with incomes of up to 500 pesos and including the first group, earned a slightly greater share of total personal income in 1950 than was recorded in 1957; that this still holds true if the categories are enlarged to include 80 per cent of the families, with incomes going up to 800 pesos in 1950 and 1,100 in 1957; and that over those seven years, only the remaining top 20 per cent—in particular, the middle class—actually increased its share.

The great majority of the Mexican population has not been incorporated into the purchasing-power brackets needed to sustain an extensive and dynamic industry manufacturing consumer goods. Available regional data indicate, furthermore, that the rural zones

TABLE 10

Personal-Income Distribution

A. Distribution in 1957

Monthly Income per Family	Percentage of Total Number of Families	Percentage of Total Personal Income
Up to 460 pesos	46.1	13.8
From 563 to 1,310 pesos	37.8	29.7
From 2,004 to 5,435 pesos	13.8	32.5
Above 5,435 pesos (class mean: 11,592 pesos)	2.3	24.0

B. Compared Distribution, 1950 and 1957

Mean Monthly Income per Family (1957 Pesos)		Percentage of Total Number of Families	Percentage of Total Personal Income	
1950	1957		1950	1957
Up to 311	Up to 304	20	6.1	4.4
From 348 to 440	From 350 to 485	30	13.0	11.2
From 504 to 788	From 632 to 1,128	30	21.11	23.01
From 989 to 12,329	From 1,658 to 11,765	20	59.8	61.4

1 The cumulative percentage through this bracket was 40.2 per cent in 1950 and 38.6 per cent in 1957.

Source: Ifigenia M. de Navarrete, *La distribución del ingreso y el desarrollo económico de México*, (México, D.F., Instituto de Investigaciones Económicas, Escuela Nacional de Economía, 1960), Tables 11 and 12.

in the center and south of the country, where half the population lives, show the lowest average family incomes. And so the problem of economic development once again proves to be centered in agriculture, where both productivity and income must be raised. Agricultural and industrial development are inseparable, however, and industrialization continues to be the chief means of a substantial increase in the national average family income.

MONETARY AND FINANCIAL STRATEGY

Monetary and financial considerations have always loomed large in Mexico's economic development. In the 1920's an excessive, but understandable, concern with monetary stability and the resumption of external debt payments probably impeded development. In any event, at that time a system of government banking institutions was established; over the years it has extended its financing to a wide range of activities and has become an important instrument of development.

This system of official banks has demonstrated its usefulness repeatedly and in many different ways. In the 1930's, when Mexico was recovering from its external-trade slump, it skillfully pursued a policy of monetary expansion that stimulated industrial growth and broadened the basic economic structure of the country. During the Second World War, it imposed monetary regulations that, even though not seconded by an adequate fiscal policy, prevented inflation of external origin from getting out of hand. More recently, it has coordinated monetary and fiscal policies and, by generally using them with discretion, has kept them from being disturbing factors in the economy. These policies have helped to create confidence, prevent run-away speculation, and assure monetary stability at the same time that they have encouraged the general growth of the country. In particular, they have permitted the diversion of financial resources toward the public sector and the channeling of long-term loans from abroad into the desired investment fields.

Nevertheless, two devaluations of the peso—if those of 1948 and 1949 are considered as one—have taken place in the last fifteen years. The second devaluation, in 1954, was drastic, unexpected, and had immediate social consequences that were nearly disastrous. From 1955 on, monetary policy has been cautious and the rate of overall growth has slackened somewhat, in part because of weak international markets. Must Mexico choose either rapid development, with devaluations, or a relatively sterile stability? Must it serve the dictates of financial policy, or can it use financial policy for purposes of a more positive development?

The monetary and financial operations of economics are extremely deceptive, for they veil the reality of the resources, production, organization, and labor that lie behind them. In development, the function of monetary and credit policy is not to maintain a given volume of money supply or a predetermined figure of foreign-exchange reserves, but to give the necessary fluidity to productive activity and to facilitate the required amount of public and private investment. It is futile to stabilize the money supply if there are no concurrent increases in production and investment, or to establish an inflexible foreign-exchange reserve at the expense of continued growth in the economy. The limitations of monetary policy are to be found actually in two categories of factors: on the one hand, the relative elasticity of output and, on the other, the proportion saved out of total income.

The first of these categories involves all the complexities of economic development. Although elasticity of production is largely determined by past investment, it is also affected by the composition of present productive capacity, the interrelation between the different sectors in which capacity has been raised, the incorporation of technological innovations, the efficiency of productive processes, and the relative availability of labor. From this point of view, the function of monetary and financial policy should be to reinforce the points of flexibility and, of course, break through the bottlenecks. This assumes that the government uses qualitative or sector credit control rather than quantitative regulation of the supply of loan funds to expedite its development plans. The government alone can judge how credit can best be directed to achieve the desirable goals of development. For example, without the existence of well-endowed official banks, the credit requirements of Mexico's agricultural economy could never be satisfied.

A country's capacity to save should also guide domestic monetary policy. In principle, saving might appear to be a given and invariable factor. It is said that monetary policy cannot create savings for development. In an income distribution like Mexico's, the capacity to save is restricted to the small percentage of the population that enjoys high income. Therefore—so goes the argument—a policy of monetary expansion would not necessarily absorb this saving and would, moreover, create additional demand, which, in the face of inelastic production, would accentuate the inflationary bias inherent in development. But the savings of individuals are only a part of the savings of a community. The savings of business enterprises can be stimulated by a flexible and well-oriented credit policy. Industrial enterprises, because they lack access to bank loans, frequently are prevented from expanding and thereby creating their own savings. This may lead to a concentration of savings in enterprises that are good credit risks but are less in need of expansion or less important to economic development. The banking system and monetary regulations have to take positive action on this problem in order to meet the demands of economic development.

Monetary policy alone cannot be relied upon; it must be aided by fiscal policy. A good tax system would reduce much of the luxury consumption and even investment carried on by higher-income sectors, increase the overall rate of savings, and transform part of private savings into public savings. Budgetary expenditures made from increased tax revenues would improve income distribution, promote a larger domestic market, combat the rigidities of supply that inhibit monetary policy, and ensure sufficient funds for the official banks that play a special role in economic development. Fiscal policy, through adequate tax measures, can also induce business savings and thus raise the capacity to finance industrial expansion. A tax system can be severe and still stimulate development and enterprise.

Tax reform would have incalculable consequences in Mexico. In addition to the foregoing benefits, it would make monetary policy more effective and would offset some of the handicaps under which the central bank operates. But, above all, it would give the public sector renewed vitality with which to attack the problem of development.[3] It would even be instrumental in securing a greater volume of foreign credit, should this become necessary. By increasing tax revenues through general reforms, external monetary stability could be guaranteed without hindering economic development. Unless there is an adverse, violent, and prolonged fluctuation in the international economy, the external equilibrium of the Mexican economy clearly will become progressively more dependent upon a compre-

---

[3] A basic tax reform began to be carried out in 1962 under legislation enacted in December, 1961.

hensive economic-development policy implemented through well-coordinated measures. Growth involves great structural changes. Demand rises, and if the economy does not respond with higher output and productivity, demand will turn to the rest of the world, that is, to imports. The intensity of the increase in imports depends upon income distribution, tax policy, the promotion of agriculture, the stage of industrialization and, in general, the soundness of the development program. If all these factors are combined harmoniously and directed toward a single objective, they will constitute the best support of Mexico's currency. Furthermore, they will enable Mexico to secure more prompt and effective aid against any contingency that may arise in international business conditions or against an unforeseen or fortuitous fluctuation in Mexico's foreign-exchange earnings.

THE NEED FOR AN OVERALL APPROACH

If Mexico is to accelerate its rate of progress, it must recognize the interdependence of all the different aspects of economic development: improvement of agriculture, expansion of industry, growth in public and private investment, broadening of public services, correction of unequal income distribution, replacement of imports, promotion of exports and tourism, better orientation of monetary and financial policy, tax reform, and social advancement. These are elements that support one another, but they are not directed by a natural law that will necessarily produce harmony and optimum results.

Mexico is not and never will be independent of the world economy, nor can it isolate itself from the trends and fluctuations in international trade. Mexico's economic system must accept them as an exogenous variable and be prepared to adapt itself to whatever displacements they may originate. At the moment, the prospects of world markets appear rather uncertain. They could improve as industrial trends in other countries are revitalized, or as the demand for primary products increases in nations that until now have hardly participated in world commerce, or as effective international measures are adopted to regulate prices and the balance of world supply and demand. But, until one or all of these occur, the Mexican economy will receive less impetus from abroad than it did in the past.

The structural changes in its economy have placed Mexico in

a new situation. Industry has already entered a phase so diversified and complex that only a more complete integration will enable it to reduce progressively its share of the country's imports of intermediate products. A greater coordination of industrial development and, where necessary, of public investment will make it possible to fill the most important gaps. Agricultural output must become more flexible in order to meet the growing industrial demand for its products and the food requirements of the population. Progress in agriculture would attack the problem of income distribution at its base, but it must be accompanied by a higher rate of industrialization to absorb surplus farm labor.

Although Mexico is not precisely at a crossroads, it perhaps has reached a turning point where the experiences and difficulties of the previous journey grow dim, whereas along the road ahead the obstacles that may slow down its pace are not yet clearly perceived. If up to now it has achieved a certain degree of success in formulating and executing its economic development, it must do even better. If, on calm reflection, it finds many things that are not satisfactory, it must remedy them. Mexico must liberate itself from the past and commit itself to the future.

APPENDIX I

STATISTICAL DATA AND PRINCIPAL SOURCES

The sources of the tables in this essay and of other data cited in the text are as follows:

National product, main sectors of output, public and private investment, imports, exports, and tourist expenditures: derived from data published by Banco de México, Nacional Financiera, Secretaría de Agricultura y Ganadería, Petróleos Mexicanos, and the U.N. Economic Commission for Latin America. National-product series as revised in September, 1963, by Banco de México, converted to 1960 prices.

Population and labor force: Dirección General de Estadística; 1960 data from population census.

World trade: imports of primary products, 1876–1880 to 1913, and 1938 to 1953, from P. Lamartine Yates, *Forty Years of Foreign Trade* (London, George Allen and Unwin, 1959); Mexican exports, 1879-1911, from *Estadísticas económicas del Porfiriato: comercio exterior de México, 1877–1911* (México, D.F., El Colegio de México, 1960).

Industrial output in developed countries: from United Nations, Statistical Office, *Patterns of Industrial Growth, 1938–1958* (New York, 1960, U.N. Publication No. 59-XVII-6).

Public sector: Combined Mexican Working Party, *The Economic Development of Mexico* (Baltimore, The Johns Hopkins Press, for the International Bank for Reconstruction and Development, 1953); Banco de México, annual reports; Centro de Investigaciones Agrarias, *Los distritos de riego del Noroeste: tenencia y aprovechamiento de la tierra* (México, D.F., Instituto Mexicano de Investigaciones Económicas, 1957); and Secretaría de Recursos Hidráulicos, Secretaría de Obras Públicas, Petróleos Mexicanos and Comisión Federal de Electricidad.

Income distribution: Ifigenia M. de Navarrete, *La distribución del ingreso y el desarrollo económico de México* (México, D.F., Instituto de Investigaciones Económicas, Escuela Nacional de Economía, Universidad Nacional Autónoma de México, 1960), a portion of which appears in this volume of essays.

Index

agrarian-reform program: effects of, 51, 57–59, 117; nature of, 181. *See also* agriculture; land-reform policy

Agreement of 1922 (with International Committee of Bankers): 121

Agreement of November, 1941 (with U. S.): 120

agriculture: output of, 3, 8; land redistribution in, 8; and industry, 8, 24, 53, 180, 181, 183, 184–185; political consensus in, 9, 16; and economic development, 24, 57; nature of income from, 136; investment in, 179; in underdeveloped countries, 180; mechanization of, 184–185

—, European: and industrialization, 46

—, Latin American: growth of, 3; exports of, 8

—, Mexican: income in, 6, 49, 50, 134, 138, 139, 140, 154–157, 186, 196; in P.R.I., 9; growth of, 26, 27, 28, 34, 46, 50, 51, 57–62, 72, 173, 174, 176, 179–183; productivity of, 26, 43–44, 48, 60, 61, 123, 143, 182; effect of Revolution on, 28, 29, 50–51; effect of Depression on, 29, 31; and Second World War, 30, 31, 185; and industry, 36, 198; and imports, 39, 182; before the Revolution, 46, 47, 107; after the Revolution, 46, 50, 51, 57–62, 181; and agrarian reform, 51, 57–59, 117, 181; influence of geography and climate on, 53, 61; investment in, 54, 72, 77, 80 n., 82, 83 n., 86, 94, 96 n., 101, 193, 199; government support for, 56, 58, 59, 110, 117, 181, 182, 191; and urban development, 59; proportion of population engaged in, 72, 175; mechanization of, 73, 118, 187; and economic development, 118, 198; importance of exports to, 181–182, 187; development of, 181–182, 182–183, 187, 201–202; and domestic market, 182; training in, 183; mentioned, 201. *See also* credit unions; entrepreneurs, agricultural; farmers; workers, agricultural

Agriculture, Ministry of: 43

Agriculture and Livestock and Poultry Raising, Guarantee and Development Fund for: 78, 83

Agriculture and Livestock Census: 136

Aguascalientes, Mexico: income distribution in, 146, 147, 149

Alemán, Miguel: 59

Alliance for Progress: effects of, 12

Anglo-Saxon law: influence of, in Mexico, 96

apartment houses: financing of, 98

Argentina: agricultural output of, 3, 8; social policies of, 8–9; politics in, 9; labor market in, 16

—, economy of: growth of, 3, 12, 15, 16; history of, 5–8, 10, 13; government participation in, 8–9, 10; saving in, 13

automobiles: manufacture of, in Mexico, 176, 187

auxiliary economic organizations: types of, 88, 98–100

avio loans. *See* loans, *avio*

Baja California: income distribution in, 146, 147, 149

balance of payments: of underdeveloped countries, 39–40; and industrialization, 184

—, Mexican: 32–38, 176

bank, central. *See* Bank of Mexico

Bank Experts of the American Continent, VI Meeting of Central: 77

Bank of London and Mexico: foreign control of, 115

Bank of Mexico: economic policy of, 17–18, 75–76, 116, 125, 200; data compiled by, 44, 68, 133, 162, 164; function of, 71; and economic development, 72, 78–79, 86–87; establishment of, 74, 115; and National Banking Commission, 74, 86; jurisdiction of, 74, 80, 81–82, 83, 85–86, 93–94, 117; and reserve requirements, 75–76; and securities market, 79; financing of government by, 79, 120; and rediscount operations, 82, 84–85; and foreign-credit operations,

mortgage loans: 86, 102–103
mutual funds: 103

Nacional Financiera: establishment of, 8, 115; financial activities of, 14, 120, 126; and trust funds, 83; and industrialization, 119, 122; and foreign loans, 121; mentioned, 81 n.
National Banking Commission: authority of, 74; and Bank of Mexico, 74, 86; control of financing by, 85; and *financieras*, 86, 94; policies of, 116
National Bank of Agricultural Credit: 115
National Bank of Mexico: 113, 114–115
National Insurance Commission: 119
National Mortgage Bank: 97
national product: and economic growth, 23, 25; and investment, 24–25; analysis of history of, 27–33; and exports, 38–42; and income distribution, 133. *See also* gross national product
National Savings Board: 119
National Securities Commission: 91, 97, 119
National Urban Mortgage and Public Works Bank: 115
natural resources: exploitation of, 24, 36, 37, 48; foreign investment in, 48; public investment in, 58; and economic development, 127–128. *See also* raw materials
Navarrete, Ifigenia: 196
Nayarit, Mexico: income distribution in, 146, 147, 149
North Pacific Zone: income distribution in, 145, 146, 147, 150, 151, 152–153, 154–158; industrialization in, 154
North Zone: income distribution in, 145–146, 147, 150, 151, 152–153, 154–158; industrialization in, 154
Nuevo León, Mexico: income distribution in, 146, 147, 149, 150

Oaxaca, Mexico: industrial loans in, 83 n.; income distribution in, 146, 147, 149
Oceania: industrial output of, 178
oil industry. *See* petroleum industry
Organic Law of the Bank of Mexico: terms of, 75–76; results of, 119
output: and investment, 192
—, surplus: utilization of, 35

peso: devaluation of, 9, 117–118, 120, 198–199; Bank of Mexico promotes, 87. *See also* currency; money

petroleum industry: in underdeveloped countries, 41
—, Mexican: foreign investment in, 7, 48, 108, 116, 118, 127; growth of, 26, 28, 30, 31, 34, 50, 51, 62, 63, 175, 176, 186; production of, 26, 43, 44; effect of Revolution on, 28, 29, 50, 51; and Great Depression, 29, 31; early plans for, 46; under Díaz regime, 48, 108; and national economy, 49; government support for, 56, 58, 191; expropriation of, 118, 121
political development: and economic growth, 23, 24
—, Mexican: 45, 127, 177, 130
population: and economic development, 4, 24–25; and income concentration, 145
—, European: and industrialization, 46
—, Mexican: growth of, 14, 50, 68, 174, 202; effect of the Revolution on, 28, 50; distribution of, 52; social classes in, 170; figures on, 175
—, Mexican rural: changes in, after the Revolution, 50, 52–53, 62, 182; migration of, to cities, 52–53, 73, 140, 174–175, 184–185, 186, 187, 193, 202; real income of, 60, 195, 196–198; and agricultural productivity, 61; standard of living of, 61–62; and industrialization, 202. *See also* demographic structure, Mexican; farmer, Mexican
—, Mexican urban: growth of, 52–53; improved conditions of, 62; income of, 195 Population Census (1950): 158
poultry raising: 83 n., 86
Poultry Raising, Guarantee and Development Fund for Agriculture and Livestock: 78, 83
President, Mexican: power of, 10 n.
P.R.I.: popular support for, 9
prices: stability of, 17, 36; control of, 38; and income, 166; changes in, 12
—, world: stability of, 40–41, 178, 179
primary products. *See* natural resources; raw materials
private enterprise: and economic development, 45, 190, 193–194; under Díaz regime, 54; areas of, 62–63
producer-goods industry: growth of, 66, 122, 166 n.
production: and inflation, 36–37; and monetary policy, 101, 199; and economic development, 179
—, Mexican: and capital formation, 33–34; structure of, 35–36, 176; inadequacy of, 37; public investment in,

Lightning Source UK Ltd.
Milton Keynes UK
UKHW03f0753270418
321742UK00001B/71/P